First published 2003 by Mackintoosh. Ltd.

MACKINTOOSH. LTD.
Elsham Hall, Brigg
North Lincolnshire
DN 20 0QZ

ISBN 0-9545026-0-4

Copyright © Robert Elwes 2003

The right of Robert Elwes and Chocolate Mountain Chronicles title to be identified as the author of this work has been asserted by him in accordance with the Copyright, Designs and Patents Act 1988.

All rights reserved. No part of this publication may be reproduced, stored in or introduced into a retrieval system, or by any means (electronic, mechanical, photocopying, recording or otherwise) without the prior written permission of the publisher. Any person who does any unauthorised act in relation to this publication may be liable to criminal prosecution and civil claims for damages.

A CIP catalogue record for this book is available from British Library.

Printed and bound in Austria.

This book is sold subject to the condition that is shall not, by way of trade or otherwise, be lent, re-sold, hired out, or otherwise circulated without the publisher's prior consent in any form of binding cover other than that in which it is published and without a similar condition including this condition being imposed on the subsequent purchaser.

The Chocolate Mountain Chronicles

'Barking by the Bodensee'

By Robert Elwes. Esq.
'The Silver Spoon Schuhplattler'

Chocolate Mountain Chronicles Index

CHAPTER ONE:	The Great Escape to the Chocolate Mountains	1
CHAPTER TWO:	Ducking, Murmeltier and Hunting for Schools	15
CHAPTER THREE:	Bavarian Cowboys, Appenzellerland Wandertag and Crazy Choristers	32
CHAPTER FOUR:	The Butcher, the Baker, the Fireman and the Candlestick Makers	42
CHAPTER FIVE:	A deadly silent School Reunion, Painting Cows and Saving My Soul	51
CHAPTER SIX:	München, Mourning and Kirsch Drinking with Hemingway's Ghost in Montafon	61
CHAPTER SEVEN:	Rapping to Chaucer, Montessori, the Martinimarkt and Smiling Santa	72
CHAPTER EIGHT:	Clinical Clowns, Chocolate Cows, Catawauling and Cunning Dachshunds	79
CHAPTER NINE:	Sonntagsessen, Damüls Protocol, a Pet Physician and a Newspaper Heroine	87
CHAPTER TEN:	Saint Nikolaus, The Twenty-Four Hour Bürgermeister and Jassen Jokes	97
CHAPTER ELEVEN:	Schmugglen, Pumpeulusisch, Red Mary and the First Snow in Damüls	104
CHAPTER TWELVE:	The Phantom Plumber, the Secrets of the Priest and smelly Swiss Cheese	112
CHAPTER THIRTEEN:	Ice Dancing, Ancient Chronicles, Eisstocks and Christmas Traditions	120
CHAPTER FOURTEEN:	A City Christmas of Cribs, Curious Culture and Circus Krone	129
CHAPTER FIFTEEN:	Das Silvesterklausen, a House Fire and Silvester Traditions in the Alps	136

CHAPTER SIXTEEN:	*A Seductive Schrammler, Liechtenstein Walsers and Georgian Handball*	143
CHAPTER SEVENTEEN:	*Three Kings Day Birthday, Haunted Hohenems and Angelica's Lost Letters*	150
CHAPTER EIGHTEEN:	*A Fasching Clown Medal, Schwarzenberg Surprise and Skateboarders*	159
CHAPTER NINETEEN:	*Andelsbuch Cheese, a Phantom Rolls Royce and a Blue Police Light*	167
CHAPTER TWENTY:	*Landesbibliothek, Ski Jumping and Longing to belong to an Alpine Lilliput*	174
CHAPTER TWENTY-ONE:	*Felder the Free Writer and Felder the Stool Maker's Bregenzerwald Beauty*	181
CHAPTER TWENTY-TWO:	*Ghost Train Spotting in Fairytale Feldkirch and a Rankweil Revelation*	186
CHAPTER TWENTY-THREE:	*Landeshauptmann, Skateboard Kings, Snow Zebras and Ketchup Borders*	191
CHAPTER TWENTY-FOUR:	*Laughing in Lech, Snow Riding on Haflingers and Beck in Brand*	198
CHAPTER TWENTY-FIVE:	*The Final Chapter of a Chronicler's Midlife Quest*	203

Map of the Chocolate Mountains and Photographs loaned by Special Permission. Copy of the Official Endorsement Letter from the Landeshauptmann of Vorarlberg.

Extract from the Second Wild Man's Quest in a Fisherman's Gondel on the Bodensee.

"AUTHOR AS ANGEL"

Dr. Herbert Sausgruber
Landeshauptmann

Bregenz, 31st of January 2003

Mr Robert Elwes
Rebgarten 14
6973 Höchst

Subject: Preface/foreword for book

Dear Robert,

I hope that your book on our chocolate mountain paradise of Vorarlberg will encourage visitors to dig a little deeper into the heart of our wonderful world of laughter and in famous alpine hospitality. I know that we have so much more to offer than skiing with sunglasses and dancing in alpine meadows as people will doubtless discover in your book etc. etc.

Yours sincerely,
Landeshauptmann and Höchster

PS: I'm glad that you chose my village of Höchst to write your opera and humorous book.

Chocolate Mountain Map.

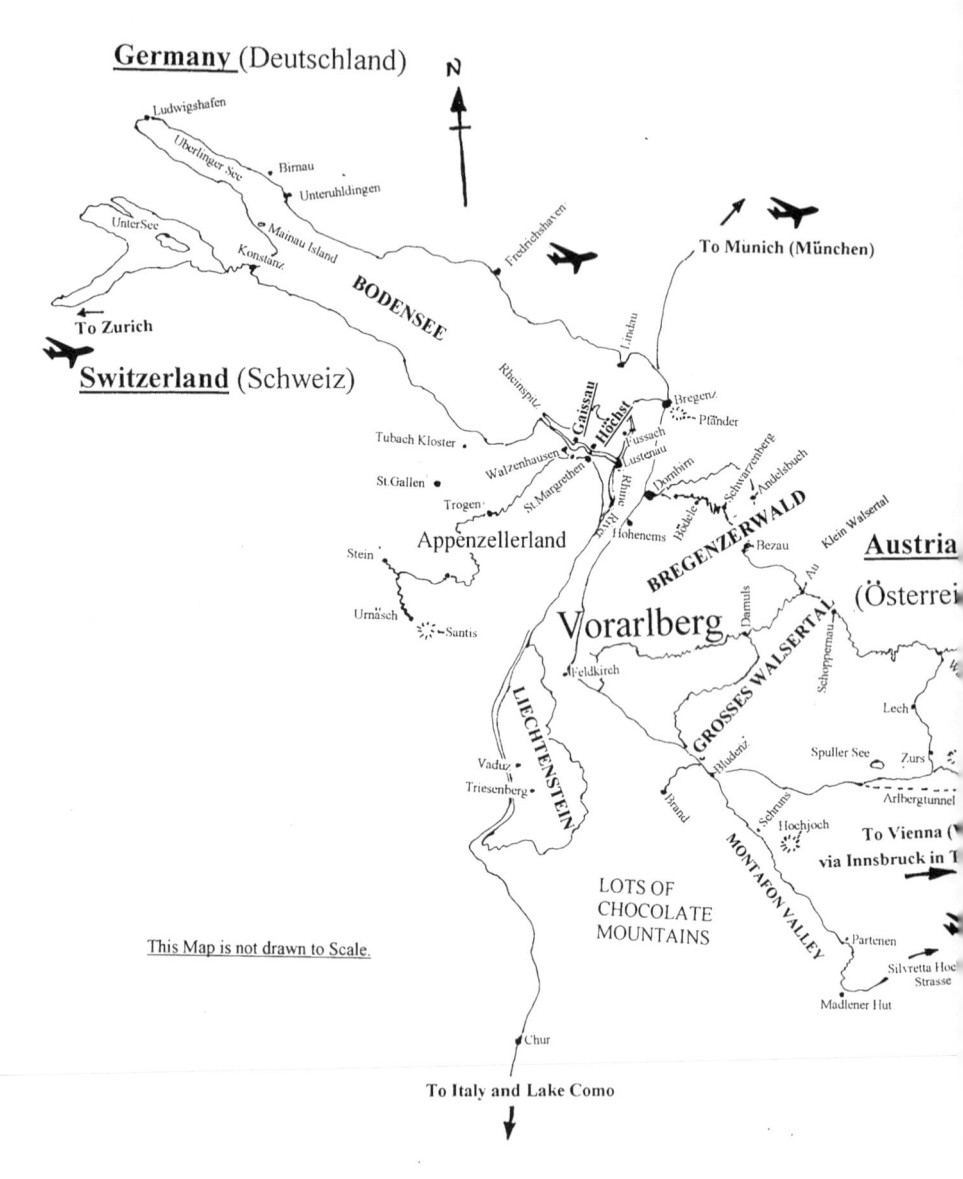

THE GREAT ESCAPE TO THE CHOCOLATE MOUNTAINS

We held each other tightly as we reaffirmed our decision.

Out of the window the barley rippled in the wind. It was as though two despondent lost souls were standing throwing stones into a vast green lake of corn that stretched out beyond the horizon. The landscape of the Lincolnshire Wolds was not necessarily flat but every tree or building seemed to break that boundary between the fertile earth and the great blue cloudless heavens above. There was certainly something romantic in the feeling that mankind was just one small part of this huge natural panorama so insignificant to the naked eye yet so important in its creation.

No matter how much we tried to farm nature's seemingly limitless resources to feed an ever increasing population there was no denying that nature was wiser than man. History was about to repeat itself as Father Time re-balanced the pendulum of evolution. The time was right and as had happened many times before in this green and pleasant land, another agricultural depression was about to envelop our lives.

Contrary to the catastrophe of the crop failures, wars and rebellions or the bubonic plague that had disrupted the region in previous generations this impending disaster was caused by simple economics and the technological advancement in the wider world beyond our fragmented island nation. Over twenty eight thousand agricultural workers had left the land in the past two years in the United Kingdom. The erosion of employment was more than any other industry in the European Union and the English factor was further damaged by the Foot in Mouth crisis of those same politicians. Over two thousand family farms had disappeared from Lincolnshire alone in the past twenty years. This was more per square mile than the Great American Depression but with the fundamental difference that this was not caused by dust bowls but by man himself in search of free trade in a world of supermarket monopolies and cheap imports.

We sat defenceless against the unnatural elements of monetary exchange, political expediency and potential bankruptcy. The brave new world of agriculture was moving irreversibly towards contract farming or diversification from wholesale food production. Big words from even bigger banks but being realists we had already seen this wind of change blowing through corn two decades ago.

The barley no longer whispered sweet nothings to our bank manager for we had followed his cautious advice in times of peaking yields and falling prices. We had decided like many others that the romance of threshing corn with clapped out combines was reserved for the records of social historians. In fact the decisions made to diversify into farm tourism and other quite unrelated rural businesses were now paying dividends. The agricultural depression was not the motive that drove us to opt like hundreds of other midlife hippies to seek a good life in some godforsaken best forgotten foreign land.

The ideals of struggling to fight nature in some deserted part of the globe cut off from human contact in the solitude of self-satisfaction did not appeal at all to us. We had no desire to re-colonise abandoned farms in the isolated parts of the European Union or indeed to encourage the Common Agricultural Policy to pour more failed subsidies into some fruit farm in the middle of a place of otherwise wild untamed natural beauty.

We lived well and intended to live better and not without the creature comforts of home. Our home was probably in the top ten list of city dweller's escapist fantasies probably somewhere between the one about the Englishman's home is his castle and that rose covered cottage that always seems to bloom throughout our otherwise quite inclement summers. It was of course a home which we had lovingly restored and improved to live in such a climate. Somewhere our children had grown up like the many generations of shrieking and laughing children that had echoed within the confines of its four hundred year old stone walls. The swallows had nested here in its pan-tiled eaves for far longer than its anthropomorphic inhabitants but they had long since adjusted to our nesting needs.

It was not the urge to migrate from a place of firm historical family roots. Although the birds that flew south probably had more sense than my ancestors. It was not a decision to nest elsewhere as we were well past the nesting stage and almost beyond the brooding stage.

There were of course moments when we felt that our children were our world and reproduction certainly had its pleasant aspects. We missed them when they weren't running around our feet and confessed to have completely forgotten about them when they were far away enjoying boarding school. Home is home with or without the finger murals on the freshly painted stairways or the broken pieces of toys that send you hurtling down those stairs after being unwisely distracted by the painting abilities of your offspring.

We both had jobs which ideally suited us and which most management consultants would describe as intellectually challenging, financially rewarding and extremely flexible to the needs of the family unit. I had a job where one minute I was wearing a cod piece within a play of my own making and the next minute I was sampling a cod piece to be served in a restaurant with similar freedom of culinary expression. My loving wife and long suffering partner in this new career sabbatical was also happy examining artefacts from times past as it was something she had spent her life doing in the far flung deserts of Egypt and subsequently in the greener pastures of Lincolnshire.

It was not the monotony of work that drove us to jump off the platform of stability and security into the lights of the oncoming ghost train from hell and probably employment damnation. In fact we both found work in England a huge source of infinite indulgence. Quite probably we had much self gratification in the satisfaction of our achievements and our ever improving knowledge and experience in matters we both found rewarding in our separate ways. We both often worked beyond the call of duty into the long hours of the night and, until we both reached forty, we had no complaints on this front with much to look forward to and much to be proud of which cannot be said of many jobs these days.

There was the question of mid-life crisis but we both had never really had a straightforward life to become bored. The chemistry of sexual fantasies about liaisons with film idols wearing strange garments on tropical islands had much to appeal to both of us in our middle age. There was the adventure but our past lives had crossed over these bench marks and carpet burns no longer attracted us in quite the same way as it had before we tied the knot twelve years ago. Even if we tied knots in memory of the times we had tied knots to hypothetical beds in our wildest imagination it was not going to bring on a sudden wish to seek out another life with that screen idol that we kept secret in our wet dreams.

Our social life did not make us particularly want to escape to some desert island despite the above prospect of realising our inner most concealed carnal fantasy. There was much fun still to be had in the surf and the tide was definitely not out on the party scene. We knew that we would miss many like minded friends from the arts, country pursuits and professions for which we were clearly not qualified, but which held our utmost respect. The champagne had flowed like fountains and diamonds were definitely our friends best friends.

"We must be totally stark raving mad!" I said watching the sun drop below the vast expanse of green which was now turning into a grey mass of nothingness.

"Let's just enjoy the madness of the moment" Marina replied huddled under the summer duvet probably thinking of a warmer climate.

The double king sized four poster bed was comfortable and practical in a house situated on top of a hill open to the four winds. In fact it was comforting to shelter under its dense canopy knowing that we were going to cast its finely carved wood aside for a life changing experience in a foreign land where neither of us had ever really lived let alone put down any roots. There were many stories it could tell us but somehow we felt safe and secure knowing our story was now a part of its long family history of silent slumber.

"Are we giving up our lives for the sake of our children or is it so that we can have one last regression into childhood before senility sets in ?"

"Dreams are only dreams unless you wake up and try to make them come true."

She smiled as though she knew it was some corny line from a now forgotten Hollywood black and white blockbuster. Whoever wrote the line knew it could only be delivered in such a perfect scenario from the pouting lips of a screen idol but it seemed to fit our situation too. After all we were going to escape into our small screen dream world that had finally begun to eclipse the sunshine of our lives in Lincolnshire. It felt good immersing ourselves again in a moving picture dream where we were the moving stars in our own movie.

"Well I prefer the simple explanation of our children."

We looked at each other and laughed. It was a deep dark humour born from blacker moments of distress but somehow it was a bond of sarcasm that had formed between us which even our closest friends failed to comprehend. It wasn't the lonely chuckle lent to something amusing on the television but a manifestation of laughter that was from the deepest part of the lungs and indeed the heart. No wonder our friends could never understand our jokes because the punch line was somehow left unsaid.

"We're just going off to the chocolate mountains!"

****

The idea was as simple as our children had explained it to their various classmates and teachers but putting it into practice had been harder than we could have possibly imagined. The books that summarise the move to some far away paradise with a simple by-line have never really recognised that moving is in fact as stressful as a bad-tempered divorce or the funeral of a nearest and dearest. These experiences all seem to blend into one never ending nightmare which quite understandably can easily end in divorce or even an early grave at the hands of a packing knife.

The whole project had taken two years to plan yet somehow it seemed we had overlooked all the most important things until the last minute. We did manage to let our home to a warm hearted family who underwent an interview in between frantic packing of boxes, an infinite flow of contractors and friends, and for the most part with my head in the dishwasher.

We also managed to pack away our furniture into two rooms which was quite a feat considering we had five years of detritus spread over twenty rooms.

Finally we said goodbye to all the pets and took them to their respective new homes, that is, all bar the white rabbit that died of a broken heart just before we could catch it. It was ceremoniously buried at the bottom of the garden along with the long line of other rabbits that had mysteriously died in our care including those that our dog had patiently retrieved from their attempts to escape certain death. Despite the fact that I had spent most of my adult life working in a family Wildlife Park the roll over of rabbits in our custody would make the executioner on death row check his score card.

The classic tips from all the books on midlife migration include the purchase of a worthy looking vehicle so naturally I purchased a gas powered long wheel base Landrover Defender and stuffed all the most useless survival gear and broken toys into every possible orifice. Packing the roof rack was fun in the pouring rain and the nostalgia of British engineering coughed and spluttered as we set off to catch our ship from Hull to the continental culture of Europe. We only just made it into the wrong cargo hold adding to the vast array of dents and scrapes already suffered by this miracle of motoring history.

Small wonder we were accosted by a Dutch Landrover enthusiast in a Service Station who wound down the window of his immaculate version of our rust bucket to comment on the unique specifications our original classic car. We laughed at the prospect of accepting his invitation to join him at a rally in the Swiss mountains as more pieces of our classic car fell off in my hands. The Swiss Family Robinson who were reputed to have lived on a desert island constructing everything from their surroundings could have built a better mode of transport powered by flatulent goats. In fact the leaking exhaust grew so loud and nauseous that we gave up communications and prayed to ourselves to survive a truly exhausting epic journey across the heart of Europe.

If there are any tips to be truly passed on about setting out to explore one's inner being on an expedition into the great unknown then the survival of a ride in the beast from British Leyland is one recommended not to go onto the list. It certainly flies the flag and can take on the roughest toughest terrain. However even a gas guzzling Rolls Royce can do that with the bonus of not having bone breaking suspension, constant worrying electrical failures in mountain tunnels, oil leaks in embarrassing places and unidentifiable pieces falling off all parts of its rusting, stale chocolate brown coloured bodywork. Its only advantage was any street furniture you failed to see from the rear window was simply flattened like a tank.

We still cannot understand the fascination of every single mechanic, of which there were many, but we put it down it's historical significance as the first vehicle that had four wheels that drove simultaneously powering the first British biscuit tin for passengers with no sense of smell, hearing, feeling and definitely no sense of style. Unless of course you enjoy the latest fashion in biscuit tins which perhaps explained why grease monkeys in well oiled boiler suits seemed to be transfixed by it as it graced their garage workshops on an all too frequent basis. It's cult status as the pin up of the workshop belies the fact that it has no beautiful design features whatsoever and certainly nothing attractive to male heterosexuals.

Perhaps it is the heavy duty look associated with beasts of burden that has encouraged hundreds of would be world wide free ride hippies to choose it as their number one choice. Farmers and gamekeepers swear by it but for my part I can only say that our children learnt more unintentional expletives from my swearing at it. Just buy a nice simple car with standard air conditioning, electric windows, power steering, antilock braking system and a decent radio unless of course you have a huge macho masochistic urge to experience the dark ages of four wheel drive posterity and an equally large well cushioned posterior.

"Thank goodness we didn't buy that new Volvo four wheel drive or we would have missed out on this truly British experience" said my exhausted wife.

The children laughed as we broke down for the third time at the traffic lights causing several frustrated Mercedes and BMW drivers behind us to sound out their disgust on their horns. We had all got so used to the German horn music that our naughtier children would lean out the window and conduct the concert which we all agreed was still better than listening to a Wagner Opera. In fact our children always seemed to lighten the situation as travel to them was simply a matter of when not if we would arrive at our destination.

"Well when are we going to get there?" the children chorused again and again from the back suffocated by the surplus baggage we had accumulated during our four day journey.

"There's the lake" said our oldest daughter, Emily.

"There's the border" said our eldest son, Maximilian.

"And there's the chocolate mountains" said our youngest son, Leopold who had somehow managed to smear chocolate on every part of his body including his toes.

The mountains seemed so surreal yet undeniable rising sharply up from the Lake of Konstance. The lake was in fact known as the Bodensee as it was one of the largest fresh water lakes in Europe and we had arrived in Bregenz which was over thirty miles across the water from Konstance at the other end of the "lake". The Bodensee was as calm and refreshing to look at as a cool glass of mountain water on a hot summer's day. The ferry boats which resembled miniature paddle boats were all waiting by the quayside to carry the never ending stream of summer tourists across to Lindau and onwards to the many towns dotted along its well populated shores. Bregenz is the unassuming capital of the Austrian region of Vorarlberg. In fact Austria has only a very small part of the 76 km long Bodensee as all of its flatter northern coast is the southern extremity of Germany and much of the remaining 72 km long southern mountainous shores belong to Switzerland.

The small 27 km stretch of Austria was well developed with small villages now pretty much becoming suburbs of Bregenz. We were heading for the last village of Gaissau at the most Western tip of Austria known locally as the "last elbow" as it was right on the border with Switzerland separated from it by the old Rhine river. The village had survived over development because it was separated from Bregenz by the New Rhine which luckily had two very congested bridges that deterred commuters as the roads were filled with cross border traffic from Switzerland. The other reason for its survival as a pretty mainly agricultural village was its proximity to a protected nature reserve on the lake and as we were to find out its own traditional brand of village community. This last undeveloped but enlightened village was to be our new home on the flood plain of the Rhine at the foot of the Chocolate Mountains.

Well that was our plan but nothing quite works out as expected and a midlife adventure would be pretty dull without a few hard hitting facts to overcome. When romantic dreams start to become reality it is often wiser to turn over the pillow and sleep on them.

"Where are we going to live?" enquired Emily.

This was actually a fairly important question that had not only been concerning our rather more sensible than sensitive teenage daughter. We had planned to live in a rather pretty nine bedroomed traditional Austrian farmhouse with an adjoining Cider House and Dairy set in a lush green film screen mountain meadow. However we had not quite understood the tenancy laws of the Vorarlberg region. Unfortunately it was currently occupied by the owner of a curious Chinese Restaurant which was a converted paddle boat moored indefinitely on the Austrian bank of the old Rhine. Our house was full of his catering staff who found it an ideal sleeping quarters within easy walking distance of the Restaurant.

We had acquired our dream home some two years earlier with an astute Swiss mortgage in Japanese Yen on the condition of having a Chinese tenant. This was complicated enough and we had overlooked the long notice period of six months which effectively meant we had arrived six months too early to occupy our new home.

"Well darling, luckily your mother has the same maiden name as half the people in Höchst and your sister has leant us a flat." Marina looked so relieved.

This was going to be an interesting cosy family experience as the flat was essentially designed for holiday occupation with two bedrooms, a living room and a bathroom. We were extremely thankful to find a home in Höchst but it was quite apparent that swinging cats in shared bedrooms was not on the home recreational agenda although pillow fights would probably become a regular occurrence.

Eventually we all settled down into a hearty supper of 'Maultaschen' soup and began to forget the problems of the pending arrival of our worldly goods. We had read many books on other Midlife Migrants struggling with rat infested ruins or tropical rainstorms and even worse refugee stories so our situation was more a mild case of indigestion than deprivation or starvation. So we struggled against the elements with a glass of wheat beer and watched the sun go down over the mountains.

"We finally made it" I said, slapping an indigenous insect inhabitant that had taken a large bite out of my neck.

"Summer in the mosquito invested flood plains of the Austrian outback does have a certain ring to it. We will soon be enjoying the avalanches of winter but worst of all I have a strange craving from the gale force winds and torrential rain of Lincolnshire."

The English are one of the few races of the world that can laugh in the face of adversity and worse still can also laugh at themselves in the face of a catastrophic disaster. This is probably why for much of my first month in Austria I seemed to the local inhabitants to be an eccentric curiosity to be treated with respect lest I implode in self embarrassment. The television had somehow stereotyped the quintessential English humour as a mixture of silent slapstick comedy and complete insanity. It was further complicated by my inability to speak the local language and my often misinterpreted sign language.

"What shall we do with this gorgeous summer ?" said Marina thoughtfully.

" We could always enjoy swimming in the lake and then there is the question of finding work to feed the nestlings."

The moon settled over the distant snow capped peaks and we tried to pick out the different star formations in an unusually dark sky. The emptiness and silence had been a part of our lives for so long in England but the sound of the church bells and cow bells gave us a feeling of calm even if it was probably just before a storm. Suddenly fireworks shot up into the night sky flickering over the wooded hillsides and illuminating the towns and villages over the Swiss border with all the colours of the rainbow.

"What are they celebrating over there ?" I asked astounded by the sheer volume of noise and fireworks.

"It's Independence Day for Switzerland."

I could see her faint smug smile lit up by the flaming, sparkling rainbows that were showering down over Höchst and I hugged her shoulder like a warm overcoat.

"That's appropriate, although I bet they are just as dependent on the European Union as we are to sell all their wonderful cheese."

"Cheese and chocolate, darling" she said with a contented smirk.

It was sad to have left farming behind but the dependency on agricultural aid was probably going to lead nowhere in England. The farm in Austria that we had purchased was in reality an early casualty of European policy in that the Dairy had been built but no one had ever milked a cow in it. To cut a long complicated farm subsidy story short the building capital was mostly from the European Union but the cows lost their subsidy and the grass they ate was more valuable as hay sold to the non European Union country of Switzerland. This situation with the Common Agricultural Policy is so complex that if you take away subsidy the effect means smaller farms would disappear but also if you increase subsidy the same thing would also occur and most probably on a larger world wide scale.

All that we knew was that farming in Europe was now only for the very large companies or for the slightly eccentric idealist. We fitted into neither category and simply preferred to pursue the romantic middle ground occupied by increasingly penniless aristocrats and those whose family history bore some hopeless fascination with the land. It was interesting to meet several European farming families over the summer who felt the same way and who asked like us what was the point of cheaper European food production whilst half the world population were still starving. This was yet another unresolved anomaly which like the Common Agricultural Policy was impossible to ignore yet probably better dealt with by actually having more expensive food in Europe.

Whatever decisions were to be made there was something that had drawn us to the Chocolate Mountains that was not financial, ethical, political or even sensible which generations of indigenous Bodensee inhabitants had seen before us. The Bronze Age settlers had lived from the fishing, mineral trading and fruits of the soil in their wooden houses on stilts along the lake shore. Roman Empires, and even Swedish invaders had seen the merits of this fertile ground and pleasant climate. We were just another tribe of English invaders and now we too were being seduced by the mountain air.

The children joined us to watch the fireworks and torches on the slopes of the mountain opposite lit up outlining the Swiss Cross. It seemed odd looking across the old Rhine at a country celebrating its independence from Europe and yet it was about to join Europe again. But the torches seemed somehow to enlighten us all about our freedom until a love bite from another particularly large opportunist winged demon drew blood from our naïve aspirations. We retreated into our cosy living space to take the best course for all philosophical dreamers; a good long sleep after a very long journey.

****

"Wake up you boring adults before we loose the sun!"

A pillow flew across the room followed by toe tickling, tummy jumping and if all else failed then screaming and shouting at guaranteed ear drum bursting proximity to the unresponsive adult. Offspring like pets are loving but demanding of their masters and the excitement of a new day made their crowing more irritating than a half strangled cockerel with a passion for reciting Wagner at dawn.

The first of many long summer days began with a breakfast of fresh Brot and several different sliced meats and strange cheeses. The children still insisted on exploring the various breakfast cereals mainly to fight over the free promotional pieces of plastic enclosed with every packet. Of course gradually they were seduced by the continental style of breakfast by delicious jams, mountain honey and chocolate spread and they lived up to their reputation for spreading sticky messes over lips, fingers and almost every wooden surface around the breakfast table.

I still craved for my farmhouse breakfast of bacon, fried eggs, Aga oven cooked sausages, and freshly gathered mushrooms. That was until I began to appreciate the difference between expensive spongy cardboard English supermarket sliced breads produced for mass consumption and the fresh, sweet smelling local loaves served by jovial ladies speaking wonderful farmer's dialect. There was also my romance and deep love affair with the amazing variety of coffee making machines which whirred, gurgled and panted in the extraordinarily early mornings making continental breakfast more bearable.

This love affair was so passionate that I always received strange looks from bewildered house-wives when I attempted to seduce their coffee making apparatus. The machines were quite simply the most beautiful pieces of technology I had ever set eyes upon and our relationship was heated by the noises and steam that gasped from them as they brewed aromatic, titillating and quietly arousing and uncontrollably sensuous fresh coffee. Several coffee machines had been so designed to attract insomnia driven authors with cute slim sophisticated external functions, pouting nozzles and rhythmic grinding noises that would make cheek to cheek flamenco dancers weep with ecstatic joy. The sweet smells and clicking noises that drew me towards them almost made me want to jump up onto the table and tap my feet and flick my fingers in the air.

The idea of a cup of instant coffee or perhaps a filter coffee made me feel like Romeo lamenting the death of Juliet but luckily I knew that these machines could be brought back to life at the soft touch of a button. There was no need for me to take poison when the elixir of love brewed before my tear filled eyes. This emotional union became so intense that my wife refused to have a machine on the grounds that we were moving house but secretly she confided that she feared I might pay it more attention and forget my conjugal duties. However she soon realised that the tiniest cup of expresso coffee could keep a fully grown man awake and attentive even after the longest Schnaps sessions. Luckily for my health these sessions were relatively infrequent as the meaning of the saying coffee will keep you awake all night only ever dawned upon me as the sun rose over the mountains.

But the days began at a reasonable hour during the summer holidays although the working and school times were centred around the sun. As the dawn woke up the village along with the church bells just outside our bedroom window we too began to rise at an hour normally reserved for bakers and dairy farmers. Shops opened their doors as early as six o'clock to catch the commuting workforce who started work an hour later and no matter whether the weather was inclement, torrential rain or freezing cold this never changed. The days of nine to five, bowler hats and umbrellas, and office etiquette at eleven seemed so remote to this workforce of smiling dawn treaders and traders.

Most authors, artists and those involved in the theatre like myself would never consider the prospect of starting work at such an unearthly hour but soon I too was treading the neat fresh swept paths to tread the boards of the local Opera House. It was not exactly a normal Opera and could not really be described as a House as the Bregenzer Festspiele was a performance space like no other in Europe. During the latter part of July and former part of August over 200,000 Opera fans converge on Bregenz for the most spectacular opera set on a stage built on stilts on the Bodensee.

I was privileged to be invited by Kaufmännischer Director, Franz Salzmann for interview to volunteer in assisting promoting the Festspiele to the great British public who despite losing English National Opera's Director to this festival still did not really understand the benefits of travelling abroad for entertainment. The professionalism and high standards of all of the company was so impressive and so much more technologically advanced than English regional theatres that I felt immediately at home especially with the computer and office facilities which were years ahead of even the best London theatres.

The Festspiele is a gigantic four week opera festival which in this instance featured twenty three open air evening performances of La Boheme by Puccini. The scenery was built on stilts on the water and represented an enormous café with five chairs rising to twenty five meters high and three tables forming the three main performance stages. The largest stage was a table of over 50 meters in circumference and underneath it there were various rooms for the Wiener Symphonic Orchestra and two choirs. I met several of the singers some of whom were from England and all of them said it was an experience they would never forget performing on a floating stage to an amphitheatre of over 7000 visitors. I had attended most of the performances over the past twelve years including classic operas like the Masked Ball and Rigoletto as well as contemporary opera like Porgy and Bess but every year the performances just seemed like a magic dream. Something that an Opera lover cannot experience in the intemperate climate of England.

The sun would set over the Bodensee in the first hour of the performance and the lights of Lindau on the opposite shore would twinkle across the water but this backdrop was merely a distraction from the stunning visual and lighting effects spanning over three stages. The audience were quite simply mesmerised as all their auditory senses were filled with beautiful arias from the very best tenor and soprano voices. It was also a spectacle with hundreds of extras carrying anything from multi coloured Christmas trees to giant match sticks that glowed in the cool summer night air. If it rained there was an indoor Opern Halle and another Studio Halle which also promoted performances of other playwrights during the Festspiele and throughout the rest of the year. This was something a young director from a small provincial theatre like myself found particularly attractive. Soon I too was drawn into writing a play fired by the enthusiasm and inspiration of this sparkling jewel in the cultural crown of Vorarlberg.

Whilst waiting for my interview for the Festspiele I had my revelation in more than one sense of the word. A local television crew were filming by the empty stage and requested a volunteer to jump into the water to show that the

Bodensee was still warm enough to swim in and that it was an ideal place for summer holidays. I had time to spare so I willingly removed my suit but when they discovered I was English I was replaced by a bikini clad blonde. What I did not realise was that the technicians café overlooked my performance and as I returned to await my interview appointment I kept getting strange looks and comments on my long legs. It was only when I was having coffee in this café that I realised that my revelation had stimulated more interest than intended.

Moreover I was seduced by this cultural tourism to venture up into the Bregenzerwald to the small village of Schwarzenberg. Some years earlier I had become fascinated by the story of Angelica Kauffmann who had always claimed to have her roots in this tiny village despite spending most of her famous career as a painter in London and Italy. In my humble uncritical opinion, she was to women artists what Mozart was to Austrian music. She was certainly born around that time when being a child prodigy was like being a Hollywood film star except at Royal Court rather than the public picture house. Her paintings adorned the village church alongside her father's work who became her managing agent. She, like her latter day Hollywood stars, slipped up with her fascinating personal life in London. This gripping tale of love, intrigue, and heart break drew me to her and my first play in a foreign language. With encouragement from the village museum and theatre who bore her name, and a charming 'Sachbearbeiterin' from the Landesregierungsamt of Art and Culture, with a broad Yorkshire English accent, I began to write a musical play about her.

The summer was occupied by swimming with the family in a variety of swimming venues by the lake whilst I wrote sitting in the cafes with my treasured soul mates the indispensable cup of coffee and a wheat beer. We basked on the grassy shores of the lake and the children enjoyed the wide variety of diving boards, wooden rafts, playgrounds, treasure ships, water trampolines and slides. The family chose to explore the Bodensee swimming areas as the lake was a wonderful freshwater swimming pool in its own right so we travelled all along its shores in Germany and Switzerland trying out an ever increasing number of even higher diving platforms in search of the ultimate childhood adventure feeding their limitless bouts of vertigo and adrenaline.

The inexhaustible number of new swimming experiences then began to spread to the mountains where we hunted out new swimming pools with spectacular views of the mountain ranges. We would lie in old apple orchards watching mountain eagles soaring high above in the mountain breezes and several would be copycats hurling themselves off cliffs with their multicoloured paragliders. Nature and tourism seemed to adapt well in these surroundings and even the very smallest mountain honey bees enjoyed feeding on the remains of our picnic which always included an abundant selection of local fruit.

"We have all become mermaids" said our now extremely proficient daughter as she dried her dark tanned skin in the suprisingly hot sun.

"Speak for yourself. We're sharks!" replied the two boys as they wrestled on the grass and bared their teeth at each other like wild tiger cubs.

" Well we could go on holiday to Sicily as an old friend has invited us to see his Orange Farm. He's actually from near here in Bavaria and he chose to move further south to enjoy the sunshine" I said watching their excited faces.

So like hundreds of holiday migrants we spent the last two weeks of our summer holidays exploring ruined Greek temples and amphitheatres, Roman villas, Mediaeval cathedrals and Hill top towns with our resident archaeologist. Of course the sea, sun and sand were always going to be popular with children but it was not long before we started to miss the clean streets, orderly traffic and cool alpine ether of Vorarlberg. The oranges and lemons were somehow not as seductive as that first apple in our alpine Eden and we all missed that sweet seductive taste of the Chocolate Mountains.

The volcano of Etna with its blackened dry slopes of cooling lava was such a stark contrast to the green meadows of the Bregenzerwald dappled with hundreds of wild flowers. We could all enjoy the pleasures of swimming in the sea and building sand castles but we soon discovered that most of the rest of Germany, Holland and Italy wanted to also share this indulgence. The almost deserted villages of the Chocolate Mountains were so much more friendly and exclusive and we yearned for peace and quiet.

The small town of Erice set up on top of a high mountain to the west of Sicily had all the qualities we had found in Austria. It was only visited by day tourists coming from the beach resorts so the hotels were able to offer us beautiful views without the hazards of noisy discos and rude guests asking for ridiculous things. I still fail to understand why holiday makers require their own food and drink to be served in another country and use swimming pools when their hotels are on the beech.

The Bregenzerwald was being gradually eroded by this sun seeker madness and it offered so much more service and often cheaper holidays in temperatures more amenable to these types of tourist. It might be considered reasonable to ask for sea, sun and some exploration of differing cultures and cuisine but the people we seemed to meet looked like half roasted dumplings and constantly complained about the cooking. Being a great fan of eccentric hotel owners I enjoyed the Sicilian hospitality especially when one completely harassed manager simply swore at his guests and took to the bottle.

That would never happen in the mountains where even the swimming pool attendant knew what you wanted before you asked for it. Toes in the scorching hot sand full of cigarette ends huddled under expensive sun canopies was a far cry from the immaculately clean orchards of a mountain swimming pool or indeed the grassy shores of the Bodensee. We enjoyed jumping off treacherous cliffs into the clear blue ocean but it was most definitely a holiday experience not a way of life.

"We can see what drew you to this island life."

I said looking out over the green swathes of orange trees and over the pale brown sun burnt plains towards Mount Etna. The evening breeze cooled the pink tiled veranda and the bats and lizards hunted the mosquitoes and dragon flies. The sun had finished painting bright oranges in the cloudless blue sky of another hot summer's day and I could just make out a few lemons shining in the first rays of the full moon.

"I love it here but sometimes I miss the green fields and cows" said Rudolf, our host.

"We seriously thought about moving in next door but ..." I sighed.

"The Chocolate Mountains" interrupted my wife with a giggle.

The plane took off from Catania circling for one last look at the beaches where the children had rolled in the white sand and surfed on blue ocean waves whilst we burnt in the sun. It was a holiday that suited everybody yet it was just a holiday. Doubtless there were photos and happy memories but soon it would be forgotten like most travels abroad and the souvenirs broken or consumed. I turned back to my aeroplane breakfast thinking of black fresh ground coffee, warm soft bread from the baker and thin sliced smoked ham. There is no better feeling than that of a hungry man returning home.

"What are you day dreaming about now, Daddy?"

"My Chocolate Mountain breakfast."

"Well, if you don't want your chocolate I can give it a home."

Max smiled as he munched my chocolate and we flew home.

"PLANE + VOLCANO"

DUCKING, MURMELTIER AND HUNTING FOR SCHOOLS

The social life by the Bodensee was considerably different from our social circles in England although many of the country activities still featured in the calendar of alpine events. There were several gatherings of village communities that we attended over the summer months not least were the vast array of Dorf Fests.

These festivals were all of a fairly standard formula where the adults sat at long benches consuming grilled sausages and meats and drinking vast quantities of beer and Schnaps whilst the children ran ragged around them. Normally the local band would play Volksmusik sometimes accompanied by a variety of strange local instruments like stringed Zithers, brass Schallmeienguga and even the rare long alpine horns from neighbouring Tyrol. The singers would occasionally deviate from the more popular drinking songs and tell ballads about the cow herders and strange happenings in the woods. Mostly these deviations were heckled until the band returned to drinking songs unless they were sung after the beer had run dry. However that in itself would be cause for a ballad as the massive glasses never ran empty for fear of a village lynching. Fortunately the bar staff were mostly beer bellied football players, firemen or local farmers and quite capable of literally throwing out unruly elements.

It seemed that any excuse to have a party was taken up with great fervour and customary enthusiasm by the local Bürgermeister and his willing crew of volunteers including world poverty, centenary celebrations of village landmarks, and even when they brought the cows down from the mountain pastures. The latter of these celebrations had the added attraction of traditional 'Tracht' or village costumes, flower clad cows and sheep and huge cow bells as well as vast quantities of beer and sausages.

"We're going to take you to see the cows coming home for your birthday this weekend" announced my loving spouse arriving back from München with a slightly better new generation Landrover for my birthday present.

"I'm sorry but I have a prior engagement as I have been invited to go hunting" I said somewhat disappointed not to be able to take up the offer of yet another fascinating 'Stammtisch Abend' in the company of other like minded farmers.

"Well then I suppose it's Weidmanns Heil." She giggled in the full knowledge of this customary hunting greeting whilst I scratched my head thinking of how to be polite to wide men whilst staggering up a narrow path on the sheer face of some treacherous mountain peak in pursuit the elusive mountain goat.

We had made the acquaintance of many long standing friends over the years and one such friend was the son of a local industrialist who shared my passion for the outdoors and country pursuits. The banning of hunting foxes was very much on the agenda in England and many Austrians sympathised with the loss of this traditional country pursuit. But many more had an affinity with deer stalking and pheasant shooting as hunting on horses was not really practical in the mountains. His profession tied him to a desk for most of the day but any excuse to go hunting with its associated customs and rituals made us like minded soul mates. The age old practise of hunting drew us together with a common purpose.

"It's your birthday so let's go hunting" Lothar whispered as we climbed out of his car armed with shot guns and a good supply of tobacco.

"What are we going to hunt at this hour ?" I asked thinking it was just about teatime back in England. A time not normally known for hunting but more for a time of relaxing after the chase with a good strong cup of tea.

"Just follow my lead and you'll soon find out."

We strode out across the meadow below the flood banks of the Bodensee following the course of the drainage canals until we arrived at a crop of maize that towered above us. It hissed and rustled in the gentle early evening breeze as though it was trying to say in soft hushed tones that I also must be pretty green in my ignorance of the quacking that could be heard beyond the corner of the field. The yellow corn cobs grinned at us out of the browning tops of an impenetrable cattle fodder crop. The cheeky yellow smiles would soon be devoured in the name of autumn milk production along with the sweet smelling fresh cut grass being gathered for silage by a tractor across the meadow.

A heron flew up into the pink sky and then there was a huge fluttering of wings and duck calls rang out like jeering crowds at a particularly vocal hunting debate. We contributed our speech to the argument with barrels blazing as the flights of mallards and teal flew over us towards the relative safety of the Bodensee. The waterfowl was abundant and extremely well managed and carefully conserved in the nature reserve like the finest of English duck flights. As we stalked along the drainage canals enjoying the hunt I imagined the Bronze age settlers living from the waterfowl, fish and berries around us.

Following in their footsteps was difficult as the landscape and hunting techniques had changed dramatically in the Rhine delta since the seven kilometre long New Rhine had been constructed in the latter part of the nineteenth century. This combined with extensive flood and drainage canals had effectively turned a landscape of flood meadows and reeds into prime agricultural land. Over 1600 men had toiled for five years to divert the course of the old Rhine to a new course between Fussach and Hard after the flood disasters of 1888 and 1890. Where once there was flooded apple and pear orchards, sour meadows and reed beds there was now hay and silage meadows, maize, and, nearer the villages, vegetable crops and apple plantations. The latter intensive cultivation of fruit in long vine like fields was more prevalent on the German side of the Bodensee and in the foothills of Switzerland. Gaissau was left with withered old apple and pear trees scattered around the landscape like sad lonely shadows of the past agricultural system of grazed orchards.

The very tip of Vorarlberg is a long wooded spit called Rheinholz at the end of the old Rhine which had been designated as a nature reserve where even the dreaded motor car was exiled. It was a haven for all types of wildlife with its sour meadows being carefully managed by controlled mowing only once a year. There was also an ancient woodland habitat where we could see Roe Deer basking in the last of the sunlight and we could just make out their knarled stumpy horns to tell us their gender and maturity. The light began to fade as we walked by some fisherman gathering in their nets from their motor boats and a local angler excitedly showed us his wriggling catch.

Fishing had always been a part of life here changing little since the Bronze Age and Felchen and Schleie fish were still the bountiful fruits of the Bodensee. I had once had a strange experience with fishing when we came to visit to purchase our farm. The Bank Manager had interrupted our paperwork with the time honoured 'Mittagspause' which was a two hour lunch break in the middle of the working day. He politely said that he would bring the paperwork to us and that we should go and enjoy the invitation of my wife's cousin, Gerhard, to visit his hut by the Bodensee. Sometime later as we were bathing in the lake a small motor boat came around the reed beds steered by our Bank Manager and his wife. He proudly stepped ashore holding up an enormous pike and his brief case. Then he proceeded to cook it on the barbecue with Gerhard. Fishing was a hobby not to be confused as business.

I told this story to my hunting companion whilst we stood admiring the countless shades of fleshy pink, orange skin, indigo yellow and crimson red colours of the sunset. He laughed and tried hard to encourage me to actually shoot a birthday duck. The bats were diving and weaving all around us chasing the moths who were trying to navigate by the crescent moon. The white swans bobbed sleepily on the lake with their white plumage shining like the ghosts of past fisherman who had been lost at sea. These great monarchs of the water birds only needed to crane their long necks to show that they not man ruled the Bodensee.

"Well we have got quite a good bag and now I think I hear a birthday party going on at Gerhard's hut so let's go and cook them for supper."

We walked out over the reed beds on a narrow footbridge to the hut which was situated on an island in a small copse of willow trees. We proudly showed off our modest bag of teal and mallards to Gerhard and carefully butchered them for the frying pan. I discovered that I shared my birthday with his daughter. We joined the party sitting on long benches talking and drinking until well into the night under the light of flickering candles and that lucky crescent moon which smiled down upon our happy throng.

"If you think that was fun wait until tomorrow" Lothar said as I fumbled with my key in the early hours of the morrow. "I'll pick you up in five hours time and be sure to wear some walking boots and a good coat."

"No problem" I said falling over the threshold of our humble dwelling.

The morning was like any other Summer Saturday morning. The birds and the church bells had begun their dawn chorus with a cacophony of sounds that vibrated around my sore head. I managed to rise focusing on the thought of a new hunting experience and wondering why my socks seemed to always be the wrong way around. Having struggled not to slice my cheeks as I mowed the stubble of a long night away I imbibed several cups of sweet smelling and hangover quenching fresh coffee. My thoughts and body refreshed I jumped into my four wheeled biscuit tin and drove towards my next adventure.

"You made it in good time" Lothar said loading a rifle and binoculars into his car whilst I chatted up his wonderful coffee machine again.

"Where are we going this morning ?"

"We're going up to Lech to get a Murmeltier."

I had no idea what a Murmeltier was but I did remember once being honoured after a long drinking session by the Bügermeister who had given me his card with an invitation to go 'Murmeltier Jagen'. At last, I thought, I might actually come face to face with this legendary animal. But after being given a 'Wolperdinger' in a München Beer Garden I remained cautious in case it was some kind of practical joke. For the uninitiated hunter the 'Wolperdinger'" is impossible to find in the forests of Bavaria. Those who know the Victualien Markt (a famous market in the centre of München) would easily be able to purchase a stuffed "Wolperdinger" as it is made up from the feet of ducks, fur of rabbits, wings of pheasants and horns of roe deer or similar fictional combinations designed to fool unwitting visitors who boast too much of their hunting achievements.

We drove up towards the mountains collecting an old friend of Lothar's father and quite accomplished taxidermist who was to be our mountain guide. He had one of the rare hunting areas above a mountain lake near Lech and his home would make the London Natural History Museum of taxidermist specimens look quite bereft of exhibits. Every space on the walls, ceiling and floors was taken up by roaming grizzly bears, grazing alpine Steinwild and Gams, swooping mountain eagles and of course the infamous Murmeltier.

It looked rather like a beaver with big buck teeth, four fingered claws on its upper arms and five fingered claws on its larger hind legs. It's fur was pale brown almost grey and it lived in colonies high up near the snowline and was noted for it's strange whistling calls. We were after a larger buck male which required patience, stealth and a good shot normally over 50 metres as they could easily catch human scent and dive into their burrows. We had a very good shot with us as rashly I had lost a bottle of whisky to Lothar during shooting practice as he managed to hit the bulls eye with his last bullet.

The car climbed up the mountain passes past the last Dutch and German camper vans of the summer touring season. We drove past the empty hotels of

Zürs which would soon reopen to the throng of the rich and famous, and past the puffing mountain bikers some of whom cycled across the mountains from Germany to Italy. We even passed above the empty ski lifts that would soon resound to the swish of skis and snowboards. It was sad to think that most English tourists had never seen these beautiful mountains without them being smothered in snow as even in late summer the brightly coloured flowers carpeted the landscape. The mountain pass was cleverly conserved by a system of automatic barriers preventing the inexhaustible invasion of the motor car by requiring tourists to use the buses or two wheels or two legs.

Our permitted vehicle climbed on past the Lechersee and a huge Hütte Hostel than slept over three hundred walkers and bikers during the season (which was basically when there was no snow to impede their ever growing numbers). Eventually we stepped out of the car at an old alpine cow shed high above the tiny houses of the highest villages in Vorarlberg which were clearly visible below the wafting mists. The cows had just been taken down to the lower pastures and we found ourselves alone.

It was like those first footsteps on the moon except we could breathe in the fresh unpolluted mountain air, filling our lungs after conquering the world that lay far below us. We were standing so still on a misty daydream moon which was formed from mountain cheese making but I was floating like an alpine astronaut above the unadulterated Arlberg.

The feeling of achievement might not have been as physically demanding as lunar walking but I was breathing real oxygen and it was being quickly absorbed by the blood that pumped adrenaline around my ecstatic body. I would probably never experience moon walking but there was a momentous feeling of gravity in that moment of perfect silence.

The sound of silence was quite spectacular. You could only really experience such stillness if you locked yourself away in a darkened sound proof room yet here we were looking out over rocky crags down at civilisation like the Gods of Mount Olympus. As we walked to the sound of our own heart beats along the alpine pathways, the excitement was magnified by this bizarre noiseless atmosphere.

The hazel walking sticks like the very practical hunting boots, feathered hats and loden coats were tried and tested hunting attire. I pitied the poor Ice Age man nicknamed Ötzi who they had found frozen in the mountain snow as he had only animal skins to protect him from the elements. We were luckier than him as the summer sun still warmed our pale skin but many others forget that the weather can change very quickly in these mountains. Sensible walkers, bikers, climbers and hunters always wore rucksacks with provisions although it would seem that Ötzi had lived from the land and might well have died from the elements too. The pass led up a sharp incline through stunted scrub pines looking out over main central valley of Vorarlberg with its arterial motorway and tunnel system that connected the Bodensee area with Innsbruck and Tyrol. The immense valley was the main connection for this region with the rest of Austria unless you struggled over the mountain passes that snaked painfully sometimes up to over 2000 metres all around us.

At first faint sound of bells from the last cow herds moving down to their winter pastures broke the stillness but then we heard strange whistling noises all around us. With binoculars we could see mountain Gams looking down at us as their baby kids played in the brushwood and circling above us were two Steinadler, the great symbols of this rocky wilderness. Eagles were considered by many civilisations to not only be the masters of the mountains but also to give hunters great vision as their eyesight was greater than our meagre binoculars. They were also the great predator of our quarry and the Murmeltier whistled warnings to each other of the danger in the skies above.

If only they had foreseen the danger of the approaching hunters as we carefully crawled into a suitable vantage point behind a rocky outcrop. Lothar carefully raised his rifle and aligned the cross hairs of his telescopic sight on an unsuspecting male who was standing up on his hind legs to survey for predatory hunters. It was too late and the shot echoed around the steep mountain cliffs. The hunter drew back the bolt of his rifle and the empty bullet case bounced against the rocks. The hunted fell backwards as the bullet entered his heart at a range of eighty metres never again to whistle sweet nothings to his exuberant harem who scurried into the safety of their burrows.

"Weidmanns Heil" said our guide who then proceeded to dissect the fallen prey with the precision of a casualty surgeon.

"Weidmanns Dank" said the vanquished hunter as he looked down at his prey with that strange mixed feeling of guilt at ending a life yet jubilation at being able to take a life in such an effective and efficient manner.

The hunting customs in Austria are wide and various but there is always time for the hunter to honour his quarry. The Murmeltier's soul was now rising up to the great Murmeltier heaven high above its mountainous earthly home but the ceremony of giving the empty corpse the 'letzte Asung' or last meal was performed with great deference. An oak twig still bearing its green leaves know as a 'bruch' was inserted carefully into his buck teeth and another 'bruch' smeared in his blood was taken by the hunter and inserted in the rim of his hat. The guide and the hunter shook hands and complimented each other on a good kill.

Higher up on the grassy slopes the Gams looked down at us with their white cheeks with black blazes making them look like grinning goats. Instinctively they knew the human hunter's written rules of this alpine wilderness that it was not their time yet. The black crows circled waiting to feast upon the intestines as we sat on a grassy hummock eating dried sausages appropriately known as 'landjäger'. The mists of time floated past obscuring the valley far below as we followed in the tradition of generations of hunters before us.

"Do you want to go hunting again ?"

My host said tying his trophy up to his large walking stick to carry it back down the mountain. The Murmeltier's starry eyes glinted in the sun staring at the heavens as it swung by its feet like a captive circus trapeze artist.

As the Murmeltier was making its last performance in the circus of life and death I contemplated this interesting question. It required some quiet deliberation as my mind ran over our experiences again. There was no question of ethics here like in England as it was simply accepted that man had always hunted since he could stand on two legs. The arguments about cruelty doubtless raged where ever humans considered wild animals like their domestic pets but I was looking at one of the wildest places in the Alps unscathed by skiing and untainted by man's urge to develop every part of the planet. The economics of hunting no doubt helped the dairy farmers of the High Alps who paid rent for every four legged beast (a calf counting as two legs) but generated most of their income from hunting rights. There were walkers, bikers, and climbers but they did not support all of these farmers especially in these remote areas which deserved some protection from tourism.

The world of agriculture producing good wholesome victuals for the table seemed so far apart from the demands of tourism especially with the abundance of food and leisure time. It is easy to forget the past when hard cheeses and soft butter on black bread was the staple diet of this region especially when you can even order Chinese noodles in mountain top restaurants. The hunter seemed to compliment the farmer in this last wild preserve of nature. As we passed hundreds of walkers going home to their cosy houses in the valley I wondered who really cared for the Alps after the holidays were over. We stopped to view a proud and handsome bronze steinbock on a rocky plinth with a plaque about the reintroduction of their species thirty years ago to this region; a reminder that there was a place for the hunter here helping to conserve this Alpine paradise.

"Yes. I think that was the best birthday present I've ever had."

"There's more to come" said Lothar with the experienced smile of a hunter that somehow was the same all over the world. The eagles soared high up above our car on the updrafts looking down upon us. They were the natural hunters and could see far beyond human ethics and politics. We only shared their mountainous hunting ground but it was in our blood too. I quietly saluted them wanting to stand high up on a cliff top and cup my hands to cry out my allegiance to this wild place. I swore to come back again. So it was a wild man had found yet another passion beyond his affair with the coffee machine.

****

The summer holidays were over and it was time to spend time hunting for schools for our equally wild children. The education system in every country is different and there was a marked difference between the English and the Austrian school hierarchy. After the tampering of the past half century it was no longer clearly defined in the English system which type of school might suit which type of child as the comprehensive ideology based on the old fashioned principle of all-embracing blanket education of the masses had suffocated individual choice. The rest of Europe had not seen this communal ideology in quite the same way and offered different schools for different pupils on the assumption that from an earlier age than sixteen children could find a happier specialisation that suited their individual choice, talents and aspirations for the future.

The argument about choice has many loop holes. For instance if the state equipped and improved all schools equally then every school could offer such specialist services. Unfortunately the demands of health, welfare and other political expediencies make such an ideal almost impossible and this does not optimise resources or account for individual needs. The system in England was becoming more realistic in its aspirations but we were now living in Austria which was much more along the European formula.

Vorarlberg children left their pushchairs at the age of four to attend Kindergarten until they were six years old. Then they then graduated on to a more formal Volksschule where they began a more formal general education.

This lasted until they were ten years old. It was at this stage that streamlining began based on the ability, potential and wishes of the children and parents. The Hauptschule suited pupils of mixed abilities and those who wanted to go on to study at a Handelsakademie, Handelschule or Polytechnik. The Gymnasium tended to be appropriate for more academic pupils wanting to go on to do the matura at eighteen or go on to university.

"We're not going to stinky Austrian schools!"

"What are we going to do with our wild bunch ?"

"Well, let's start by visiting the schools and hope that they think we've tamed them" I replied as a pillow flew past my ear and my two tiger cubs sprang on my back sending me tumbling onto the painfully hard wooden floor.

The school hunt that followed was exhausting but like all the best animal acts the taming of our tigers was the highlight of our visits. We would try hard to stop them from fidgeting, rolling on the floor or giving the unsuspecting teachers groin injuries. Despite these distractions we managed to secure places for them all in very impressive well equipped and clean schools. It was so far removed from England where under funded schools fell apart before your eyes and parents were required to bail them out with fund raising on an all too frequent basis. Admittedly the schools missed that air of traditional dilapidation that ran right through the English system which was associated with Harry Potter films. However we did manage to find a monastic boarding school that retained this idiosyncratic charm for our eldest son, Maximilian.

"They call it Mehrerau and my father used to go there" said Marina as we walked into the courtyard past an ancient soft barked American Redwood.

"In fact I think several of my ancestors attended the school as it has been around for three hundred years in one form or another"

The monastery and abbey of Mehrerau was run by thirty-three Cistercian monks with the usual rounded bellies and jovial smiles. In the eighteenth century there were in fact originally two schools run by Cistercians on the Bodensee at either end of the lake. The Collegium St. Bernardini was the Austrian boarding school in Bregenz whilst Salem was the more famous German counterpart near Konstanz. However Salem became a lay boarding school after the monks were forced to leave in the nineteenth century. They both offered an Internat education like English boarding schools. Salem boasted more famous pupils including the Duke of Edinburgh and accordingly charged exorbitant fees for pupils aspiring to become future escorts to English monarchs. We loved both beautiful schools but Mehrerau was only four kilometres away on Austrian soil. We could not see that our son Maximilian was going to ascend to the throne of England. More realistically he might descend from yet another terrifyingly high ski jump or diving board.

"Cool. It's a boys school with absolutely no annoying sisters."

"It will mean dormitories but they let you out on Wednesday afternoons and for the weekend after Saturday morning school."

We were shown around the monastery which was originally founded as 'Kloster Bregenz' by the Benedictines in 1092. At its peak the monks owned land from the "young" Rhine near Sargans to the "young" Donau near Sigmaringendorf which was a huge area by any stretch of the imagination. The long history of various different orders who had run the Kloster was only interrupted by the occasional dispersal of the monks by angry monarchs, wars and more recent dictators with short moustaches. Each exile was soon followed by reconciliation and rebuilding but the last such World War Two abandonment had taken its toll and the monastery was busy rebuilding and renovating the extensive buildings.

The dwelling house for the school was a mixture of modern architecture with large glass windowed classrooms on three floors and half timbered medieval dormitories. The extensive facilities bore all the hall marks of a well worn, tried and tested boarding school with over two hundred and fifty years of traditional highly disciplined monastic education. The wider monastery also had a farm producing fresh milk and a butchers shop with traditional fresh and smoked meats. There was also a sawmill and other offices for wood products including a "tischlerei" or woodworker and an architect specialising in distinctive modern wooden living spaces.

The monastery also boasted an unusual vaulted wine 'Keller' which was a popular restaurant serving hearty meals and some local wines and beers fit for hungry monks. There was also a hospital and an exciting new theatre project was under construction.

Most interesting was the boys swimming facilities which took advantage of the Bodensee. This consisted of a traditional wooden bathing hut set in the water on stilts where the children changed and then a set of wooden steps was lowered from the floor of the hut into the water. The swans were enjoying the last of the summer sun and the swallows dived and darted after the flies on the lake which was so calm that it looked like frozen ice.

"Well, ice swimming will toughen you up in Winter."

"Actually the boys go skating when the lake freezes over."

There was a sigh of relief from Maximilian who was imagining having to break a hole in the ice to take a compulsory early morning plunge.

"But what about my school ?" said Emily looking enviously at the vast array of sports grounds and the pony stables.

The hunt for the next school was more difficult to find in fact it was so difficult to find that a kindly lady rode in front of us on her bicycle to show us the way through the winding roads of Lustenau. The school was nearer our village than Bregenz yet so much more difficult to find in a maze of poorly signposted streets.

The New Gymnasium was only two years old and its modern streamlined facade of glass and technologically improved stone-like concrete was an impressive sight as we walked into the atrium. It was adjacent to a huge outdoor swimming pool with diving boards and so many other sporting facilities that a hotel specifically for sports had been built next to the school. It was so far ahead of the crumbling Comprehensive Schools of England with huge open spaces and classrooms with specially adapted furniture more resembling a swish office than a place of adolescent study.

"Welcome to our school it's quite new but we have a long reputation."

The headmaster was wearing a track suit which made us look somewhat over dressed but you could see Emily's eyes light up at the thought of no uniform. Whilst her mind was roaming through clothing shops we went through the more mundane business reserved for parenthood of registering our daughter in her chic boutique of learning.

"Do you have any questions to ask me ?" said the smiling headmaster.

"Well" said Emily sheepishly. "Can I wear anything ?"

"We don't allow our pupils to come to school without any clothes on."

The school was a hit for our normally passive sofa and television prone soon to be teenage daughter. In fact we hardly ever saw her in the weeks to come as she set about grasping the new found freedom of education and consumerism with a vast array of girl friends. Occasionally we would receive mobile telephone calls telling us whose house she was visiting and when she was planning to cycle or roller blade home for some food or pocket money for yet another shopping expedition.

"You adults always forget me. Where's my school ?"

It was tough being the youngest, sweetest and most ticklish child but our wildest son, Leopold was looking forward to his school too. He had found the language barrier most frustrating and hated speaking deutsch except when it resulted in an ice cream or better still, some chocolate. It was true that the youngest child was always the hardest to let go from the parental bonding process but he too needed to go to Volksschule to be tamed after the wild adventures of the holidays. He had been christened in Höchst where Marina's cousins lived and so we registered him at the nearest of the two Volksschule by the church.

"Daddy, they've got a playground and mini golf."

The older children laughed but it was quite true there was a mini golf course with all kinds of hoops and obstacles in an orchard at the end of the school grounds. The idea of future professional Austrian golfers must have been going through the minds of the constructors of this almost brand new edifice to junior school education. Pictures in the library books in Höchst showed black and white photographs of children sitting with their arms folded at their desks in 1934 with a teacher carrying a large cane. But the old school house built in 1836 was now a café, jewellery shop and local government offices.

Another more spacious new purpose built glass fronted school had replaced the dark days of village schooling and the days of the nuns and spectacled grey suited teachers with hats on. A teacher from the pre-war years once told me just how difficult it was to get parents to send their girls to school as they milked the cows and their tiny fingers threaded the famous lace machines that were still running in the village. Luckily the times had changed in favour of other industry and sadly the number of dairies and 'Stickerei' had been dramatically reduced. But without them child labour was now a thing of the past.

The new era of twenty-first century enlightenment even extended to a surreal parental meeting sitting in a circle with a candle whilst the teacher asked the parents to approve her timetable. Soon smiling children with brightly coloured satchels and clothes skipped, hopped and jumped their way to school along with our wild son, Leopold. The good old days of pinching tomatoes and dodging the teacher's cane had disappeared in this suburban ideology of t-shirted teachers with computer laptops. Now low energy school glasshouses grew the next generation of television tomatoes. But we accepted that this was the new way forward for future space and time travellers and nostalgia could become their first science fiction holiday.

"Well that's a relief" I said not quite comprehending the difference in the new Austrian school time which soon began to dramatically change our daily routines.

Schools started at dawn with breakfast at six o'clock which was at least three hours earlier than English schools even allowing for one hour for Greenwich Meantime. My working routines began to change rapidly from working all night to a new pattern of dawn rising with the church bells and screaming children being dragged from their happy slumbers. The nine o'clock drop at the school gate was now seven thirty Austrian time and I soon began to wonder if I would ever see the stars coming out again.

Dawn is a very special time all over the world. Whether you are waking from a freezing cold night in the desert or shrouded in damp mist in a forest or jungle. There were always bird songs. Austria differed slightly from England but 'Singdrossel' or thrushes still sang outside our bedroom window in late summer. The starlings or 'Stars' of the show flocked together and then disappeared in September. I would sit by the window listening to the birds and trying to match them up to 'Landvögel'. Autumn began to change the foliage and the apples and plums fell from the trees and I now missed their familiar calls.

My attachment to my coffee machine began to grow into a caffeine addiction quite out of proportion to the alkaloid stimulation normally associated with these ground beans from continents below the equatorial divide. Like smoking, alcohol or sex addiction I decided that it was time to escape from this affair which was obviously going nowhere. There were meetings on various theatrical projects with composers, directors, sponsors and advisors as the work on Angelica Kauffmann moved painstakingly slowly towards fruition. But I needed to get away from the seductive aroma that reminded me of fire dancing in Africa or sambas in South America. I needed group therapy so I signed up for the church choir.

The Kirchenchor was one of two choirs in Gaissau that met in the Rheinblickhalle. This was a large white village hall built in 1991 and true to its name it overlooked the old Rhine. Gaissau was two kilometres from Höchst and was soon to become our home. It was very different from the bigger well developed village of Höchst with much of the orchards and old houses still clearly visible with their great gable beams and shingle clad walls reminiscent of giant upturned wooden galleons beached beside the old Rhine.

I was early and having squeezed in seven tiring appointments for my project I decided to walk across the covered wooden foot bridge past an old wooden hut that I later discovered was the old customs house. Rheineck was on the other bank of the swollen river with the Swiss flag flying from an old castle sited on a hill above the town. I walked along the tow path watching the cars and trains flying past en route to St Margarethen to the east and St Gallen in the west. Eventually I climbed the steps back onto the concrete bridge which had replaced the old covered wooden cart bridge in 1962.

"Where is your passport ?" said a Swiss border guard with a tight fitting red beret as I approached the strange nineteen eighties Zollamt.

"I'm English and I've been out walking along the river" I replied in astonishment. It was like a Cold War movie set. The checkpoint was made of a suspended glass and steel structure looking like five green house roofs floating over six oversized lamp posts. I expected soldiers to rush out of the customs house at any minute like the Berlin Wall movies but the border guard just strolled over to greet me with a grin on his face. He repeated his question studying my every move.

"Well I'm terribly sorry but I'm English and my passport is over there in the car as I have come here for choir practise" I said further disconcerted by his brusque manner.

"You need your passport to cross the border" he said grinning like a Cheshire cat from Alice in Wonderland.

This cat and mouse game was often played out by border guards in this quieter part of Vorarlberg but at one time it had been a serious matter especially during the second war when refugees were fleeing to Switzerland. The majority of them were Jewish refugees but at the end of the war they included generals from Vichy France and the Third Reich. There were also many stories of gold, coffee, saccharin and silk stocking smugglers but I suppose I didn't fit the brill creamed hair and brown overcoat identity normally associated with the black market 'Schmugglen' of those wartime years.

Later I was told stories of suspicious murders amongst the smuggler gangs and local people joked about houses full of piles of carpets and mysterious rags to riches legends of the local fishermen. The river was often passable on foot too in times of low water encouraging refugees to head for Gaissau and Höchst as a place to ford the river often with calamitous results including drowning or worse shooting. The border was indeed also quite confusing if you had no local knowledge and I had crossed the line.

During the Second World War the local adjutant painted a large Swiss cross on a field on the other side of Gaissau to confuse allied pilots hoping to ditch their planes in the safety of neutral Switzerland. One unfortunate British crew crash landed on the field hoping to be offered Swiss chocolate and a nice cup of coffee only to find themselves prisoners of the Third Reich. One can only assume that they never got the coffee but the prisoners were well treated in Austria with plenty of Red Cross tea parcels. Austrian prisoners of war were not always quite so lucky some surviving terrible conditions in Russia returning home up to six years after hostilities had ceased.

In fact an off duty border guard had occasion to mention to me that the more lucrative traffic in people into Switzerland was more important than anyone coming back out into Europe which was already saturated with illegal immigrants. The more modern problems of drug smuggling on other borders never really affected this border. This was far more notorious for people smuggling but nowadays normally long haul trucks rather than fishing vessels were the preferred bulk transport of the twenty first century.

Fortunately the Austrian border guard with a better fitting green peaked cap joked with his Swiss colleague about challenging people on his side of the road entering Vorarlberg. We then chatted about the wet weather and I passed on back to my choir school thinking I might enjoy their long historic profession of guarding the last Austrian frontier crossing.

I soon rejected the idea as it seemed now to be too similar to traffic wardens. I later learnt several nicknames for 'Grenzer' which were not always polite. However I might add that I always found them begrudgingly helpful. I made a point of always asking them directions whenever I passed over to the other side of the border in case they lost touch with those charming ghosts of their past who used to salute carriages as they thundered over the old wooden bridge. It was not always easy selling motorway passes to frustrated foreign motorists and checking the passports of thousands of the guest workers that crossed into Switzerland every day. It took a very special kind of person to be the first line of a nation.

"Welcome to the Kirchenchor!" said two charming ladies grabbing me tightly under my arms and walking me down the steps to their practise room. "You come with us not the Männerchor as they are old men and we sing in English too."

In fact we sang in Dutch, German, French, Hungarian, Italian and of course Church Latin which still always reminds me of incense induced sleep in a cold church on hard wooden pews. It was definitely a step in the right direction and singing in the bath or in such company is a great stress relief after a long day. Lungs full we sang until we burst.

More of interest to those seeking company was the 'apres choir' adjournment to the large double decked paddle boat beached on the Austrian bank old Rhine and used as a Chinese Restaurant by the same family who were renting our house. It was an amazing restaurant averaging over one hundred guests per night from both sides of the border and I had eaten there many times always impressed by their duck pancakes and noodles.

We sat and discussed the problem I had with coffee machines and once the group had familiarised themselves with the knobs and nozzles we soon passed far beyond therapy into the realms of fantasy. Like many Austrians they were soon into the less subtle intricacies of sexual encounters with puffing and panting machines but more suprising was the reactions of normally coy female contributors to the group. I was most taken by their attraction to vibrating hand held mixers and thought perhaps some food therapy might well be the answer to my coffee addiction.

****

"What a pity as I was just going to buy you a really wonderful top of the range model" said Marina as we sipped yet another coffee together recovering from the early school hours. "I might try out your new vibrating mixer gadget as it sounds exciting and perhaps a little more titillating to my taste buds."

That was enough encouragement for any strong willed man and so I resolved to take some time out of work from the play to play with food. The risk was that I might get fatter but being tall and thin in Vorarlberg only ever got you strange looks in supermarkets and at alpine agricultural gatherings.

I was once eyed up and down by a farmer and his wife after a conversation about their dairy stock at an agricultural gathering. They told me that they admired English bulls but the wife gave me a pinch and wondered if they had enough flesh on them for harsh winters. My day dream of proving my virility in the hay with an alpine dairy maid from the purple cow advert was spoilt by the reality that I had other pressing engagements. Marina pinched me before I fell into my breakfast.

"But first you promised the children to go to school."

"Alright, I'll go that Volkshochschule you keep pushing in Lindau."

"It'll be alright, Daddy. They're German and your school is on an island across the lake. You could go by one of those paddle boats, or the bus, or the train but, knowing you, you'll take your brown biscuit tin" said our smiling daughter.

For the uninitiated in the finer details of Austrian, Swiss or German transportation it is true to say that Vorarlberg is probably one of the few places where transport planning has overtaken the need for motor car commuters. The buses were always clean, pretty much on schedule and reasonably frequent certainly to serve the needs of commuters. The trains were better for longer distances being equally spacious, tidy and punctual to the point of arriving early (especially those servicing Zurich and Munich) but with the added benefit of extraordinary on board service. The planes from Zurich, Munich and Friedrichshafen also serviced the region quite well so I found life relatively easy with most destinations easily reached within a maximum of four hours travel to London.

The German border near to Lindau no longer had the same customary 'Grenzers' standing waiting to check passports. The European Union had opened up like the United States. But unlike the highways of America there were plenty of police present to take their place tucked behind signs and waiting to stop unwary speeding travellers. In fact I saw several accidents on my travels to Lindau notably pedestrians, cyclists and even a police car with an absolutely livid policeman cursing a foreign driver. Considering the separately marked cycle paths, wonderful pedestrian crossings especially for school children, road calming speed bumps, roundabouts, speed warning signs and bus lanes this surprised me as I had driven in Sicily; the land of the suicide driver.

"Welcome to our School for Deutsch" said my seemingly stressed out teacher in a Swabian English accent. "We do not speak English here."

She had to contend with so many languages that she could have rebuilt the tower of Babylon although this biblical reference might be lost on her mainly Turkish Muslim class.

The recently restored barracks made a comfortable school and gave me an excellent insight into the problems of Bodensee immigration. I once wandered up to the social service office in search of coffee to be greeted by kindly staff who spoke excellent English yet rarely had the opportunity to meet English immigrants. The majority of immigrants were still from Turkey which had a long tradition of 'Gastarbeiters'. In the nineteen fifties industrial recovery meant that factories were short of essential workers and at first workers migrated from Italy and further afield over the Alps. By the early sixties they began advertising for workers in Turkey offering free mopeds and accommodation as well as wages up to sixteen times greater than in a mostly agricultural based Turkish economy. The situation gradually changed to saturation point now with whole families and a naturalised generation still disenfranchised but forming well settled communities throughout Germany and Austria.

As in England the cultural differences tended to separate the communities despite over forty years of integration but the xenophobia was still present especially with increasing unemployment and no real need for politicians to care about over ten percent of the actual population as they still had no mandate. My classes never ceased to impress upon me just how difficult resettlement could be and that perhaps I was lucky to retain a popular national identity despite the conflicts of the twentieth century. It was this conflict that had highlighted this ancient problem not only with the Jewish population but also with many German speaking minorities in Poland, the Ukraine and the Czech Republic who had in fact been also originally sold by their Dukes as 'Gastarbeiters' too.

History always reverses nationalism but understandably such pride unfortunately goes down well with beer and Schnaps over a game of Jassen. The price of alcohol is a much more important vote winner not that I preferred Raki and a game of Tavola. Over the next few months I heard many stories of the horrors of persecution and racism as well as jokes about other refugees as there was always somebody feeding the bottom of the immigration ladder. But the school impressed me despite its limitations on my personal need to understand the local dialects of Höchst and Gaissau.

Lindau island was one of the prettiest places to go to school as the town wisely discouraged traffic offering parking outside the old town. I had several occasions to visit the town on business and found the local authority helpful and interested in the history and culture of the Bodensee. The harbour has a stone Löwenmole Bavarian lion sitting on the wall of the harbour opposite an old lighthouse reminding visitors that Lindau was in fact the Freistaat Bavarian claim to the lake not a part of Swabia which claimed the remaining part of the northern German coast. It was always nice to watch the mist rising as the sun rose over the water and the Ferry Boats sounding their horns as they avoided the fishing and sailing boats. The swans simply ignored them all as they paraded around the harbour basin.

Strolling through the cobbled streets I enjoyed the market stalls and two adjacent churches. Most of all I loved the Theatre which was noted for its puppet shows and the bench by the strange old Rathaus which was my favourite haunt. The summer tourists left and the streets became quieter and I could sit starry eyed by the tall Diebsturm watching people rushing to work whilst I awaited my school to open. The Casino at the end of the town was probably the only sad but conspicuously twenty first century alteration to an otherwise quite unspoilt example of a sensitively modernised mediaeval island town. The island town of Lindau was truly an unspoilt living landmark on the Bodensee although all around it the invasion of intemperate industry and its associated atrocious architecture was just one short swim away from despoiling my Mediaeval day dream.

"What do you like about our town?"

I was interrupted from my early morning contemplation by an official looking lady carrying a board. It was a difficult question as I loved most of it from an architectural perspective and the scurrying citizens were generally charming but perhaps a little short of Bayern time to reflect upon her Swabian statistical survey.

"I suppose it must be the timeless silence" I replied nonchalantly in English.

"I'm so sorry to disturb you" she said a little confused by my response.

"I mean I love it all but especially the stillness in the morning" I emphasised.

She smiled and tip toed away on her high heels to interview a less ethereal tourist.

"TIP TOES"

BAVARIAN COWBOYS, APPENZELLERLAND WANDERTAG AND CRAZY CHORISTERS

The end of the summer holidays often leaves adults at a loose end and it is the ideal time to enjoy Ausflugs or outings from the many and varied clubs in Höchst and Gaissau. There were many clubs to choose from and I tried several of them. My favourite was a Vorarlberg Cowboy Club which was called quite appropriately the Pro-Western Club.

The two villages used to boast over thirty seven guest houses and bars. The motor car and the associated laws on driving whilst at least thirty times over the limit had reduced this number. There were now less than twenty although newer farm diversification grants had enabled new local Gaststube selling farm produce to replace some of them. However there was one saloon bar that stood out amongst all the rest simply because it was so unusual and almost certainly unique to the two villages and most probably Vorarlberg too.

The Saloon lived up to its name in every detail from the swing doors right through to the clomping cowboy boots on the wooden floors. It was open on two nights per week all year around and it was always full with would be and wannabe cowboys and cowgirls. The bar was next to a large riding stable and there were always different events but the most enticing attraction was Egon the cowboy, often confused with his brother, Lothar the hunter.

He had virtually grown up in the saddle and had decided to bring back some of his American riding experience to his home village. He started the bar in a barn with parties after his western riding shows in the early nineteen nineties. He was so renowned for his western riding skills that he was once called in by the fire brigade to lasso a loose cow that had strayed into the waters of the old Rhine which ran past his bar.

Time overtook him and he soon hung up his saddle as the bar grew into two bars. Like all good cowboys he then took up the guitar to entertain his fans. I had seen other Bavarian Cowboys like Fred Rae get even more inspired converting stables into cowboy towns and singing wild west songs whilst mounted on a horse with no reins. But Egon was a much more modest Vorarlberg Cowboy preferring to swing onto the saddle of a large motorbike like many modern cowboys of the really wild west and play a good tune.

The image of galloping cowboys chasing wild steers with lassoes had been long since replaced by Harley riders in sun glasses riding through the mountain meadows to the sound of country music and cow bells. However just occasionally it was fun to revisit those wild western legends and both my two sons and myself were most definitely not going to miss the club's annual visit to Pullman City.

"Will we see real cowboys and will they speak German ?" said Max excitedly.

"It is in Eging am See in the Bayerischen Wald so I suppose they'll speak Bavarian but I bet they think they're real cowboys" I replied sipping a wheat beer.

It was a long way to near Deggendorf in our borrowed red fifty seat stage coach but we were in fact both wrong. Pullman City was far better than the real thing in the United States where I had spent some time travelling in the nineteen eighties. It was admittedly a special weekend for Trappers and Indians but it was far more fun than the arid hot sweaty plains of Texas and who cared if it was set in the far more beautiful green and pleasant Bavarian countryside. Everybody looked at you strangely if you spoke English as real cowboys spoke 'Bayern Sprache' even the Indian Chief spoke 'Canadian Hoch Deutsch'.

"Ninety percent of illness is in the head and meditation and affinity with your natural environment will cure your spirit" said Hunting Wolf sitting in the middle of his huge Mandan Earth House. He played his wooden flute to an entranced audience of want to be Wild Indians from the Eastern Block.

"See your spirit and respect everything around you just as I am still learning from my Buffaloes" he said to an entranced assembly of assorted Salvic speaking Sioux Indians.

We later saw his buffaloes charging down the main street in a very comprehensive American History Show with sword fighting Civil War cavalry, stage coaches, steer running, comely dressed Trappers in their firs, hides and skins and of course superb Indian dancing in eagle feathered costumes. We lived, breathed and ate all the Wild West of beautiful 'Bayern' could offer us and then drank in some more.

The town was in itself an experience with huge saloons with live music and several restaurants serving anything from spiced Mexican dishes to Indian horse or buffalo steaks. The merchandising opportunities were not lost on the children who were armed and ready for action within minutes. The accommodation accounted for every possible taste with a huge modern Holiday Village, Caravan Park, Wooden Block Huts, Indian Tipis, Fort Pullman Barracks and even an original Palace Hotel in the Main Street boasting a whirlpool spa in place of the old tin bath tub. Being a Bavarian cowboy could be as uncomfortable as you wanted but we opted for a luxury holiday house.

"So you are a brave ?" I said cautiously to a scalp hungry Indian.

"Our club is based on the early settlers and we try to dress the part" he retorted.

He certainly looked like a truly wild brave with a woven hide jacket, his beaded shoes and emasculate handbag, and the mandatory bear claw necklace and feathered head band.

"I joined the Hunting Wolf meditation yesterday and finally saw my spirit" he said looking out with glazed eyes across the crowded smoky saloon bar. "It was an Eagle flying high above and I could see into my soul."

"Do you have any Indian blood or genetic links with any of the tribes?"

"He is from near Vienna" said his girlfriend clad in a huge brightly coloured woollen rug dripping with wonderful beads and carrying a beaver skin hand bag.

It was easy to see the attraction of this hobby as it was a pleasant mixture of nineteen sixties peace pipe flower power and a politically correct excuse for wearing of furs and jewellery. I enjoyed my infinite supply of jugs of beer and admired the wide variety of scrupulously detailed costumes right down to the hand made shoes and regimental buttons. Staggering out of the darkened den of iniquity I nearly fell over Marshal Big Joe whom I had seen in several other cowboy theme parks in the past.

"It is so professional here" I said trying to excuse myself.

"I love it here. They treat actors professionally" he replied brandishing his gun at my groin.

I hoped he was not referring to me as I had rather overlooked him in the stampede for the little men's room. He was a well known dwarf actor whom I respected for his unselfish commitment to live wild west entertainment rather than being seduced by the more lucrative world of television and films. He smiled at my obvious embarrassment as being his size had several advantages in his profession as nobody failed to remember him and everybody wanted him to rise up to the zenith of his chosen comedy career.

I wandered down to the Mandan Earth House to listen to Hunting Wolf again talking to two presenters from a German television station. His speech was rather wasted on the young modest presenters whose minds and spirits were elsewhere dreaming of starring in their own spaghetti western. The fact that Hunting Wolf too had not succumbed to the media impressed me far more than the media hype of the shows that day. I was happy to enjoy the blatant commercialism of purchasing autographed cards from the real actors and even from the excellent Blue Ridge Mountain Band that night. It was the physical affinity with my childhood Cowboy and Indian dreams that I was buying not a television repeat.

The long night of singing and line dancing was rounded off by the campfire listening to real live wannabe Bavarian Cowboys breaking wind on another Ausflug from their village fire station. One of them caught an escaped white rabbit and held it over the camp fire by its scruff toying meancingly with his hunting knife.

"We could cook it and use its pelt" said the proud catcher.

"Let it go we've got soused herring and Schnaps" said his companions. "We eat white sausage not white rabbit for breakfast."

As we drank our way home to Austria listening to the folk songs sung by off duty members of the church choir, I day dreamed about watching the Indian dancers and sitting by the campfire under the stars. It seemed so far away from the huge open prairies that those early settlers pioneered yet I knew that nobody except them could live that experience and the dead cannot speak except through their spirits. We had all experienced something at Pullman City and imbibed a considerable amount of their spirits.

"Let your spirit run freely !" I toasted as I enjoyed another high spirited Schnaps.

We passed München where the "Wiesen" or Oktoberfest was in full swing with the Sunday 'Trachtenumzug' parade with bands, dancers and shooting clubs in their village or town 'tracht' costumes and horse drawn carts with floats depicting traditional crafts and church yard scenes. This was the Ausflug that most tourists see in Bayern but I smiled to myself thinking Bavaria was more than just "Lederhosen". It was a Freistaat where you could be whatever you wanted, wherever you wanted and probably with others who wanted the same dream. After all its last great King Ludwig had built fairy tale castles which attracted thousands of tourists every year. Pullman City was simply an extension of the Bavarian ability to not only realise but also to enjoy living and making their dream come true.

****

"The Wandertag begins at eight o'clock by the school"

The lady on the end of the telephone was the parent organiser for our son, Leopold's class outing. It soon became apparent that male parents rarely organised anything to do with their offspring as the villages still very much cultivated a male bread winning society. We were going to Walzenhausen in Appenzellerland where it was only a few decades ago that women had finally secured the right to vote.

There were also more practical reasons for the division of parental responsibilities as many mother's explained looking at me as though I was a gay transvestite or worse, possibly a bisexual closet mother. These included the reality of the school hours which were definitely not helpful to working parents especially the 'Mittagspause' for lunch of up to two hours right in the middle of the working day and also the totally unpredictable afternoon school hours. The idea of house wives was very much a cultural part of the two villages but in contrast to some Mediterranean countries the men were not allowed to sit out in the sun during working hours, at least, not where a spouse might see them.

"But you're a Papa!" said one of the children in excited anticipation of the long awaited Autumn Wandertag. There was plenty of giggling at my recently acquired cowboy hat and strange rubber wellington boots when I told him to fall back into the line.

Our small group of two classes of twenty five children set off on the bus to the border at Gaissau and then over the old Rhine into Switzerland to the railway station at Rheineck. As we waited on the railway station the teacher pointed to a small electric train comprising of a single carriage with an elderly smiling driver standing beside it polishing the windows. It was hard to smile after thirty eight years as the driver of the "Zahnradbahn" when you considered the literal translation involved teeth, bicycles and trains and everybody then joked about your teeth. We avoided these tired jokes and clambered aboard. I enjoyed the views and the incomprehensible vernacular of the local driver's commentary. Steadily we bit our way up the almost perpendicular track on its rotating metal teeth climbing to over six hundred and seventy metres above the Bodensee.

This small village of Walzenhausen had become a popular escape for our family on wet or foggy days as it boasted some of the most spectacular views of the Bodensee and more importantly was often in the sunshine when the clouds covered Gaissau and Höchst far below. The Hotel by the station was a hidden treasure as it was never full and had a four star view and a deserted indoor swimming pool that the kindly manager had permitted us to swim in above the clouds on wet days during the summer. Leopold and I looked smiling at its strange mixed architecture of a typical Victorian Spa Hotel and a seventies concrete apartment block. But our hopes were dashed by the jolly voice of the teacher who had spent sometime exploring the foothills of Appenzellerland and was determined to take us walking in the fresh Swiss mountain air.

"We're off to walk to St Margrethen which is opposite Höchst through the woods."

We strode off around the hill admiring the stunning one hundred and eighty degree views across from the Pfänder towering over Bregenz to the pretty island town Lindau in Allgäu round to Friedrichshafen in Swabia. There were in fact several other excellent walks including a trail known as the Witzweg or Joke Walk in the opposite direction towards Heiden which was marked by plaques with very old and dated Swiss jokes on them. The Swiss are most definitely not known for their humour but this two hour walk linked up to another interesting little Bergbahn train to Rorschach and a small ship took an hour to ferry you back along the Bodensee to Rheineck.

However our hike went the other way through the forest and woodland playgrounds stopping for "Pause" or lunch at a hut overlooking a vineyard. During lunch I watched the grape pickers moving along the vines picking the green grapes and leaving the red grapes for a later harvest. I had visited several small vineyards in this region and much of the wine never reached the supermarket shelves mostly being consumed by hobby farmers or Swiss nationals as export taxes prevented wider foreign appreciation. But it was the small poster that attracted my attention pined to the log cabin which advertised a cow show in Walzenhausen.

"We'll take all the children again" said Marina as we read the leaflet. She had attended the Returning of the Cows from the mountain pastures in Schwarzenberg in the Bregenzerwald and had enjoyed the traditional costumes and floral decorations.

"It'll be fun and certainly a bit more ethnic than the cowboys but they wear similar hats and you won't understand their dialect at all."

The school trip wound its way down through the wonderful hardwoods to St Margrethen whilst I made hazel whips and stone axes for the wilder children. St

Margrethen was the rather dull town opposite Höchst that always seemed fast asleep. It had little to offer except a summer swimming bath and winter health spa. We even passed over the border without encoutering a single soul let alone a friendly acknowledgement of our feat. Back safe on Austrian soil we made our excuses to the teacher in the knowledge that the next day we would be back in Walzenhausen for another family Wandertag at the 'Viehschau'. At last I could meet real farmers again and enjoy Appenzellerland discussing the future of the dairy industry in the Alps with fellow livestock lovers.

However the large plastic cow staring at me across the dewy meadow the next morning was a sign of just how little I knew. We parked in a large cow pasture near Lachen another one hundred metres above Walzenhausen with an extraordinary panoramic view over the Bodensee. It was so different because we couldn't see anything of the lake as it was as though it had gone to sleep under a duvet of soft fluffy luminescent white clouds. We were definitely far above Cloud Nine notorious in literature for being the place of reference for lunatics and eccentrics and there we sat for most of the show milking a huge plastic cow surrounded by indigenous cowmen chewing crooked 'Krummer Hund' cigars.

We were actually in cow heaven where they all had to pass their final judgement. This judgement was not quite the same as in purgatory but it was a deadly serious affair with much cow slapping and teat pulling. Some of the men chose to wear their traditional red flower embroidered waistcoats and black boater style hats garlanded in flowers. Their silver chains twitched as they checked their equally elaborate flower enamelled time pieces waiting for the judges decision for the best milking cow. Something so important that it had drawn them all out of the beer tent where they had been merrily laughing and jodeling over their bottles of "Most".

This apple cider drink was quite potent and suprisingly there was no other fresh apple juice despite being the apple harvest time. So after making do with some goodly samples I too wandered out to watch the spectacle. I watched the final cows being paraded before an attentive crowd of farmers leaning on the plastic cow which was a more steadying influence than the real thing. The judge was very particular in his choice of winner justifying his decision based on the sheer size of the udder, the position of its teats and even the quality of the milk right down to its butter fat and protein content.

I then jauntily wove my way through the crowd avoiding the large cow pats to try out my new language skills on one of the cowmen. Pretending to examine his large cow bell and ornately carved and hand painted milk pail, I opened the conversation with a slightly overt but friendly English greeting.

"How do you do. I love your red waistcoat" I slurred trying not to look at his earring lest I be misinterpreted as being overtly forward.

The rest of the farmers halted their intense argument about the cow that had clearly won because it was heavily in calf and studied me inquisitively.

The young cowman looked at me as though I had come from another planet examining my clothing and somewhat bandy legs as the alcohol seemed to have taken away any control from my nether regions. His bright white teeth gleamed in the afternoon sun obviously matured from fine milk teeth and the large doses of calcium in his unpasteurised milk. His lips moved as he turned to joke with his friends but I stood transfixed listening to what could only be described as some form of Appenzeller Arabic.

"Sorry, but I'm afraid I don't understand you at all."

Flushed pink with embarrassment I looked down at the silver cow buckles on his black leather shoes realising that communication with the plastic cow was probably going to have higher probability of comprehension. I turned sheepishly around gesticulating towards the plastic cow with both hands making a milking motion.

This they all understood and I promptly left them listening to the echoes of their alpine laughter over my shoulder. I thought to myself that at least teats were international. Maybe if I had stayed there longer we might have gone on to 'udder' the odd familiar word but dairy quotas and yields might require the help of a translator. As I spotted my official translator heading across from the long lines of brown bovine udders, I contemplated the comedy of the cattle men's confusion if she had been translating my sign language.

"Did you see the young boy with his garlanded young heifer reciting that lovely poem about his favourite cow" said Marina as we drove back down to Gaissau.

"No I was trying to communicate with the natives" I retorted.

"Bet you had to try sign language" she said wipping off a smelly cow pat.

I demonstrated my cowman communication technique pulling hard at invisible cow teats to peals of laughter from the children. But somehow I knew that I would return to this strange land of Swiss wine and cheese. Now I had seen how the cows were milked and that cheesy cowman's grin had made me feel at home. The thought of his craving for teats and my craving for aromatic coffee was running riot in my mind. A strong cup of expresso was an excellent medicament to 'Most' overindulgence and fresh milk from the fridge was as far as I would get in practising my milking technique.

****

I now loved the mountain 'jodel' but not as much as singing with the church choir whose Ausflug was next on my list. When I heard at evening practice that the weekend was going to be in Switzerland again my heart leapt at the thought of more cheese, wine and merriment. I excitedly told my patient wife who promptly reminded me of my work but giggled as I reminded her of my new found Swiss sign language skills.

"You can go if you promise to finish your food project."

She was referring to my long list of engagements with local producers in Höchst to try to understand more about food culture in the villages. We had decided that the best way to understand Vorarlberg farming was through its produce especially as we were waiting for our own farmhouse. So I had started to learn some of the old techniques notably those which I felt strongly might die out with the onslaught of the relentless supermarket.

Actually the Swiss Ausflug was an interesting flying visit to some of the more famous vineyards in the south of Switzerland. We crossed the winding mountain passes, passing villages with wooden huts on stone mushroom stilts and stopped to sing in the echoing Felsenkirche of St. Michael in Raron (which was a huge 6000 cubic metre cavern dug out of the rock in 1974). Finally we reached the vineyards which were nestled in a gigantic valley bowl surrounded by the towering mountains of three nations of Italy, Switzerland and France. We hiked through the vineyards above Salgesch looking out over a vast checker board of hundreds of ripened vines that had been growing grapes (notably Pinot Noir) in the magnesium rich soils under the rim of the Finges woodland slopes since the Roman settlers. The region was now famous for its Premier Grand Cru most probably encouraged by the Knights of Malta who had settled there in the thirteenth century. As the bells rang out at the end of our long hike admiring the autumn leaves and ripe red grapes I felt that I had seen another side of Switzerland. The northern land of red waist-coated cowmen seemed far removed from these multi cultural, multi-lingual French and German speaking wine lands.

We were literally on the southern tip of Switzerland and the outdoor café chatter of France to the east and hard cheese pronunciation of German Switzerland created an enjoyable bizarre blend of customs and traditions. The hotel owner generously provided us with samples on our hike encouraging much singing and merriment but it was further rounded off by an evening wine tasting and cheese raclette with a Grand Dignitair in the great wine cellars of Provins. The choir sang and danced until the hotel manager dispatched us to bed but I had enjoyed the tipping of my toe in another very different world from Vorarlberg.

We cooled our hangovers early the next morning looking out at the Matterhorn from a smart hotel high up in Zermatt and enjoyed walking in the rain through the pretty resort gardens of the old spa town of Montreux by the Grand-Lac of Geneva. The French speaking regions certainly enjoyed luxury and civilisation in comparison to the wilder mountains of the North and our equally wild Vorarlberg choir. It was rather like the Saxons and Normans meeting at the Battle of Hastings to decide on the future of Britain. I sat back watching with a cup of French coffee, an English Sunday Newspaper and a German Schnaps having finally understood a little bit more of the Chocolate Mountains.

"They're a strange bunch aren't they?" said an English voice behind me.

"Yes they're from Vorarlberg over the mountains" I retorted.

"Reminds me of rampaging Manchester United football fans" he grumbled.

"Actually they sing a lot better and go to church on Sundays" I said sarcastically.

We laughed at our typically cynical deeply satirical brand of English humour and then exchanged the usual pleasantries of Englishmen abroad. Looking out over the Lac Leman towards the mountains of the French Haute-Savoie we could see a French boat steaming over the rain spotted water towards the quayside near the café.

"Looks like more French invaders coming to spoil our Sunday papers" he said sadly.

"Well I'm Anglo-Saxon. I'm off back to join the wild untamed and unashamed choir."

I smiled thinking of how many football fans would convert to Catholicism if they knew just how much fun it was in a Church Choir. Singing on the terraces of a thirty to forty thousand seat stadium certainly was an amazingly uplifting feeling but those kind of stadiums did not exist in Vorarlberg. Church Choir was the next best thing and without those nauseating total body tattooed nationalist thugs and shaven skin heads singing racist chants. Even though we were not cross dressed in copes or singing Church Latin out of key you could guarantee somebody would empathise with this chorister's 'Ausflug'. Not that this was standard Church Choir dress at all. Of all the Autumn Ausflugs, I would not have billed the Church Choir much above a school excursion but never judge a choir by their cover.

As the Schnaps was being circulated in a harvest festival basket by a smiling lady whom you might tip your hat to after church, I looked down the bus at the singing and laughing throng. The choir had sung halleluja as we swerved down hair pin bends, and told jokes that would make the priest roll off his pew in the confessional box. It was definitely a higher rating on my Ausflug top ten than the Cowboys. I smiled a knowing smile as the lady passed by again with an empty basket. The picture of her playing accordion to forty merry choristers in the vaulted cellars of the winery was indelibly stamped in my mind.

Drifting off to sleep as we swept down the Autobahn past Zurich my mind enjoyed a magic moment as I jigged along the long wooden tables to the sound of some vaguely recognisable Scottish ballad. The guitars were still strumming and harmonious voices of the choir filled my ears. Maybe I was dreaming or had it really happened in a fit of debauched euphoria. Who cared as we weren't smashing anything just singing and dancing. This was the fundamental difference between destructive football hooligans and fun loving choristers which made this Ausflug unique.

"What did you think of the choir ?" said Marina on my return.

"Well they sing, they dance and do pretty much everything."

"So it wasn't all wings and white copes."

I smiled sipping my treasured Monday Morning Coffee remembering the nun joking over the vast array of wine tasting glasses in front of her. She couldn't speak over the din of the choir so she just mimicked her joke about having angels wings. She cleaned her steamy glasses and winked at me as her wine glasses were refilled.

THE BUTCHER, THE BAKER, THE FIREMAN AND THE CANDLESTICK MAKERS

The Vorarlberg hospitality had taught me that the nights were long and the mornings were very short indeed especially as I had agreed to undertake my food project. This involved requesting various shops and indeed village personalities to let me behind the scenes to glean a few secrets about some of the food that was prepared in the two villages.

"Excuse me but I am an English writer and big and strong. I would like to help your shop" I said to the rather tired looking owner of a new local Farm Shop.

It was very early in the morning and he was sitting in his cellar with his coffee surrounded by piles of crates and so I tried to use my completely inadequate sign language to illustrate my point. This must have made matters worse as he looked at me wondering if I was intoxicated or worse still from some mysterious local Mafia or a Union lynch man.

"We have an insurance problem which I hope you understand."

I walked back home feeling dejected as I had really wanted to help in the shop as it was always staffed by kindly ladies with wonderful local dialects. But I kicked the piles of tinted leaves trying to hide my disappointment like a child looking for some fun playing with that wonderful Autumnal stomping, swishing and rustling sound. It is often at these moments that inspiration is found in the gusts of wind that pick up the leaves and swirl them around your otherwise hopelessly bereft and empty head.

"I'm going to go back to basics and go to the real craftsmen and learn from them. After all most of the produce in that shop isn't actually made there anyway."

I got a strange look from a passing stranger who seemed confused by such a long English greeting. Politely she returned what she deemed as a long good morning with a short traditional curt reply and then hastily scurried off in case I continued the conversation.

The Butcher's Shop was an oasis in a village that was changing fast into a shopping desert where Supermarkets were literally stifling the traditional shops. The warmest of greetings assailed me as I stepped over the marbled threshold and I was immediately granted my request and invited to meet the rest of the charming Blum family.

"We'll show you real butchering if you would care to join us for an hour a day this week. You can teach us a bit of English whilst we chop" offered an ever smiling Herr Blum who was in fact the son of the equally cheerful 'Opa' Blum who also was helping him butcher some fresh pork. "Today is Slaughter Day but we no longer kill the animals here since the regulations made it too expensive but we still select the best live beasts from the local farmers before they are dealt with in Dornbirn."

Over the next few days I got to know the family quite well and learnt a great deal about butchering, sausage making, and meat smoking. The Vorarlberg housewife that went to purchase meat at this butcher's shop knew that this was the place where the meat was clean and fresh and that it only served the best quality fat free products. Supermarket meats were really a waste of money and invariably of inferior quality with poorer cuts and little attention to details as the production was often mechanised and automated.

The making of white calf sausages was a very good example of this personal attention to detail that really could not be replicated in Supermarkets. The sausage meat was always selected from the best ingredients and every secret recipe was lovingly measured out with fresh herbs according to a tradition passed through the family. The sausage meat was mixed to the perfection of the butcher not down to the allotted machine time of the factory manual and all the skins were carefully selected unlike the condom conveyor belts of English mass produced branded sausages. Every string was carefully checked and hung on racking ready to be gently cooked in immaculately clean steam ovens.

"Would you like to help me today?" asked the pretty butcher's daughter.

"The whole family works here and that's the way we like it ever since we built the shop in 1962. My daughter became a Meister Butcher in 1987 but my two sons preferred to study for another profession. Not bad for a country butcher and they are all my pride and joy."

He smiled at his warm and voluptuous wife who grinned and blew him a little kiss. I assumed that the way to his heart like mine was through a plentiful fresh red meat diet not to mention the nice topping on his desert menu.

His daughter led me into the smoking room where there were two massive smoke ovens. One was the cold smoker and the other was the hot smoker with an additional gas burner to provide heat as well as smoke from the smouldering sawdust. There was also a steaming 'Kochschrank' full of 'Rouladen' and 'Schüblinge' and a 'Backofen' where they cooked 'Braten', 'Schinken', 'Leberkäse' and 'Spanferkel' which, to an untrained full blooded Englishman, sounded and smelt delicious. We loaded racks of 'Landjäger', 'Wienerle' and 'Bauchspeck' for the smoke ovens until the smoke overcame me.

"How do you survive in this smoke?" I coughed.

"Well firstly I don't smoke cigarettes anymore and secondly I don't cry as the smoke gets in my eyes" she laughed as I gasped for air at the window.

"It's a cure for meat, smoking and love" I spluttered.

"Ah, you should try baking. I married a baker and baker's have a much hotter job. Not so much smoke but plenty of sweat" she said grinning gorgeously.

Being curious and somewhat amused by the idea of a baker holding some amorous secret aphrodisiac formula that could attract such a comely butcher's daughter, I decided that I should try out the village bakery. Like the butcher's shop the choice was reduced to two shops from a potential four shops up until ten years ago. I decided that once again small shops were a better option as they were much more likely to have more handmade quality and choice than the large baking factories. I rode off on my bicycle in search of fresh air and a baker with that extra special sex appeal.

****

"Welcome to our humble bakery" grinned Alfons Bereuter as he packed his pipe for his pre baking coffee time smoke.

It was two o'clock in the morning and I had been humouring his two assistant bakers as they mixed and pounded dough for the baker to bake in his antiquated but trusted four tiered oven. The two assistants were both experienced at their job which required the speed and accuracy normally attributed to only the finest Manchester United centre forwards. They had huge bakers hands that could chastise naughty children and I joked about my two sons being like the naughty fairytale characters of Max and Moritz who were spanked soundly by a baker. Just as they had worked up a sweat preparing over fifty different types of dough mixes and proving them on rolling trays for the oven, the baker had made his entrée with their welcome Kaffee pause.

"I have finally found some soul mates who understand my craving for coffee" I said trying to translate my pigeon English into discernible early morning deutsch.

"The best morning coffee is always at home after work."

The assistant bakers laughed and winked in the direction of the baker who grinned and puffed on his pipe trying to focus his mind on the job ahead of them. This was a small bakery where the personal touch was not just in every single fresh bread and cake that he baked but like the butcher the pride ran right through to selecting and sorting the finished products for his shop and hotel customers.

I followed the process throughout the morning until finally my eyes began to close from the lack of sleep and heat of the oven. I watched the baker adeptly slide his long "schaufel" into the oven with precision timing always bringing out the bread perfectly baked and landing them like hot coals on the long wooden "brett ". Being tall I often had to duck as the assistant bakers carried these uncommonly large and heavy boards to the cooling room slung over one shoulder like waiters at an early morning feast.

"You have kneaded and rolled over one thousand pieces of dough and your hands are so huge. I bet your wife enjoys your massage technique."

"That's what we meant about morning coffee" said a merry baker clapping the flour off his hands. "Why do you think the Meister has had seven children?"

I smiled to myself as I walked home in the rain just as the sun was beginning to cheer up the miserable dawn and the colourful Autumn leaves floated cheerily in the puddles.

I hugged my bag of fresh 'Semmel', 'Igel' and the baker's 'Nussbrot' speciality which the jolly Meister Baker had given me for entertaining the unsung workforce of the night. The baker's work was normally only acknowledged begrudgingly by hungry children at the breakfast table or perhaps on feast days when he baked 'Nikolas brot', 'Königskuchen' or 'Osterhasen'. I had enjoyed watching him make so many other things with wonderful names like 'Pärle', 'Mischbrot', 'Kornbrot', 'Jausen Schindel' and 'Nusskipfel'.

Out of the corner of my eye I caught 'Puschel' the baker's cat watching me keeping it's sixteen year vigil looking after the mice for the Meister. Alfons Bereuter was the twenty third baker to own the bakery since its construction in 1904 and doubtless knowing cats and their nine lives there was probably a similar tradition of baker's cats. It lovingly licked its tiger stripped fur. I wondered just how many bakers kittens there were now in Höchst. It disappeared under the flour sacks but not before giving me a Cheshire Cat grin. I pulled up my collar and skipped home looking forward to my 'Kaffe' and a roll in bed with honey.

****

"So you want to join the Feuerwehr" he said studying a strange Englishman.
"I understand that I can volunteer as it is Freiwillig" I respectfully responded.
The Kommandant looked at me probably wondering what his fire crews would make of an Englishman who spoke no local dialect and extremely poor deutsch. There were over eighty firemen many of whom had served the station for their entire lives. They manned six quite modern fire tenders and a charming original wartime tender that had seen service in Africa. The Fire station was well equipped and I was given a guided tour meeting several smiling firemen who had just returned from a practise run.

"We don't have many fires but we do get quite a lot of calls for flooding. Our worst year was nineteen ninety nine when the Bodensee over spilled its banks."

The papers signed we sat down in the wonderful refectory and over a cold beer he told me about some of the history of the station and its many activities including shooting, football and the odd social occasion. It seemed not too strenuous and I was pleased to join something that clearly meant a lot to the people of Höchst.

"So besides fires, floods and car accidents what else do you get called out to here?" I said expecting a long list of technical incident reports.

"We get the odd cow call."

He smiled knowing that my mind was spinning trying to guess whether this was some local code for an alarm call. The old Rhine was not just a flood problem but occasionally the odd cow wandered into flood dykes or got stuck in the mud. The only way to handle a one tonne mooing and clanging alpine cow was for the farmer to call out the Feuerwehr with their special crew of rope pullers. It was apparently an experience not to be missed especially in the rain and mud and always cost the farmer some "milk" in the form of bottled beer for the often exhausted participants. It sounded much more fun than the running of the bulls in Pamplona and I could not wait for my first "cow call".

Actually my first call was on my wedding anniversary but being a willing and able fireman I rushed to the station looking forward to my first incident. I was promptly provided with my white fireman's helmet, fire coat, long trousers and customary wellington boots and I climbed aboard a small fire truck.

"You are verletzt so go to the third floor and lie down."

Obediently I climbed the stairs of the local old people's home and lay in the corridor with another fireman. It was a long wait and a charming elderly resident came out to chat with us. We chatted about my wedding anniversary and of course jolly old England and then she disappeared into her room to fetch us a bottle of champagne. This was so typical of the friendly manner of Vorarlberg where nothing worth celebrating should pass without some cheery mellifluous commemoration.

"Can you walk ?" asked a fireman in a gas mask roped to two of his colleagues. I didn't think the champagne was that strong but I did my best to act my part.

The fire crew then strapped me into a stretcher but instead of carrying me down the stairs they took my out onto the rain soaked balcony.

"You like heights, Englishman?"

Before I could tell him about my troubles with the three metre diving board in the swimming pool, I was slid onto a teleporter ladder and we swung out over Höchst. The fireman from Lustenau smiled as he guided his joystick control safely to the ground. I thanked him politely but could not help thinking of those poor victims of the twin towers who were out of reach of any such assistance. Luckily Höchst had few other tall buildings and there was enough living space to avoid the death traps of sky scrappers. This practise was a joint exercise with Swiss fire ladders from St.Margrethen and Lustenau and was being extremely capably commanded by the Höchst Kommandant with over twelve fire tenders and sixty firemen in attendance.

"I'm sorry to miss our dinner darling, but I spent our anniversary riding down on teleporter ladders in a stretcher in the pouring rain. I suppose I did see some unique romantic panoramic views of Höchst by night."

"Well tomorrow is my birthday and we can go to the Linde."

This was always a treat and over the years Marina's cousin Gerhard had taken great trouble to cultivate our taste buds at this temple to Austrian cooking. He had once taken me to meet the chef who was making ice sculptures for a wedding decoration and it was to our gourmet cousin that we owed so much to the understanding of Haute Cuisine. The Linde was a large hotel in the centre of Höchst and had three restaurants all serving the very best cuisine often for guests from Switzerland which was a great compliment as Swiss people valued only the finest cuisine, admittedly at more affordable prices than over the border.

"So thirteen years is a good innings especially considering the stress of these past months here in the chocolate mountains."

"Well I could have stabbed you these past couple of weeks over the translation of your blasted Angelica Kauffmann texts."

Luckily the charming waiter, Hubert, was in attendance and he bought in a huge copper frying pan. He lifted the lid to reveal a beautifully presented selection of game meats with assorted dumplings and vegetable tips. The smell engulfed us and we set about stabbing carefully selected pieces of tender venison and mountain hare treating ourselves to a very special anniversary and birthday dinner.

"Wait until you see what I have got planned for you."

My loving wife played with her new coral necklace and we thanked the kind experienced and attentive waiter for the excellent service.

****

The increasingly full diary she had planned was probably becoming an administrator's nightmare as everywhere we went people invited us to visit their clubs, hobbies and various charitable organisations. There was also the media and production work during the day not to mention the children's indoor tennis, horse riding, football, swimming and endless amounts of homework.

"You can help Leopold by going to his evening classes."

This was actually much more interesting than simply being the parent who was allocated to drive a taxi full of screaming ungrateful offspring as it always involved parental participation. Many parents are prepared to sit in their cars awaiting their child or more serious parents might sit in the spectators seats, but I was "daddy two shoes".

"That was fun, now I'll watch a video whilst you tap dance."

So over the months I learnt that I had two left feet as I took up Line dancing on Tuesdays and excruciatingly painful tap dancing on Fridays. With the choir singing, the fire brigade, and the occasional sortie to attend concerts and even "Schuhplatteln" my evenings were rarely without adventure. Marina too explored the strange positions of yoga and other even more strenuous evening fitness clubs. We became fit parental idols to our offspring.

Some of the clubs like the Kirchenchor had special events which involved visiting other towns to join up with other like minded singers in concert halls or churches. This was always an impressive affair as the sound of a huge choir singing a Latin mass with separate music for soprano, alto, tenor and baritone required a significant amount of practice and rehearsal. This was invariably quite tedious and often involved some travel but the conductor always had a huge turnout as the post practise social incentive always involved the visiting of local taverns. Only the Welsh choirs have quite the same social integration but many of them are single sex which often spoils the apres choir amusement.

The traditions of the various choirs became of some interest as many of these choral clubs had a long unbroken genetic history. The Gaissau choir was very much based on this principle giving mothers, fathers and grown up children a chance to interact socially which was something normally only reserved for family occasions like Christenings, Weddings or Funerals. However the latter of these occasions often excluded the unfortunate deceased member of the family so the weekly choir practise enabled the generations to laugh and joke together without the emotional detachment attributed to these formal events.

The choir consisted in many cases of brothers and sisters, mothers and daughters and several cousins making it strong in intimate humour yet open to new blood especially from England. There were often funerals which were generally sad affairs honouring a lost member of this extended family but always politely toasting them into their new heavenly abode. There were also weddings where strange rituals like the playing of throwing and catching crockery over a blanket were undertaken with much laughter and smashing of plates. But most interesting of all was the massed choir of two hundred men and women with an unforgettable sound so uplifting as to give anyone with agnostic inclinations a good shot up the backside. However it was not the concert which was so interesting but the extraordinary circumstances and venue.

The concert was set in an exhibition hall in Dornbirn as part of a huge show called Gloria which was not quite as one might expect in these godly circles. It was in fact a huge trade exhibition for the church in Austria and was part of several such European trade exhibitions included on a church trade circuit in Poland, France and Italy. There was everything you could imagine from restoration companies, pilgrimage holidays, bell campanologists, host bakers and, of course, candlestick makers.

Whilst I was waiting for the church television interviews to finish before the concert I strolled amongst the trade stands to see what industry had to offer the christian faith. I thought that I would feel like Jesus felt over the traders outside the temple but actually my scepticism was overtaken by sheer fascination. The world of church shopping was like many other trade and industry requirements with an estimated value of over one million pounds per annum to European industry.

I was shown the very latest organ technology where the organist was no longer required and the wind was replaced by computer originated resonant sound technology saving up to nine tenths of the costs of restoring traditional wind driven organs. Then there was the tourism potential of the shrines of Europe consortium where Lourdes, Loreto, Fatima, Czestochowa and Altötting had grouped together to promote religious tourism. I had attended several pilgrimages as a Knight of Malta and found this glimpse of the religious tourism industry serving over ten million tourists annually a truly enlightening topic, especially as it was an industry with a two thousand year history.

There were several charities serving all parts of the globe which was always popular in Austria as a wealthy, philanthropic and deeply religious nation. I had enjoyed several charitable functions notably for a six hundred thousand pound children's hospital in Gomel in White Russia planned by my wife's cousin, Gerhard and built by the generosity of the people of Höchst. Every town and village supported projects in the third world and in turn this had created a vast industry of support workers and equipment suppliers. The three year old exhibition was a chance to see everything under one roof and was not so much in aid of 'white collar' workers more to encourage them to support the wider economy.

"Well how was your first concert?" enquired my wife as we ate breakfast.

I had stood conducting a line of cows at the Höchst cow show the day before with the children and doubtless they all expected a poignant remark comparing the lowing cows with the caterwauling choir. But for once I was lost for words still in a world of designer church door mats and shining religious kitsch souvenirs that literally lit your way home.

"I have seen the butcher and the baker. I have joined the firemen but that was a most extraordinary candlestick maker."

****

"What are you talking about daddy? Come on we're going to shoot sausages and if you don't hurry up we'll miss them" said Max pushing me out of the door.

I giggled to myself impressed with my children's unwitting sense of humour and strolled after them wondering whatever it was we were about to do nothing would surprise me anymore. The idea that anyone could think of Austria as a land of handsome agile skiers in sunglasses or even as an alpine region full of girls in pigtails skipping across meadows to the sound of cow bells was quite ridiculous. It was concept devoid of real time experiences as I had started out watching sausages being made and now I was going to shoot them. This was after all the chocolate mountains that the true underground tourists should experience not so much a sausage eating country of farmers and skiers but more a sausage shooting nation of authentically fully armed Austrian eccentrics.

"We would like to shoot some sausages" I asked the munitions man.

"How much ammunition do you require?" he said counting out hundreds of bullets.

"I'm not sure. How much do you think it takes to shoot one?" I said quite bewildered.

The surreal conversation was being conducted through a glass window in the Höchst Shooting Club surrounded by several happy shooters sitting with their beers in a room full of trophies and painted targets.

I decided to simply hand over some money to the efficient and polite looking gentleman as I could see the language barrier was once again becoming confused by my lack of diction and he had several weapons at his disposal.

"Come on Daddy. This is a blast!" said Max grabbing the bullets.

My mind focused on bursting sausages and judging by the number of bullets I had been given it was going to be a massacre. I had hunted deer, kangaroo, elk, pheasants, ducks and even murmeltier but sausages were altogether a different target. I wondered if they wobbled or passed before us in long strings like fairground targets. This was definitely going to be a blast of combustible proportions and I entered the room with explosive expectations.

"But Daddy, they're shooting targets" said Leopold sadly.

"Don't worry just hit the black bit three times and you win" I retorted encouragingly.

Actually we spent the next two days lying on tables firing rifles at fifty metre targets to win delicious 'schübling' which we ate until we could eat no more. We had also shot at fairground targets to win plastic flowers or synthetic toys but somehow the idea of shooting for something you could eat was so much more relevant to our natural hunting instincts. There was however no courageous story of the animal's last moments and indeed no trophy to indicate the prowess of the hunter just a large string of sausages from a pig that might have once snuffled in an orchard before it took its last taxi ride to the slaughter house. But somehow it was still an adventure which hundreds of past members in their navy blue 'Schützenrock' and silver buttoned uniforms in the fading photographs on the walls must have enjoyed since the club's foundation in 1846.

For children it was a dream come true; shooting real rifles rather than toy guns and actually seeing where the real shot had hit the targets. Almost every town and village in Austria and Germany had some kind of shooting club and they did not experience the horrors of mad gunmen in Scottish Primary Schools because their children were taught to use guns safely and in these specially adapted clubs. England was under represented in gun sports at the last Olympics because of the new gun laws banning pistols and effectively ruining the medal hopes of future generations. I felt that England could learn a great deal from these 'Schützen' clubs instead of the emotionally driven media politics of Parliament. In this small shooting gallery there was even a picture of a high ranking politician painted on a wooden 'Ehrenscheibe' target. I looked down my sights with no imaginary Political target in mind just the wish to win more harmless, delectable and highly digestible sausages.

"Daddy I got a bulls eye. Do I have to eat it ?" said an ecstatic but anxious Leopold.

A DEADLY SILENT SCHOOL REUNION, PAINTING COWS AND SAVING MY SOUL

The Autumn in Austria is one of the most colourful times in the natural and supernatural calendar. The trees loose their tinted tones as the mighty winds and unrelenting rain strip them bare of their leaves. Their naked black trunks turn into waving shadows on the mountain slopes exposed to the elements like thousands of soldiers turned out on parade in a thunderstorm without their uniforms. It is a time of both sadness and joy for the two villages in their festive and religious expression of the end of summer and the beginning of winter.

"Allerheiligen is the most important date in the catholic calendar" said Marina as I frantically unloaded my baggage from the new baby Landrover.

"Well then we must try to make a special effort on Halloween and All Saints Day so that we don't miss anything" I replied as I climbed aboard the early train to Zurich Airport. "I have to go to England now so count me in if the plane gets back in time."

"Daddy. You're supposed to be taking me fox hunting before the government bans it. So please get on the train or we'll miss the plane" said Emily agitatedly.

We left the Chocolate Mountains as the sunrise was beginning to warm the cold rainy night and joined the hundreds of dawn commuters who migrated daily from Austria to Switzerland in search of better pay and working conditions. I had met many guest workers from Vorarlberg on this train and none of them were entirely happy with this early morning migration especially with the very efficient but constantly overcrowded trains. This morning was no different but a few hours of travel by train, plane and automobile was a small discomfort to be endured considering that it gave me the chance to live with my children in such an unfamiliar but pleasant land.

London was as ever damp, dirty but distracting and different. Harrods glittered like a beached cruise liner and my daughter beamed like a spoilt but ecstatically happy film star riding the bow waves of consumerism. Meetings in ancient dusty gothic offices that always smelt peculiarly of polish and leather came and went by the tick and the tock of finely balanced antiquated grandfather clocks. But I was actually anxiously anticipating a boarding school reunion after thirty wild years where I expected to drunkenly confess some of my most hidden childhood secrets of my monastery incarceration. I was distracted momentarily by the wind rushing through my thinning hair as I galloped by the last light of the moon on a sweating horse across the stubble fields after the fox hounds. England will always be a memory of "Good Old Blighty" where real gentlemen wear stocks, tweeds and leather riding boots and the foxes wave their fine brushes as they too enjoy the glory of the chase.

Times were changing more rapidly than many pundits had expected and it was clear that the government were using the emotive issue of hunting and dethroning aristocrats as a distraction from a failing economy and a crumbling autocracy. The turn of the twenty first century would be remembered as the beginning of the end of the socialist utopia that had sold out everything that was quintessentially British for an almost communist ideology of "populist progress." England's green and pleasant land was fast turning in the direction of another Nineteen Eighty Four world of Big Brother with an even bigger Primeministerial Blairite grin smiling out of every media orifice. At least I was honest about where my personal colours stood and I was still proud of the Crown and Country even if our sovereignty and freedom was being sold out for short sighted political expediency.

I had been on the March for the Freedom of the Countryside but unwittingly I had also joined a May Day March, courtesy of the police who were rather over anxious to please these political masters and actually cordoned off some shoppers in Oxford Circus. I knew that both these opposites were unpopular extremes and ideal for political manipulation. I stood up a traffic bollard in the May Day March telling off the black masked troublemakers and threatening to tell their mothers of their physiognomy which they failed to comprehend to the amusement of the annoyed and bored crowd. However I had gone to the Countryside March with the intent of joining a just cause, admittedly dressed as a white rabbit, but standing up with people with whom I sympathised. The difference between the two extremes was quite clear as both marches were for freedom, but the government only seemed to react to the violence of the May Day radicals, not the peaceful protest of country folk.

"Well what have we all done these past twenty five years?" said our old monitor.

The conversation at our school reunion dinner had travelled around the dining room table with a large bottle of malt whisky. It seemed that many of my school friends now living in America and fashionable parts of London had become teachers, computer programmers, photographers, lawyers and city slickers. What could I say for myself, aged forty plus living in a foreign land as a hippie good lifer? The bottle swished inexorably and inevitably around the table to my empty glass and the room focused hazily on my response as I shakily refilled my trembling tumbler.

"I'm afraid I'm a bit of a drop out as I just said sod it to socialism and went to write a musical in the Chocolate Mountains" I slurred.

There was an uncomfortable deathly silence worse than my nightmare stage appearance as a compare for a heavy rock band at a mediaeval banquet for students. This paranoia would always haunt me as there were many mistakes in my seventeen year long rather chequered career as the producer and director of theatrical productions in Lincolnshire but that went down as my darkest minute. It was not the fact that the students had turned out to be pensioners and they were expecting mediaeval lute and flute players but it was the whisper in my ear backstage twenty seconds before going on that they only spoke German.

Suprisingly the show didn't bomb altogether as one wheel chair bound high spirited aged Graduate Student started banging the table with his dagger in time to the band's version of 'Rocking with the Devil'. Whereupon the whole room rose from the nearly dead into an electrically recharged dance hall of spinning Zimmerframes and rocking wheelchairs. But there was that dark minute when the rock band surveyed their audience in their black leather outfits wearing plastic reindeer antlers and their thoughts turned towards tar and feathering the compare. Luckily I had remained composed enough to use my only two phrases in German and thankfully to this day that band remains oblivious of the appalling mistranslation.

"From the Kellers of Hell I bring you the Walking Dead. So enjoy your last rock in England before you rock with the devil" I announced to a stunned silent room.

Actually the bottle of whisky was not going to save me either as I had spent too much time filling in for the many actors and musicians that had chosen to sink a few too many in their dressing rooms. One outstanding case being the drunk knife thrower who missed the balloon between the legs of his equally inebriated assistant and nearly gave him a new, probably safer career as a soprano singer. He certainly saw double top that night.

My malt whisky reminiscences were cut short as the silence was broken with the immortal words uttered when nobody had anything else to say.

"Well let's drink to that!" And we did until we all passed out on the floor.

****

As promised the diary was full when I returned to the relative calm of the Chocolate Mountains. There are many holidays in the church calendar and Vorarlberg is a very Catholic country which in fact suited me as a Knight of Malta and Protector of the Pope. I avoided mentioning this locally as it seemed out of place in a village where the 'white collar workers' functioned perfectly well without errant knights.

I did make sure that I attended the many religious festivals over the summer months including the spectacular harvest thanksgiving. The church in Höchst was decorated with hoops of ivy hung with corn cobs and wreaths of yew and red flowering heather and the altar was decorated with green, grey, yellow and orange gourds. But this artistic reference to Halloween was just a preamble or taster of the All Saints and All Souls Day Festivities.

"First you have to take the children out trick or treating" ordered my spouse.

That was easy enough and I piled various masked and face painted children into the old biscuit tin to go and ring door bells in the hope of filling their ever hungry mouths with sweets and treats. We passed several urchins pushing pumpkins in wheelbarrows and started ringing door bells where we might be more welcome.

"Süss oder Sauer" yelled the children as the door opened.

The Halloween traditions were considered to be rather American than Austrian but that wasn't going to stop my flock of children from milking it for all it was worth. They piled themselves up with chocolates, biscuits, sweets and strange looking nuts guaranteed to remove any lurking milk teeth. It was as much fun as Three Kings Day and they got to express themselves in their costumes, face paints and ghoulish screams and shouts without getting complaints from the neighbours about child cruelty.

"Good, they're exhausted, now you're late for your choir" said my colonel in chief pushing me back out of the door.

I was even later for choir as the basement where the choir normally practised was taken over by a teenage Halloween Party which had locked the passage door. The conductor was suprisingly forgiving as I climbed through the window at an appropriate interval in his infinite list of tunes. I managed to catch the last songs normally attributed to Afro-American Gospel Choirs but admirably sung by the Gaissauer Church Choir.

"We could try the party going on at the new Quo Vadis Stadel" I said apologetically.

I tried to make up for my poor punctuality by offering to sponsor the leader of the choir in a body painting competition to raise funds for charity but the choir were suprisingly recalcitrant citing that body painting was old news in Vorarlberg. This naturally caught my imagination as it was certainly unusual in Lincolnshire. Perhaps this area was so conservative that it had retained body painting from the Bronze Age settlers. I knew that there were adverts with chocolates and cows painted purple and I had milked a brown plastic cow. This was my chance to see where they painted the cows and I wanted to join the secret cult.

As I drove out into the countryside I hypothesised on what I might encounter in the corn fields of Höchst. The Klu Klux Clan with weird white hoods and burning crosses simply did not fit despite the clearly conservative politics of the villages as there were no African slaves to barbecue. The Freemasons were a very secretive organisation in England that were supposed to blindfold new members and get them to hop on one leg whilst choking a chicken. They were set up to prevent Catholics from rising again after the Reformation and so they were ruled out although chicken choking might be a ceremony from these parts.

There was nothing black or white about this Halloween as I found out as I entered a cowshed full of body painted teenage revellers. I felt a bit like an old bull in a cowshed of multicoloured young heifers and bullocks, besides life was all bullshit and bollocks anyway and it was a great party. The main thing was to find the guy who had painted all those cows and he was right up there amongst the giant cobwebs on the stage.

"Are you are responsible for painting the cows purple?" I shouted above the music.

Arno Linder was in fact the Austrian Number One in custom airbrush body painting and he had probably painted more flesh than I would ever see on the naturist beach in Fussach. (Not that I had ever exposed myself there). The concentration dripped down the edge of his spectacles as he painted strange graphics on my naked chest.

"I am the Guinness Book world record holder for painting 50 people in one painting in five hours and forty three minutes" he replied tickling my tummy with his airbrush.

I tried not to laugh as I looked around the room at his dancing paintings and concluded that it was much more fun than painting cows anyway.

****

"You are awake ? The church service is in two hours time" said my wife, chortling at what the cat had brought back from the cowshed. "I don't think that masterpiece will wash off in time for church."

"My Daddy has got a body tattoo!" said Leopold, showing a crowd of his friends who studied and prodded my stupefied corpse like a Kindergarten class of student doctors on a ward visit. "I'm sure he didn't paint the chocolate cows like that."

I looked in the mirror at the work of art now inseparable from my body despite much scrubbing in the shower. If they had painted the chocolate cows with such graphic symbols I am sure that it would have attracted a lot of attention from American scientists studying extraterrestrial phenomenon. It certainly knocked the spots off crop circles, in fact it pretty much knocked the spots off most breeds of dairy cows I had ever seen.

"Come on ! Everybody in the family is going to be there but I want you to see the other church yards first" yelled Marina throwing me a fresh towel.

We drove off to Lustenau and then on to a very pretty graveyard next to the harbour in Hard. It is difficult to understand the respect held for the dead and departed in Austria, as in England grave yards are often unkempt and certainly not places of beauty although to be fair there has been much poetry inspired by such wild, sad places. The Austrian graveyards were places of cosmetic beauty and this was the day to see some of the finest flower arrangements from all kinds of strange plants and wreaths. It was a kind of Flower Show for every family and no grave was left without a candle or a treasured token in memory of those buried beneath the raked and manicured earth. The grave stones were works of art some with smiling photos of the incumbents and others with sculptures often representing the family crafts or particularly moving biblical scenes.

In England we had Poppy Day with a military parade and ceremony at the Epitaph in Whitehall in London attended by the monarch and political and military figureheads. But the memory of the War dead was much more low key in

Austria since the Second War and children collected funds for the Black Cross at the cemetery gates instead. It was sad not to remember these war heroes with similar pageantry as they had sacrificed their lives for their country too and fascism was long gone despite recent press about the extreme right politics in Austria. But then England forgot all the ordinary people who had served their country and this tour of the grave yards almost made me ashamed at our treatment of the memories of our lost relatives in overgrown, forgotten grave yards. There was poetry inspired by wild places in England's grave yards, but no real respect for the dead.

The church in Höchst was so full that many people were standing outside and I was lucky to find some standing room at the back. There were far more people than had attended the Christmas Service and it was as though the whole village had turned out for the occasion. There were seven thousand people in Höchst and at least one thousand of them had turned out for the All Saints Day service on the 1st November to remember the dead.

The priest was aware of the capacity crowd's discomfort and had carefully tailored the service to suit his irregular parishioners. The readers read out all the names of those who had died since the last service solemnly reading out the month followed by the family name and street. The prayers were interesting as they echoed from either side of the church as first the men and then the women said their rosary. Then the service adjourned to the graveyard where the families congregated around their respective graves.

Marina's family stood by their grave joining the other village mourners in a silent tribute to their loved ones. Gerhard, normally a jovial and talkative character, stood silently with his pretty, blonde and extremely astute wife, Edith. They were joined by their daughter, Barbara, who was a local teacher and shared the same birthday as me. There was also Gerhard's brother, Dieter, who had always had time to explore the perplexing world of computers with an English novelist. He had experienced much tragedy but seemed to share the sadness with a smile for the fonder memories of the departed kith and kin.

The stone tablet read like a family genealogy starting with their grandfather, Heinrich, who had formed the construction business in Höchst that now employed his grandsons. There was a long list of sadness and death including more recently Marina's father who was also an architect and her uncle who was also a builder and the local doctor. These latter two names struck a chord with me as they smiled in my fond memories of them and I recalled what they had both told me about marrying a girl from Höchst. I was told that I had married a mountain girl who would always return. I looked at the two brothers standing by the grave and thought how the fraternal bond might have been between these two now departed siblings had not the war driven them so far apart. Time had a peculiar way of returning them together again as from the cradle to the grave, whatever the history that occurs in between, it cannot deny the fact that a name means blood bonding to be there written in stone forever.

As ever my two sons broke the silent respect for the souls of the dead in a way that would have made them roll over with mirth as they sat watching us from the grey heavens above. My youngest son pulled my arm and I bent down so that he could whisper in my ear: "Daddy, do you think they had a tattoo too ?"

****

There had been some dramatic moments in our stay in Austria and there were other times of stress and anxiety notably when one or other of us experienced ill health. This was the time for saving rather than remembering lost souls and also a time to see behind the large voluminous paperwork of the Austrian Health Service.

If you travel to Austria from another European Country it is wise to carry appropriate health insurance as like the United States the health system in Vorarlberg is plagued by charming, friendly but prolific bureaucrats. I had spent some time travelling around North America on a motorcycle and my three month long odyssey was brought to an abrupt finale by a female 'Chevrolet' driver who 'bust' a red traffic and flattened me and my trusted steed. Naturally the experience had a marked effect on me, not to mention leaving me with a scar on my leg and a blemish on my otherwise fond memories of California.

It was not the fact that the policeman who had witnessed the accident whilst munching a sticky doughnut in the café opposite and had promptly issued the lady with a 'citation' that had marred my recollections of this dramatic collusion of my travels. Although it was certainly very confusing as in England a citation is like receiving an honour and I was rather confused that the Irish cop was giving the lady a medal for knocking six bells out of a harmless English motorcyclist. It was also not due to the fact that two different ambulance firms had arrived simultaneously and the crews had proceeded to argue with each other about who got the call first. As I lay stunned watching the scene I reached into my pocket to find a cigarette, but the carton was empty except for one last crumpled upturned lucky fag.

I slid it out whilst holding my aching, bleeding leg and placed it between my gritted teeth. The now swollen crowd suddenly stopped their heated debate and the cop in the motorcycle helmet lowered his sunglasses to finally look in my direction. His expression had changed from irritation with the riotous assembly to sheer panic as I produced the last match from my similarly mangled matchbox. Hazily I squinted at him as he raised his hands in the air and then I caught his bellowing voice.

"For Christ's Sake! Don't light that cigarette ! You're on the Gas pumps !"

Only then did the emergency system kick into gear and I was finally taken to hospital. Even then as I lay in the casualty ward awaiting treatment I was still required to complete my police statement, and to sign away my life to the doctors and my remaining funds to cover the uninsured health bills. Whilst waiting for this bureaucracy to process I did manage to laugh as the beach boy lying in agony on the trolley in the next door cubicle mumbled an almost incoherent greeting in my direction.

"Hey man you look bad but they patch you up well in here" spluttered the surfer.

"So what are you in here for ?" I replied through the curtain.

"I caught a big wave but I also took a bite outta my board, man."

His dental bills must have dwarfed my four hundred dollar treatment, but I still remain to this day unimpressed with the one hundred dollar charge for a five minute ambulance ride where the crew spent their time slanging off the other ambulance firm whilst I was lurching around in agony unattended in the back. Of course this makes you sceptical of health services that run on paper and Austria seemed to suffer from this syndrome too.

"I have managed to sort out your Krankenschein and you are booked into to the doctor in Höchst this morning."

This was all that my loving but rather unsympathetic wife had said to her mortally wounded husband who in fact was only suffering from a mild case of haemorrhoids. The long sounding often misspelled word had never really meant anything to me and I hadn't really paid much attention at the doctors surgery as my wife had spoken on my behalf whilst the doctor had toyed mysteriously with a pair of plastic gloves on his desk.

"Please go behind the curtain and remove your trousers" he said clinically.

This seemed to be a perfectly sensible request until I saw him put on the gloves. I accepted that like the many lambs I had assisted on the farm at home or the warm bloody calf I had delivered onto my lap as an agricultural student in Nottinghamshire, that it was going to be a perfectly natural experience. Then I remembered the anxious cow as the herdsman reinserted his arm in search of my missing watch. The watch turned out to be in my pocket to the humour of the herdsman but the anxiety of the poor cow. I looked at my wife and thought that I detected an avenging smirk from the birth of three children.

The process was not finished as the doctor booked me into the hospital in Bregenz for further exploration of my condition. In a world of insurance and paper led medicine I had plenty of time to contemplate whether this was going to be more like exploitation. The Austrian health system was the best I had ever seen and I had experienced hospitals in India, Africa and the outback of Australia. They were clean, well equipped and efficient beyond the boiling point of efficacy. There were no sacred cows to avoid at the entrance like in India, no queues of starving and dying children like in Africa and plenty of staff unlike in outback Australia where I had waited for the doctor to fly in to his clinic.

Even the signs in the hospital were so well organised that the sick were only permitted to enter the receptionist's office 'two at a time'. I sat in the hospital waiting area behind the red lined demarcation area contemplating the biblical reference to animals entering the Ark in pairs and decided that Noah was probably directly related to an Austrian administrative assistant. The business man next to me kept looking at his watch in between chatting with several white coated acquaintances and it was clear that we were all equal in the eyes of god and the hospital administration. The lady on the other side of me gave me a knowing smile which did not reassure me as the sign above her referred to gynaecologists.

"Ah ha" said the jovial administrative assistant shuffling her files. "An English Krankenschein, we don't see many of those here."

It was never a good idea to argue or upset these ladies as you could be sent for all kinds of unfortunate check-ups so I kept my thoughts to myself. She looked a bit like Noah's wife and I wanted to be one of the chosen two to survive the biblical flood holocaust. I knew I was condemned to something anatomically challenging and I was therefore extremely sensitive to any holocaust reference that might be misinterpreted and about the ordeal that I anticipated would follow from any allusion to the administrative signage.

The waiting was made bearable by the wide variety of outdated magazines and scientific papers. Although perhaps I could have done without some of the naturally assisted medical procedures for pregnant llamas in the foothills of the Andes so graphically described in a geographical magazine. The speaker pronounced my name as though I was Elvis Presley and I wondered if the rock star's hip wiggle was as a result of Austrian medical procedures.

"I presume you require the same procedure as my doctor ?"I said sheepishly.

"The same procedure as every year" laughed the Specialist referring to the time honoured ten minute black and white Comedy Show with an English butler and an old widow that was shown on every German speaking television channel on New Year's Eve. The humorous reference to this great piece of comedy suprisingly, as I recalled, never shown on English television, did not do much to put me at my ease as he was standing in a gown next to a chair with two large raised cradle stirrups.

"Ah ha" said the jolly jester as he checked my paperwork and then proceeded to insert various terrifying looking instruments into my rear end. "An English Krankenschein, we don't see many of those here."

It was difficult enough to hold a conversation with a dentist but much more disconcerting to try to make any articulation when such a comic orator was examining your second most important orifice. The instruments at his disposal were far more alarming than dentist's tools. I wondered if they had used his tackle in the film script for Marathon Man (when the star was tortured with a menacing dental drill) whether Dustin Hoffman would have accepted the part at all. In that movie the white haired torturer kept asking if it was safe and I clenched my bowels hoping that the Specialist was not going to ask such an incomprehensible question.

"Relax please, it's quite safe."

I was heartily relieved that he had answered that question himself but still not exactly at ease with my two legs harnessed into the stirrups. That cow was now getting its revenge on my practical joke on the herdsman about my missing timepiece. I swore that I would never threaten to paint cows again or to laugh at the sound of their huge toneless cow bells. I would even take the milking lessons on the plastic cow more seriously and be more sensitive to their 'udderances' especially during calving. On my return home I did not answer my wife's inquiry as to how the appointment had progressed but she tittered as she read my notes.

"You're getting extra colonic irrigation given only to patients with good insurance."

"DOCTOR"

MÜNCHEN, MOURNING AND KIRSCH DRINKING WITH HEMINGWAY'S GHOST IN MONTAFON

The beginning of the snow season requires significant preparation including the equipping of vehicles with winter tyres and the outfitting of children for winter sports. The snow had briefly visited the valley as early as September and it was always possible to find somewhere to slide on two planks of multicoloured and exquisitely curved wood. This operation gave us another opportunity to visit my favourite destination which most tourists regarded simply as the home of lederhosen and beer but I regarded as the cultural capital of Germany.

We left a hive of industry as the building workers had at last converged on our new home in Gaissau to create new accommodation for our extended family and our Chinese tenants. We headed North East from the Bodensee into the heart of Bayern and after two hours of smooth autobahn driving in our gas powered biscuit tin we arrived in the centre of the magnificent well planned city of München.

The first time I had visited this wonder of the Bavarian world it was as though I had fallen deeply, madly and so completely in love with its vibrant culture and beautiful architecture. I adored other European capital cities like London, Paris, and Rome and I had also been privileged to experience the most romantic towns of Venice and Florence. But this city was designed by the great often eccentric 'Könige von Bayern' who had also travelled to these great cities of Europe but the difference was that they had then redesigned München with all the most attractive and practical parts of these cities.

The town centre has the extensive subway and parks of London, the wide boulevards and streets of Paris, the domes and churches of Rome, the classical art galleries of Florence and the pretty grand canals of Venice. The city at night was as fun as London or Paris if you avoided the noisy intoxicated tourists in the Bierkellers. It had over forty of the finest opera houses, theatres, children's theatres, marionette theatres and cabaret and concert halls to choose from with shows for every taste and every occasion. We all loved the fifty or more museums and galleries especially the Deutsches Museum with its Imax Cinema and Planetarium and the various palaces and residences of the now defunct royal family.

The Brauhäuser mentality of most tourists is understandable too as each brewery had its own special guest house serving wonderful dumplings, white sausage, pork dishes and over two hundred choices of wheat and normal beers. Their large kellers with hundreds of oak 'stammtisch' (for more frequent local companies and clubs) and 'gästetische' (for irregular guests and tourists) hosted volkmusic all day and most of the night. They were often good value for money especially for families and pensioners who sat upstairs out of the smoke and music. In summer the Biergarten were filled with a stream of locals and tourists and I always enjoyed the Hirschgarten where there were deer in the Park.

The Parks, Palaces and Gardens were ideal for fresh air playing in the snow or on the hot midsummer days strolling under the shade of the long avenues of trees. Our favourite haunt was the Schloss Nymphenburg in the palace gardens with a delicious tea house and various museums and follies tucked into majestically manicured Parkland. The Zoo by the river Isar with elephants, tigers, huge flight cages and strange penguin walkers and English Garden with its Chinese Teahouse tower had always provided limitless entertainment for our children during their budding youth. The open spaces were safe, clean and invariably full of panting joggers, cool roller-bladers, challenging playgrounds, and antique carousels. In winter there were also frozen runners, shrieking ice skaters, tree icicles, 'pooh stick' races in the river, sugar coated 'mandelnuss' and 'glühwein' stalls.

The Art Galleries always hosted world class exhibitions and we never missed an opportunity to take advantage of the free entry concession on Sundays. On this trip my children avoided the car, aeroplane, porcelain, archaeological, comedy, crib, toy, and hunting museums and the vast array of galleries or Pinakothek. Except of course for the new opening of the Pinakothek Der Moderne which even they enjoyed as it was not just an exhibition of the works of twentieth century artists like Picasso, Max Ernst or Bacon but also a presentation of performance art, design and architecture. A new paradise of design displays of classic typewriters, mobile telephones, vacuum cleaners and moulded furniture was born.

"What did you like most about München this time ?" I asked the exhausted children.

"I liked the Imax cinema" said the naughty Leopold also named Moritz.

"No, I liked the Olympic swimming pool with the cool diving board" said the even more mischievous Max whilst tickling his shrieking brother.

"Well I like both of them but we went shopping too."

Our daughter Emily was growing up fast and it was true that we hadn't gone to the Circus, the Zoo or to all of the ten swimming baths that we had enjoyed on countless other summer holidays in München. We grown ups knew that this would not be the last time we would enjoy the highlights and high living of Germany's most beautiful city but we could also discriminate between teenage growing pains and exhausted noisy juveniles.

It was still my theory that if President Kennedy had visited München instead of Berlin he would have become a Münchener not a Berliner. But knowing the mature modern American and English tourist connections with the Pre War Germany and their younger spotted offspring's liking for beer and the Octoberfest, 'Munich' would still be able to cater for all tastes long after the President's great Cold War speech was forgotten in a haze of alcohol. We had found so much to do that we re-christened it "the City for Children" and wished other English Tourist Boards had thought more about families having a city holiday too.

The gas powered biscuit tin was causing amusement to our rabble of urchins as a points problem caused the Landrover to let out unfortunate gun shot noises to the anxiety of fur coated pedestrians. We stuttered and spluttered our way back to the second children's heaven in the wilds of the chocolate mountains having caused several coronary heart attacks.

****

"Would you like to play some Snooker tonight ?"said the voice on the phone.

We had enjoyed the pleasure of several male and female Au Pairs in England and were justly proud of their success as teachers and office workers in Vorarlberg where English had become the second working language. Manuel was a charming dark haired and smooth tongued Casanova who retained his foible for fast food and feckless females. We were separated by nearly two decades, but it was a friendship built on billiards and the male bonding associated with the unhindered freedom of expression in such clubs where women served the drinks or hovered around the tables in search of a Paul Newman or James Dean.

The underground world of twenty something was a distant flicker at the end of a long cold tunnel and the tube always seemed to be taking me further out of touch with fashion, flirting or even just fatherly frivolity. The idea of a dalliance with death or a foolish fancy had long since coupled in my psyche as something reserved for my youth as there was little satisfaction to be had by death or injury and certainly not at the hands of my spouse. However it was the idea of feeling the felt rather than the flesh that spurred me on to yet another adventure in the vast armoury of Austrian alternative "abends".

"We are going to the Blaue Sau" said the manicured Manuel.

This was a notorious disco haunt for teenagers in Lustenau but it also had two full sized snooker tables. Not suprisingly the name referred to blue pigs and I had already experienced blue cows and body painting so nothing really shocked me anymore except perhaps table dancing. As we drove off into the rainy night I enjoyed my lecherous thoughts on the combination of felt and flesh but then I was only feeling forty something. Frankly it felt better than any four letter words beginning with 'f' and I had experienced plenty of them.

The Billiard Clubs in Vorarlberg all have a similar design with a long bar, several dimly lit pool tables, electronic darts boards and a long legged lovely ready to quench your thirst and anything else you might desire. This club was no different except that it possessed two manicured beauties and I was not referring to the barmaid's cleavage. There were two wonderful snooker tables which I had sorely missed from my club days in England and this was my chance to hustle a bit of cue action and two club regulars also approached us on cue.

"Englishmen play good billiards, so what about a doubles game ?"

The two players had that look of club professionals but I was ready to enjoy a little friendly hustle tonight so we swapped partners to 'even out' the teams and started to play.

They were very good indeed and I had played a lot of snooker on some very fine tables in England. In fact with some exciting pink ball games we were in for a great evening's entertainment but it was then that I remembered 'table cricket' which I had picked up after tea whilst playing in a beautiful old Billiard Room at a pretty old rambling historic house in Derbyshire. The game snooker was supposedly invented by bored military officers serving the Rajh in India but there were other variations which lent themselves so much better to the skills of the cue and cloth.

"Would you like me to teach you table cricket ?" I said to save my honour.

"We have never heard of such a game" retorted the local snooker table hustler.

It was the first time table cricket let alone proper cricket had reached the outer alpine reaches of the snooker world. The rules are quite simple with two teams of two players, eleven red balls representing the wickets, the colour balls representing the runs (normally excluding the black as seven is unheard of at the Oval) and two cigarette packets strategically placed between the pink and blue, and the blue and brown to encourage accurate play (if you knock them down you have to buy another packet). One team bowls trying to pot the reds forfeiting two turns if they hit a colour at any time with the white ball. The other team bats trying to sink as many coloured balls as possible with a similar penalty if they hit a red ball at any time. The batting team score runs until ten red balls are sunk in the pockets (the eleventh ball representing the last batsman to leave the field as it takes two batsmen to play cricket) and then the other team swap and try to beat their batting score.

So simple to Englishmen reared on the summer sound of leather balls against willow bats and the yells of "howzat" to sleeping umpires. The rules did not involve leg before wicket or being caught at silly-mid-off. It was so simple that my dog normally prone to sleeping on a boundary deck chair below the score board could understand it along with fetch and do not shit on the pitch. But then who accounted for the language barrier in the cricket almanac of wisdom or was it by Wisden ? All I know is that sagacity is polite surrender when the bowler pots ten red balls in three bowls with his master cue and then proceeds to beat your batting score in three shots. But then like cricket we just changed the rules again to win.

"Well, how was your evening or were you table dancing ?" said my sleepy wife.

"Actually, we played table cricket but next time I'll opt for table dancing."

The change of sport had a certain appeal but there were also frustrating rules and not much else either. Englishmen had brought skiing, table cricket so why not pocket billiards ?

****

The Bell for the Dead tolls alone and it is For Whom The Bell Tolls that matters according to the Noble and Pultizer Prize winner for literature Ernest Hemingway. The mystery of his stay with his mistress in a Montafon Menage a Trois had begun to intrigue me.

Other authors and friends had given me their books to read on this great iconoclastic alcoholic literary giant known for big game hunting and even bigger womanising. So it was that I set off on a voyage of self discovery to see if I could learn from the 'mistakes' of Montafon that he quoted in his autobiography "A Moveable Feast" and in his letters as some of the happiest days of his life. He was famous for the immortal lines in a letter to F. Scott Fitzgerald from Montafon: 'The world is full of so many things that I am sure we shall all be as happy as kings. How happy are Kings ?'

"He is supposed to have said that to his fourth wife before he blew himself away."

My wife was not entirely correct about his controversial suicide but it was true that my icon's legendary presence in the Montafon Valley had given a whole new meaning to Apres ski with a social life still talked about over seventy five years later. 'The Black Kirsch-Drinking Christ' had become a legend amongst the woodcutters and peasants of Schruns with his snow tan, black beard and ability to drink himself and them all completely senseless. He had first spent the winter of 1924/1925 there with his first wife, Hadley, his son, Bumby, and a writer friend, John Dos Passos staying in the Posthotel Taube. It was a cheap retreat for a struggling journalist and writer from Paris where he hung around scribbling with some of my favourite authors like Gertrude Stein and F. Scott Fitzgerald.

It was this fashionable factor that eventually bought idle rich people in to spoil his 'happy innocent winter in childhood'. The rich people included his lover and next wife Pauline Pfeiffer and their liaisons at the Madlener-Haus were fascinating to a writer like myself especially at my impressionable age of forty something. So we set about preparing for our pre-ski visit to explore the valley where these early skiers and winter hikers had taken guides to walk them up into the wilderness. But before we could set out on our four wheeled expedition the legendary bell tolled for the father of a friend with whom I had become acquainted in the choir and line dancing classes.

****

The Kirchenchor often sang at weddings, church festivals and sadly at funerals and on this occasion they were singing for the soul of a soloist. The closeness of the choir had struck a chord deep inside my heart not that I could play a chord or really sing much above a dull baritone on barbiturates. I had often acted as a family representative at funerals in England which were small private affairs sometimes with additional Memorial Services at a later more convenient and convivial date. My father had such a Memorial Service in his memory in Lincoln Cathedral attended by Knights, Bishops and Regimental Trumpeters but in death there was grief and sadness whoever you are in life. This was a funeral for a friend's father and I, like the rest of the choir, empathised with him in his moment of mourning.

The church in Gaissau has suffered from the zealots of the age of modern thinking who had squandered their simplistic thought on stripping bare the Church of God in favour of a colourless and lifeless fridge. At least the first impression is austere and such nakedness appealed to the local nuns whose pew viewed only the altar. In comparison to the loving and lasting tenderness of the baroque church in Höchst at first glance Gaissau Church conveys an image of quiet simplicity, possibly too simple for some simple minds and simple folk. Yet for a place to mourn death its cold unpainted arches and seventies plain stone altar are ideal and the coffin that confronted me as I arrived early seemed somehow to fit into this emptiness.

It was so cold that my breath condensed and vaporised in the damp air but the idea of heating was too elementary and not rudimentary enough for this place of mountain worship. The organist was practising Schindler's List and I felt the cold chill run down my spine. The ghosts and gargoyles were normally on the outside of mediaeval churches but here I was in the threadbare physical presence of death. I had attended many funerals in pretty little English parish churches, not least that of a magician who scarred the hell out of me by playing a hidden recording of his last performance and I half expected him to jump out of his coffin.

Given the cold conditions I wasn't going to hang around too long to experience any likely transcendental apparition besides which I was frozen after arriving one hour too early due to my misunderstanding of time keeping. The hour in Austria was admittedly one hour in front of Greenwich Mean Time but I reckoned thad they tried to be mean with Gaissau time here too. The idea that one should say half nine but somehow mean half past eight was confusing enough but with a hangover and a fervent wish not to be late for a friend's father's funeral it was both frustrating and bloody freezing .

The doors opened with a creaking that made me wonder what might happen next. It was raining so perhaps a bit of thunder and lightening would set the scene for the grand entrance of the bride of Frankenstein. I day-dreamed about a film sequel to Mary Shelly's Frankenstein written by a mountain lake whilst chasing the handsome poet, Lord Byron. The organ pipes were now producing alarming ghoulish music and a woman in black approached me.

"Ah, Englishman. You have a nice suit but we aren't burying you today."

The relief did not trickle down my leg but I was only too pleased to assist in the proceedings in the sacristy. The church warden or 'messnerin' was a light relief from a tense moment of 'petrification'. A word which is not correctly attributed in the dictionary but falls somewhere between ossified stone cold and frozen with fear. We set about preparing the service together switching on the automatic church bells and setting the stage for the last great curtain call of the departed. I was overcome by the service and moved by the church choir's singing in the church and men's choir's vocalising in the windy graveyard.

The rain stopped for the internment and so I wandered amongst the graves of all the families from Gaissau. The nuns were buried here too with another modernist head stone that was rather like an egg shaped ship. I contemplated my mortality as various representatives read speeches by the grave side. Here lies the soloist of the choir would be his respected and popular epitaph and I wondered what they would scrawl across my wooden cross. Perhaps it might be an honourable Montafon pilgrimage plaque like Hemingway but with the words:

'Here lies that spooked out scribbler who didn't win the Pulitzer prize but had a good try at drinking himself to death. Cheers.'

It was always sad to watch friends file by the grieving family paying their last respects to the departed head of a family and a loving father. The churchyard was full as he was obviously a well known and respected man of the village. He had lived a long and happy life and avoided the dramatic tragic demise of Hemingway, passing on peacefully into paradise. As we all toasted his health in the floating restaurant I reflected on this melancholic moment and decided we were all equal in death. However doubtless his son knew that if there was a choir 'stammtisch' in heaven and then he wouldn't be surprised if that 'Black Kirsch-Drinking Christ' was also drinking this happy soul of a soloist under the table.

****

The Valley of Montafon is often forgotten in favour of posher playgrounds in Switzerland and France for the wealthy and not really famous. Ernest Hemingway was right to chastise his writing companion, John Dos Pasos, as 'an unerring pilot fish' for bringing the rich families like the Murphy's and the Anglo-American Paris set. It is now very over-developed and not particularly attractive around Schruns where they stayed in the nineteen twenties. The past seventy-five years has seen several developments and dams being built as the population has grown six fold on the back of tourism, construction and power generation. This can be said for many of the more famous Swiss and certainly most French resorts too but there are still hidden pockets which remain beautifully unspoilt. Doubtless as the idle rich dig deeper in their pockets the whole valley will disappear in a sprawl of houses and holiday flats.

However the forward thinking folk who have created this tourist valley are some of the nicest and friendliest I have ever encountered in Vorarlberg. Hemingway told terrible stories in his autobiography and letters about peasant farmers hanging lamps in the mouths of the frozen corpses of their departed spouses and that they called tourists 'tricky foreign devils'. But three quarters of a century had past and the word 'peasants' was now used as a derogatory word by unforgiving best forgotten foreign tourists. The further we travelled along into the steeper valley the more we felt like the ghosts of those first foreign holiday skiers and climbers who first visited this lost valley of Montafon.

The first glance of the Piz Buin is as spectacular as the Matterhorn in Zermatt and the nearer we went to the Silvretta Hochalpen pass at the end of the valley the more we began to feel an affinity with them. The Madlener Haus still exists by the new dam on the Silvretta Stausee and the Wiesbadner Hütte below the three peaks of the Silverettahorn (3244m), the Piz Buin (3312m) and the Dreiländers Peaks (3197m). The best skiing is still down the valley on Hochjoch (2520m) above Schruns but we drove on to the village of Partenen which was so quiet and unspoilt nestling below these spectacular mountains.

There are many great places to eat in the Alps and we had several favourite places including the Hirschen in Schwarzenberg in the Bregenzerwald where I had first fallen upon the Hemingway phenomenon as the wonderful proprietor unwittingly claimed to have entertained him at the bottom of his menu. Actually if he had visited Bregenzerwald some forty miles North of Montafon he would not have been disappointed. But then so many hotels (especially in Italy and Africa) claimed him as a phantom visitor that I was beginning to believe that his ghost was still on a seventy five year pub crawl as it would take him that long to visit all these watering holes. After much searching for all his familiar haunts in Schruns we stopped at the one Dorf Gasthof which did not boast of him as their customer although their wild game dish was probably the best I had ever tasted in Vorarlberg.

Pretty Ingrid Dona welcomed us in her working tracht to her family inn unassumingly called the Partener Hof and we settled down to enjoy a 'Sonntagsessen' of wild mountain 'gams' and 'hirsch' served on plates with traditional floral decorated wooden under plates . The Inn was probably not old enough to have been on Hemingway's list of peasant pubs but the walls were full of photographs of traditional tracht (not least those of the current family) along side stuffed hunting trophies, and the usual Voralberg innkeeper's memorabilia.

I noticed a lady with her young son sitting opposite a stammtisch full of wayward vociferous local woodcutters and rustically clothed drunk 'peasants'. When I mentioned my research I was immediately beckoned to approach her table by the waiter and being naturally curious I readily accepted the invitation.

"I am from Gaschurn and I understand that you are writing about Hemingway."

She studied me as though I was a rare phenomenon in an age of snowboarding teenagers and loud mouthed foreign skiers. I wondered what to say as she was clearly a little too well dressed for the attendant stammtisch locals opposite who remained unexpectedly deferential in her presence. Her aura of an original distinctive 'Montafonerin' obviously commanded respect possibly because she was also pretty and in the company of her young son.

"My family have the guest book with Hemingway's signature from 1925 and the Murphy's too. As a matter of fact I have just returned from my holidays in Cuba where we followed the Hemingway trail too. You are most welcome to come for tea."

In the only inn in Montafon Valley that had made no pretensions to be a part of the drinking trail of the 'Black, Kirsch-Drinking Christ' I had found somebody seventy-five years later who actually possessed evidence of the greatest writer's pub crawl and love triangle 'menage a trois' in Montafon Valley. I was lost for words mainly because I wanted to ask her why the people remembered such a legend as I couldn't remember much the next morning let alone seventy five years later.

I politely declined as my family began to become restless for exercise but I left my visiting card scribbled across a waiter's chit (and she later kindly forwarded a copy of the Posthotel Gaschurn visitor's book and some photographs too). But after she had left the restaurant like a radiant phantom from the past I thought of how much she reminded me of the photographs of Hemingway's mistress. My mind turned to the famous writer's 'menage a trois' between his wife, Hadley, and his sexual obsession, Pauline Pfeiffer. But then I was forty something and the thought was wasted on me but it had inspired me to write again.

The past has a strange way of catching up with writers as I had found with the Angelica Kauffmann librettos. My wife and myself had sat together in the Hotel Hirschen in Schwarzenberg and I had seen the menu notes and laughed about the fake claim to have hosted one of the greatest love cohabitation triangles in the history of Vorarlberg. The second most notorious love affair was in my opera and with the true local heroine, Angelica Kauffmann, and another blackened cherry picking womaniser and marriage swindler, Graf Horn. Yet Hemingway's misplaced fraudulent rampant indiscretions were immortalised on the menu whilst Angelica's seduction and cuckolding was brushed under the carpet.

It was so typical of masculine morality that I had been quite bowled over by the Vorarlberg mentality especially when the waitress had told me how difficult it was to live in Schwarzenberg as a divorcee. The idea of a male home rule had appealed to me in my midlife crisis especially in such an Alpine world where men set the standards for women. But perhaps I was cast as one of Hemingway's foreign devils or I could waiver, but only to create a legend. My struggles with the modern thinkers of the local Landesregierung increased the irony as I fought offensive after defensive to bring out the mild but moral musical of Angelica's love life. Worse still, such a story of a women duped into love with an unsuitable scoundrel was constantly censored as being too like the Sound of Music.

My beer glass was half full or half empty depending on the perspective of the drinker and the amount of Kirsch Schnaps that accompanied it. I settled into chatting with the local pleasant 'peasantry' about Montafon not mentioning the significance of the coincidence on a midlife writer. I earnestly toasted Ernest's machismo ghost with another Schnaps for the road, stuffed my Krummer Hund cigar between my grinning teeth and staggered down the road to join my children in a much better snowball fight with the 'Spielplatzkönig' and his mates.

****

The Montafon Valley actually has much to offer twenty first century visitors and despite it's growth I remain firmly loyal to the great Hemingway haunt of Schruns. You can still find a small but very pretty inner 'dorf' centred on narrow streets and a cobbled square with assorted cafes. There are several museums, craft workshops and churches worth visiting besides the central church of St. Jodok although it's strange devotion to an animal loving saint depicted in the ceiling paintings belies the main interesting feature of a two tiered organ balcony. My favourite Montafoner church and village is just above Schruns and it is well worth climbing the steep winding roads to visit it.

The beautiful baroque church at Bartholomäberg enjoys some spectacular views being sited on the huge valley rim and the interior is as magnificent as the view from the graveyard (which is incidentally full of some of the finest scrolled wrought iron grave crosses in Vorarlberg). The church has been well restored unlike the sad sloping church of Tschagguns opposite Schruns which remains bereft of much of its former glory. If you have time to visit Bartholomäberg be prepared to be impressed as you sit in it's very narrow pews admiring gilded angels and cherubs and the extraordinary array of ornately carved church procession staves for every feast day and occasion including an ominous funeral staff tucked behind the pillar of the organ balcony. The church dates back to 1100 although the current Barockkirche is from around 1700. There are three superb altars but the exciting find is that it still has a rare carved Knappenaltar which opens up to reveal figurines dedicated to St. Anna.

Instead of returning directly to Schruns it is worth visiting the village of Silbertal which has a tiny museum set in an old wooden house dedicated to the miners of the valley. The tale goes that villagers always had to ensure that everything and everyone was secure after dusk as otherwise they disappeared never to be seen again. This included children who were often stolen to help in the mines where their tiny bodies could squeeze through the cracks and crevices seeking berg crystals. In fact we had attended a promenade play encouraged by the Bergkristal Hotel in the summer which was a wonderful fantasy fairytale worthy of inclusion in the collections of the Brother's Grimm. Other summer visitors may also wish to take a tour of the mines by lamp light but be sure to take great care of your children.

However despite all the detective work, invitations and books the infamous Hotel Taube is still recognised world wide for its extraordinary 'stube' where Hemingway was supposed to have played illegal poker with Herr Nels, the hotel owner, and his ski guide, Herr Lent, at a pretty, round, classic Montafoner table. The unassuming little corner remains a shrine to a great gambler, womaniser and alcoholic with some sparse but significant photographs of the participants and several other skiing parties too. Mrs Nels kindly showed me the photographs but the table was a much more fascinating inspiration as its smooth polished black slate centrepiece and exquisite ghoulish green marquetry just felt right to a ghost hunter. It probably wasn't the original table but I felt certain that it would be fun to hold a séance to raise those errant card players back from the dead.

'Is there anybody there ?' might be a good starting point for such a pretentious gathering of pen friends of the peculiar but revered Pulitzer prize winner.

'Yes but now shut up and deal' might well be Hemingway's irreverent response.

"HEMINGWAY"

RAPPING TO CHAUCER, MONTESSORI, THE MARTINIMARKT AND SMILING SANTA

The Christmas or 'Weihnacht' season is a time for greedy gluttons and ghastly gifts but there are many traditional differences which remain in Vorarlberg to the confusion of American merchandisers unfamiliar with Austrian festivities. The standardised consumer world of the plastic bass playing Santa is confused in Austria with other seasonal characters like the bearded Sankt Nikolaus and the devilish Krampus and even different festive feast days.

The festive season is further disordered in Höchst by the announcement of 'Fasching' or Carnival at eleven o'clock on the eleventh day of the eleventh month of November. The 'Narrenschiff' or colourful Bodensee 'Gondel' fishing boat on a tractor trailer is driven into the village centre carrying the 'Faschingsprinzenpaar' accompanied by the 'Schalmeienzug' playing strange brass instruments and marching girls of the 'Funkenmariechen'. The long winded 'Vorsitzender des Karnevalsvereins' reads out an equally incomprehensible parchment wearing his weird but wonderful 'Narrenkappe'. The church dedicated the day to Saint Martin and they often eat geese in Germany but it is really an excuse to start partying.

There are also several other even more peculiar religious festivities including 'Sankt Nikolaustag' on the 6th December where the children are saved by the Saint or spanked by Krampus. Good behaviour is rewarded by gifts and sweets and naughty urchins are chastised with sticks by his assistant, Krampus. The spiritual calendar then moves forwards with high spirits ever closer to the more famous 'Weihnacht'. However the strangest of the local Vorarlberg pre-Christmas festivities centres around a market in Dornbirn referred to by locals as the 'Martinimarkt'.

The town of Dornbirn had prospered especially from nineteenth century industrialists who had left their mark on the town centre by building a rare Vorarlberg example of a classical church with a painted façade and row of Ionic columns. This strange misplaced palace of worship resembled the architecture of the great Victorian English philanthropists and it dwarfed the surrounding earlier, more comely half timbered buildings dating back to the pre-industrial history. The Church of Saint Martin was built around 1840 by an architect called Martin von Kirk although the central font and altar are curious 1960's additions. It contains a wonderful fresco of the three kings above the choir by Kasparo Rick and several ceiling paintings about Saint Martin's life by the Tyrolean painter, Franz Platner. There is also a mosaic pediment by Josef Huber which unfortunately can only be appreciated in dazzling sunlight. But most spectacular in my humble opinion is the organ with over 5000 pipes and 72 registers built by Martin Behman in 1927 which I had enjoyed on many occasions from the dark anonymity of the choir balcony. It was easy to see why a church built by so many Martins and dedicated to a Saint of that ilk should also host Martini Market in the church square. There was a surprising absence of the famous James Bond Martini cocktails but plenty of other more traditional alcoholic stimulants to shake or stir up sodden visitors.

The town hosted the 'market' or rather 'drinking party' annually on St.Martin's Day. The market dated back to the agrarian times when farmers came into town to sell off their surplus livestock, to pay their dues to their wealthy landlords and to stock up with supplies before winter snows closed the mountain passes. The rain did not stop the townsfolk from dressing up in their version of Victorian 'tracht' with black tail coats and top hats for the rich, prominent menfolk and fur stoles and lace fan bonnets for the fashionable ladies. It was like a version of Charles Dicken's 'Scrooge' but combined with strange local Volkmusik and ample stalls serving copious amounts of warm 'Glühwein'. It was a merry evening of singing in the rain. I stood soaking wet with my dank family under the shelter of the ancient timber eaves infamous 'Rotes Haus' watching this strange mixture of fashionable personages parading like the Royal Enclosure on Ascot Race Day and wondering whether horses would race into the square. In fact the only animals present were some soggy geese in a caged handcart and even they gaggled together like the gossiping crowd. As we struggled through the torrential rain to the shelter of the local cinema to see the latest Harry Potter movie I stomped in the puddles along the cycle lane. My dreams of dance stardom were tempered by my ever practical wife.

"I think you are a great dancer but can you make a living from it ?" she smiled.

"Alright I take the hint. I'll go and teach English but only if you dance with me."

****

There was an infinite number of willing pupils, businessmen and artistes. My wife's convivial cousin Gerhard shared his wonderful office with me along with an endless supply of French Ribonnet wines from a vineyard that he had helped to syndicate and develop in Southern France. I had found time to purchase him a replica early English chess board from Harrods as he was a great internet chess player but somehow I felt that I could do more for him whilst his crew of builders reconstructed my new home. The offers of lecturing grew not only in Lindau where I rose rapidly from spotty student to learned lecturer but also in other schools around Vorarlberg including my daughter's school in Lustenau. This gave me a chance to learn about the aspirations of younger 'Vorarlberger' teenagers and to raise funds for the Russian Children's Gomel Hospital charity project planned by Gerhard and built by dedicated doctors, industrialists and crafts folk from Vorarlberg.

My skate boarding son, Max, was not quite so easy to place at his Monastery School and he was relocated to the Hauptschule in Höchst after a slight confusion with deutsch and his dyslexia. In fact this diary is partly dedicated to persons suffering from this incapacitating and frustrating literacy problem which causes words to become jumbled and even more incomprehensible in an unfamiliar foreign language. I suffered terribly from this debilitating and demoralising genetic disease which requires therapy and disciplined tuition, (so much so that I ran away from my school much to the horror of my parents). Unfortunately Max popped too like a shaken champagne bottle and later apologised for calling his music teacher a fascist.

My wife struggled with the children's various remarkable sports and dyslexia physiotherapists, sociologists, 'kinesiologe', ergonomists, logopaedists, osteopaths, tutors and teachers and kept a weary eye on the building construction. Whilst I was dispatched to school to try out some of my language presentation and director's techniques that I had acquired in the theatre in Lincolnshire. This was a chance to delve under the skin and into the psyche of teenagers to understand more about the new wave of sex, drugs, morals, music and the other East meets West culture of Vorarlberg. It also gave me some inspiration and fresh enthusiasm to help my family to settle in this bizarre but beautiful mountainous land.

"Today we are going to discuss Chaucer and rap to Chantercleer" I announced.

I started by nervously surveying a group of bright young teenagers from Lustenau Gymnasium who sat in a semicircle in separate groups of girls and boys looking hormonally hazardrous to my health. I awaited the first heckler which was always a good cue to engage them in conversation about literature, opera and music.

The classrooms I visited were better equipped than the North of England with the latest computers and projectors, video equipment, and with wonderful views looking out over the shinning snow capped peaks of the chocolate mountains. The pupils were taught between the school bells which amused me in a land full of herds of 'campanologically' challenged cattle but they rose to the provocation of this different style of teaching with excellent musical shows and dramatic dialogue. I was not a good teacher nor was I really trained in teenage tangents and temperament. The paperwork had swallowed up the time of front line teaching staff and that 'Mrs Noah' from the petty hospital bureaucracy now regulated the school photocopier. However I enjoyed riding on the underground of spotty adolescence and for a brief moment my tube train for midlife commuters stopped to revisit the subterranean secretions and glandular graffiti of youth culture. I realised why I hated being a teenager.

We also continued to strive to find schools and teachers for our complicated children. My considerably more academic wife explored the subterranean educational assistance for dyslexia which was also extremely advanced in Vorarlberg. She attended an endless number of conferences, seminars and workshops and even persuaded her reticent husband to leave the world of the writing desk to visit various specialist schools.

My favourite such occasion was a visit to the pretty middle valley village of Altach, where some profound and populist alternative parents had turned a disused knicker factory into a hippie haven for Montessori edification. The principles and ideology of this Italian celebrity and pedagogue were not written in stone which appealed to more ethereal 'Eltern' parents wishing that their youth had been freed from the restrictions of curriculum based learning. At least my first impression was given to be somewhat superficial and cynical as I was greeted by some eccentric ethereal parents enjoying a Christmas Bazaar which at first glance bordered on the bizarre.

Such Sunday afternoon school events in England might involve Santa's Grotto, a drum tombola, and perhaps the odd mince pie stall but that was only when mainstream parentage decided to fund raise for under funded education. The early twentieth century Montessori philosophy turned convention upside down, painted it psychedelic and then stirred in a little adult and childhood fantasy. The eclectic recipe of anarchistic and anti-authoritarian tutelage was remarkably successful resulting partially in the popular adoption of the ideology in state education for Vorarlberg. The word 'Green' had become synonymous not with the outlandish spectrum of parental hair colourings at this campfire classroom but with the devout wish to politically and socially harmonise with the natural instincts of human nature.

The smiling happy faces of wild 'persons' enjoying a bazaar based on the theme of fire was something akin to a parallel parent paradise where opera lovers like myself were able to climb into their wildest dreams and act out the fire trials of Mozart's Magic Flute. The sound of concerned children hammering wrought iron and the smell of nonchalant immaturity burning blobs of dough on hazel sticks over open log fires had far reaching implications upon the principles of disciplined and static government institutional instruction. My children plunged headlong into the myriad of moving and mind provocative activities making multi-layered candles, enjoying fairytales from genuine witches, and writing their names in the true sands of time. We enjoyed this surreal school system and joined in the technicolor transpiration of the vaguer vapours of Montessori minds. I toasted 'Mrs Noah' with my green tea in her absence and the stale state pedagogic system overlaid by her monolithic bureaucracy.

"We've been to Beatle Heaven" I murmured as the car radio played the original scratched vinyl version of Sargent Pepper's Lonely Hearts Club Band.

"You should see where they held the Yoga and the Menopause conference last week. I'll drive you there whilst you sober up from that Green Tea" retorted my happy hippie wife.

We climbed up a long and winding road to the sound of the famous lyrics to the now disbanded monastery of Viktorsberg high up above the 'green' plains of the mystical happy hippie valley village. The view was enhanced by the substance of my mind or perhaps it was the unidentified essence of the herbal tea. The speckled shadows of the cumulus clouds lit by the setting sun tickled the plains below as the breeze played with them like those ecstatic frolicking untamed children I had witnessed at the Bazaar. Nature was reflecting the worship of its bounty and on a panoramic scale befitting of earthly seasons and cycles. I had borne witness to the thanksgiving for nature like the pagan settlers who had first chosen this place of worship. Now ironically the civilised ancestors praised the headless Christian spectre of Saint Viktor that adorned the ceiling of the splendid baroque monastery chapel .

The Catholic Church in Vorarlberg had taken up a popular cause in the early Baroque period by idolising the cult of peasant apparitions as well as burning pagans, nonconformists and witches. The chapel had a shrine with a picture of 'die Mutter von Guten Rat' which roughly translated as Our Lady of Good Advice. I lit a candle to pray for wise counsel hypothesising on the Yogic hints and tips that my wife had learnt on the subject of midlife changes in the monastery next door. I had spent the morning singing the Messiah in the choir at the Gaissau Church Patron Saint's day and I reflected upon the unusual sermon on the holy Saint Otmar who had founded the great monastery and seat of learning in St.Gallen in Switzerland. The sermon had been given by an internet priest who asked the children for their thoughts and such empowerment seemed to strike at the heart of our son's problem.

The sun was setting over the valley of my youth and we all wound down from a trip into the realms of human incredulity. We descended from this pinnacle of peace and harmony and drove back down to the realities of school resettlement and I prayed for better advice.

****

A plain yellow printed note invited me to attend a 'Kulturtreff' in the Palais Art Gallery in the old quarter of Bregenz. It was a chance to mingle with artists and so different from the agrarian world I had become used to in Vorarlberg. Although the cultivating of culture had many interesting parallels as I moved from my 'green' idyll back into my 'blue' period in search of the illusive artist that had painted those cows on the chocolate wrappers.

Bregenz is the capital of Vorarlberg and it accordingly harbours much of the arts administration, concert halls, theatres, galleries and indeed resident artists. It was a small remote colony hidden from the more famous 'Kunst und Kultur' European haunts like Wien, München, Paris, London and Berlin but it was impressive and progressive. The cobbled streets of the upper old town with its walled monastery and famous church were a fitting contrast to the exhibition in the converted Palace. The show would have certainly turned and taxed the previous occupants of this pretty residence of the Archdukes of Thurn and Taxis.

"I especially enjoyed the installation work downstairs and the performance art about Turkish prisoners with electrodes attached to their testicles" I said sipping fruit juice. "The floor upstairs carpeted with flattened cardboard boxes takes me back to my childhood days of skipping along the pavement trying not to step on a lines so I couldn't be eaten by the bears."

The gallery curator smiled and his wonderful full faced beard with a tempestuously curled moustache reminded me of a smiling chocolate mountain Santa. The marked difference was that he was wearing a white, wild, woolly tie, some matching magician's white gloves, a luminous yellow silk scarf and a pin stripped suit from an excellent tailor.

"The world of art is becoming less defined and it is more difficult to find the words to describe these works and cool is inadequate" he replied leaning over the reception bar.

He was obviously a tactful and tactile personality as this objective description of some of the exhibits was not perhaps the comentary I might have chosen. I had long since cooled my ardour for sensationalist art in my midlife fantasy but he was right that it needed new words and tangible adjectives to chastise these new challenges to our perception of art.

"Chocolate appeals to everybody's fantasy. I would love to create a chocolate cow out of the handprints of gallery spectators" I said in a moment of fruit intoxicated inspiration.

The installation artist and her English speaking pop star boyfriend from Berlin entered into the discussion about the merits of the chocolate medium. Soon we were into the realms of sensuality and the American penchant for Swiss chocolate and healthy eating.

"But Vorarlberg is the home of chocolate not Switzerland" corrected the Curator.

"You mean that purple chocolate bar with the cow in front of the chocolate mountains comes from Austria?" I asked in astonishment. "Swiss Chocolate is actually Austrian."

This was good news for my chocolate loving family and I was pleased to know that Vorarlberg was in fact the home of 'Swiss' purple cow chocolate. But my own childhood dreams of Heidi running down across the meadow with a wooden pail of creamy alpine milk to a secret dairy in the Swiss forests were shattered. The image blurred in an artificially induced haze of spiked designer fruit juice but the horror returned to haunt me later that night.

I lay in my bed trying to recollect what there was to know about chocolate. There was the cocoa seed gathered by poor tropical farmers and processed into cocoa powder. The beautiful wooden milk pails slopped around my subconscious dream and the cows bellowed out insults to my ignorance. My nightmare was further complicated by my son, Leopold dancing in his 'Lederhosen' and words were coming from his smeared brown chocolate covered lips. I couldn't make out what he was saying but sugary tears were gushing down his smooth skin like a cold mountain waterfall. He was being slowly smudged out of my nightmare and the purple cow dribbled and then licked my cheek. I woke up to find my wife snuffling gently in my face. I chuckled thinking of my bachelor days when I had been woken up by a sniffing chocolate Labrador in the dog's basket after too many 'tomato juices'.

My mind was made up and I was determined to put the record straight by going to the Austrian home of the chocolate cow. I had fallen in love with the coffee bean and it was now time to try the cocoa bean or was it cocoa seed ? Here I was living in the Chocolate Mountains christened by my youngest son who still believed in tooth fairies and Father Christmas but I knew nothing about its most famous product. As a farmer I had cultivated crops of wheat, barley, oats, oil seed rape, potatoes, sugar beet and even organic cabbages but I was completely ignorant about cocoa. I even lived near the famous chocolate factories in York with their famous tea houses and Victorian benevolent ideals of industrial model villages, churches and schools for the factory workers; so similar to Dornbirn. The missing words from my nightmare echoed around in my empty head the next morning.

"Daddy!" said a little voice shaking me awake. "Where does chocolate come from ?"

"FLYING COW"

CLINICAL CLOWNS, CHOCOLATE COWS, CATAWAULING AND CUNNING DACHSHUNDS

The work on the Opera libretto had now reached the funding stage and the musicians and arts administrators began their work leaving me free to find the answers to my chocolate nightmares before a red horned incubus stole my soul. This evil spirit or Krampus was also reincarnated in chocolate and somehow it had begun to appear with a glowering grin instead of the purple clanging chocolate cow that snorted at my stupidity. It was time to answer the question that was now beginning to haunt my subconscious daytime reverie and so I set off on another exploration for my lost city of silver foil to find the Chocolate Capital of the World.

After a little research I found out that my Eldorado was in a small town called Bludenz nestled at the end of the main Rhine valley of Vorarlberg. This originally walled and well fortified town had always fascinated me as it had harboured Duke Frederick after he had fallen out with the great nonconformist barbecue for bishops at the Council of Konstanz in 1416. I empathised with him as a penniless refugee who simply did not like the odour of burning human flesh preferring the sweeter smell of chocolate. But judging by the unspoilt but empty pedestrianised town centre, I also sympathised with the poor inhabitants whose fortunes were in fact only revived much later by twentieth century chocolate production.

I asked an off duty teenage fire juggler the way up to the famous onion domed church of Saint Laurentius and he shrugged his shoulders and pointed his fire club up a closed covered stairway. Climbing the crumbling, dark and cold graffiti-painted flights of stone stairs I caught a glimpse of the stunning snow capped mountains through the silhouette of the arches. I paused to take a breath of the fresh alpine air thinking that perhaps at last I was in that lost paradise; a forgotten cradle of civilisation that worshiped God, brewed famous beer and made wonderful chocolate. I was in the chocolate town famous for the 'Weltgrösstes Schokoladenfest' and what more could a man in his middle years want from life than sweet sucesss? The peak of my existence was a few steps away and I straightened my hat and set forth to conquer my nightmare and male midlife inhibitions.

"Excuse me" I said politely in my best deutsch trying to attract the attention of some workmen digging a huge trench around the church. "But the church seems to be locked ?"

The first slightly muddied and black moustached workman, who was clearly of local ancestry, shrugged his shoulders. I realised that it was pointless trying to explain my beer and chocolate pilgrimage to the peak of manhood to him although his obese figure showed signs of partaking of much of these local victuals. However the second mud spattered workman of foreign extraction showed signs of both English comprehension and dietary abstinence.

"Church closed, but try the pink house next door" he said pointing politely upwards.

The Gayenhofen Palace was the kind of house anyone would like next door and I carefully skirted the trench which showed signs of significant archaeological remains of an earlier possibly mediaeval church. The Baroque Palace was originally constructed in 1868 for Freiherr Franz Andre von Sternbach on the site of the previous mediaeval 'schloss' but after a checkered postwar history it had eventually been converted in the nineteen sixties into regional administration offices for the adjoining geographical valleys of Walgau, Montafon, Klostertal, Arlberg, Grosses Walsertal and Brandnertal. It was still an impressive structure now devoid of its past grandeur but with helpful staff anxious to please a lost Englishman. However on this occasion I left disappointed but with a feeling that the church could not resolve my life long quest for my chocolate Holy Grail anyway.

The message on my mobile telephone reminded me of another reason why I had come to Blundenz. My enthusiasm was rekindled and my curiosity led me further up the hill to the hospital where I had arranged to meet some very special red nosed doctors. The best value lunch in town was in fact the hospital canteen and I sat at the doctors table with the white coated specialists discussing the health service in Vorarlberg. This was a wide ranging topic not necessarily good for the digestion. The rumbling and grumbling about the lack of investment in additional winter staff for tourist skiing accidents, the LKF prolific and useless paperwork (doubtless created by Mrs. Noah), the lack of an MR facility, outdated computers and the worrying closure of other smaller hospitals was enough to give any hungry politician indigestion. However I practised my satirical smile for my next patient.

This hospital was the smallest one of four principle hospitals in Vorarlberg but it impressed me more than my visit to Bregenz. Admittedly this was because I was a visitor and not a patient about to have strange instruments inserted in unspeakable parts of my anatomy. The doctors and nurses retained the same sense of humour but there was much more patient privacy with warm, clean, modern double rooms and so much more thought about human relationships and the terrifying prospect of hospital treatment. The idea of providing an adjacent bed for mothers with sick children instead of a tattered old chair shoved into English hospitals seemed to epitomise this human rather than just clinical attention to patient needs. I had come to visit another unique volunteer programme based on the alpine philosophy of psychological patient relaxation during often quite stressful and painful treatment.

"My name is Doctor Schussel and this is Doctor SoDaLa" said a red nosed doctor.

They had white coats but that was about all that these volunteer 'CliniClowns' were wearing that resembled the standard medical attire of doctors on ward visits to 'Paediatrie' and 'Urologie'. Doctor Schussel was a teacher by profession but she had helped to found the Vorarlberg branch of the Clinic Clowns seven years ago. She enjoyed her heart felt and rewarding charitable career as a clown wearing traditional face paint, a red nose and multicoloured stockings and simply making patients laugh. Her enthusiasm was so epidemic that her 'Kollege' with his classic baggy pants and braces also completely absorbed himself in his clowning for two hours of infectious laughter and merriment.

The performances in each room were all carefully planned yet retained that spontaneous, natural and childlike humour with balloon modelling, magical tricks and memory games. I watched them as they chatted between the rooms about their success which manifested itself in the enlarged eyes of toddlers, the giggling of self-conscious teenagers, and the outright laughter of the nurses and doctors. This was so much more than the bowing and clapping of live performance and the rewards were infinitely more satisfying to the performers. It touched me as a Producer and Director of Live Theatre so much more than the great tragedies or concerts that had consumed my passion in the past.

The Theatre had been my second home for over twelve years in Lincolnshire and I had enjoyed the great pleasure of working with many gifted clowns and street entertainers at Festivals and Children's Parties. I followed these clinical clowns on their ward visits cheering up children, adults and elderly patients with sporting injuries, gastroenteritis, broken limbs and other more life threatening ailments. The laughter and naïve uncomplicated humour was completely absorbed into both the minds and souls of the patients and staff. Time after time and room after room I watched sad, often anguished and discomforted patients change into smirking, laughing, giggling, chuckling and, above all else, comforted human beings.

"I think you would be wonderful in Hollywood" I said singing their praises.

We sat down in the canteen to fill in the carefully prepared evaluation forms designed to further help the clinical rather than comical needs of the patients.

"This is so much more than the Big Screen. It's a personal thing" she responded unabashed by the compliment. "It is spontaneous laughter not scripted for an audience."

"Do you ever get caught up in the personal emotions of the patients?"

"Our naivety gives us a certain neutrality but I have seen staff rushing in vain to save young and elderly patients that I have got to know. The ward then seems to be gripped by grief, loss and sadness and of course it is not the same as our job is affected by the shadow of death. But the next visit might make a difference between life and death."

It was clearly addictive but, unlike my now seemingly irrelevant and absurd chocolate or caffeine obsessions, this was humour that was worthwhile consuming. It was not intended to fill a hole in my stomach but the gap in my heart.

It was about unpretentious and guileless humour that was transparent and yet its healing effects were both visible in the smiling faces and invisible deep down in the spirit of the human essence. It was dangerous ground for performers as the thin ice could not hold the weight of all these mortal sorrows. It was too easy to fall into the cold clinical water of tragedy and drown in the misery of death.

"I shake my 'lachsalz' and spread a little joy" she said with a face painted grin.

This statement was as naïve and neutered as it was intended. I left them thinking of the shallowness of life but not without a little clown chuckle at my official blue nose.

However, other inconsequential and petty thoughts of chocolate cows played havoc with my mind and there was still that unanswered question that had brought my quest to Bludenz. It was a distraction that any white knight seeking sleep at night could not decline and the pretty young assistant who welcomed me to the Suchard Chocolate Factory was well worth fighting dragons for as her smile also was enough to melt milk chocolate.

"Thank you for coming to the home of the Milka Cow but actually it is not blue or purple as we call it the Lilac Cow" she said in a slightly automated tone.

According to the amusingly translated brochure that she handed me along with a white coat and lilac peak capped hair net, the cow of my dreams had the macho name of 'Milki'. It had also changed colour several times before settling for transsexual lilac. I pondered over breeding real cows one day that could not only change colour to camouflage themselves but also to scare off any trespassers. However Lilac was a garish colour and it might scare off any butcher intent on purchasing alpine cows. After the television coverage of the dreadful massacre of some of the finest dairy herds in England during the Foot and Mouth crisis it was always difficult to laugh again about cows, but the image of a reporter and the Agricultural Minister in a crisis news conference played upon my tiny mind.

'We are here at the farm where it all started' reports the news hound. 'Minister, can you tell us what the government plans to do with these lilac chocolate cows ?'

'There is no cause for alarm as we are tasting samples at this moment'

England had never really recovered from the ravages caused by the crisis and I remembered vividly the damage it had wrought on farms all around us and how lucky we were that our sheep flock was spared just before the lambing season. We had lost thousands of pounds from the closure of our Farm Park and Zoo which was no laughing matter. But being English I always kept my sense of humour in a crisis created by an incurable disease and spread by politicians who constantly put their feet in their mouths and I could see the merits of Lilac Cows. At least the vets could pick out the symptoms more easily and they could eat the problem. But knowing those paranoid pyromaniac scientists they would find an excuse to melt them down too. The sad thing about Foot and Mouth disease was that the meat was fit for consumption but it was not chocolate, lilac, sticky and very tasty indeed.

Our tour of the factory was quite simply astonishing and I felt confident again to be able to answer my son's question about the origin of alpine chocolate. The cocoa beans came from the Ivory Coast, Zaire, Ghana, Ecuador, and Brazil and were fermented, roasted and then the nibs were ground and mixed into cocoa powder liquor. The secret of good chocolate was to get the next stages right. There was pre-rolling and fine rolling so important to the melting stages. Then the liquefying process and addition of the cocoa butter (and the other three hundred 'well known' ingredients) and the pre-crystallising action made this alpine chocolate bar consistently perfect for the ever changing taste buds of mostly German speaking consumers. If you followed that brief translation of the automated production of chocolate then you are either a scientific genius or perhaps even the winner of the Chocolate Nobel Prize. You should also perhaps try to get out a bit more and eat more chocolate.

"We are fully automated these days and long gone are those early days of hand wrapping and packing" she said as we admired two hunky white robots that picked up and stacked the heavy boxes of chocolates delicately sandwiching each layer with a thin card picked up by their finger-like suckers. I joked that they looked a bit like the 'iron men' on muscle beach and even if a beach boy smothered his fingers in sun cream he could not physically pick up even his 'toilette' paper like these automated anthropoids.

As we rode through the multi layered one hundred year old version of 'Charlie's Chocolate Factory' aboard the lilac lift, I thought about all those lyrics that I had written for my musical inspired by this book and that magical dancing sweet factory in the 'Chitty Chitty Bang Bang' movie. I was tempted to sing the lilac cow version of 'Toot Sweets' but decided that the sequence would require a lot more thought. I could not visualise chocolate whistles in the mouths of dancing lilac hair netted factory workers as it was too messy but delightfully sticky. The new branding was being designed in Vienna for adult chocolate addicts.

I drove back home down the Rhine Valley Autobahn and listened to a Rocky Horror Show tune which seemed to suit a contemporary 'Milki, that Cool Transsexual Lilac Cow'.

****

The diary filled with so many engagements that I was at risk of becoming an alcoholic or, worse still, a chronic invalid after my wife had finished nagging me the following morning. I decided that the best policy for the future of our marital harmony was to encourage her to join me which in retrospect was a reasonable request.

"Where are we going and why do I have to dress up?" said my angel suspiciously.

"It's a surprise and I'm going to keep my promise to take you out to all my functions whenever you want" I said feeling rather like a hopeless Homer Simpson cartoon character.

It certainly was a comic surprise as we arrived fashionably late for the Feuerwehr Dinner looking like a James Bond couple in a room full of firemen in dress uniforms. We sat alone eating near 'the Twenty Four Hour Bürgermeister of Höchst' who was as ever always entertaining. As his nickname suggested, he was always in attendance and well informed on all of the forty eight clubs and societies in his village. He kindly explained the 'Fireman's Oscars' which were presented for service of over fifty years (and some of even longer duration) and the swearing in of three young firemen as they placed their right hands on the station standard and repeated standard phonetically formidable vows to fight the fire phoenix.

We left at a tactful moment after the Bürgermeister as our next engagement was at Egon's Bar where I had promised to catch up with Egon's film festival version of the Pro Western Motor Bike Film Club. However there were no Oscars being presented on this auspicious occasion but we stood out once again in a room full of well oiled cowboy bikers. I happily chatted and joked with the line dancers and hunters that I had become well acquainted with over our extended stay in Vorarlberg. Meanwhile my wife struggled with an extremely pickled hunter who tried vainly to garble some sozzled story about our hunt earlier that day.

The hunt to which he referred or rather slurred I have recorded later for her benefit. The bad breath of this bellicose belligerent simply overpowered her and we left when he stuck his stinking socks on the table and slumped across her chair. My sincerest thanks is noted to this nameless and shameless individual for my subsequent freedom to continue my local 'stammtisch' writing engagements. I made up for my fire call in the pouring rain on my wedding anniversary with a formal dinner at the Feuerwehr but perhaps Egon's Biker's Home Movie after dinner entertainment was an acquired taste. The roaring Harley Davidsons and snoring motorbike riders were certainly an unusual cultural diversion.

"So you do this kind of thing every evening?" she said as we staggered home.

"Nicht immer aber immer öfter" I imitated a beer advert with a dinner suited man.

"Not always but pretty often made alcoholics like Hemingway" she warned.

"Actually funny you should say that as last Friday's Choir Dinner with the Bach loving priest reminded me of his nickname as the Black Kirsch Drinking Christ."

"I think I now get the picture. Don't tell me. You were catawauling with the choir in the Gwölb Keller under the Priest's House. You men are all the bloody same."

****

The Great Gaissau Hare Hunt to which the slobbering lush had referred started out more as a hair of the dog but turned into a hare shoot with a dachshund. The irrepressible and irresistible German sausage dog with its catlike attributes and fiercely independent nature was for me the star of the show. However the haunting hunting melodies blown tunefully by eight Parforce Horns and the hunting ghost stories by the camp fire were high up in the noteworthy credits of this hunting tale.

The term 'hunting' applies normally to hunts on horseback in England although doubtless the government will try to extinguish this 'distinction' before too long. However in Austria the term is not so 'distinguished' and these hunters were mostly local led by their 'distinguished' organiser, Julius Blum. He was a wealthy, shrewd but benevolent local industrialist of few words and his welcome to the assembled guests was modest, moving and memorable as it was to be his last time as the 'Kapitän' of the hunt after twenty six years. Nevertheless on this occasion even he could laugh as his rueful remarks were overtaken by the humorous events of the wag's tale of hopefully not the last Gaissau Hare Hunt.

The hunting of game around Gaissau and Höchst was extremely carefully managed despite the constant poaching and proximity to other recreational pursuits. There were nearly thirty hunters armed with shot guns and the beaters performed well with a variety of interesting hunting dogs including Labradors, German Spaniels, 'Shaggy Schnautzers' and the infamous 'Sausage Dog' or Dachshund. We hunted for pheasants, jays and hares in a fashion similar to England although the smaller amount of wild game was relative to the shooting territory and the abundance of foxes and other predators.

Standing in the woods on the Old Rhine Spit I giggled at the guile of the Gaissau Pheasant that cunningly perched up a tree thwarting all efforts by the beaters to dislodge it. The hare that hastened in my direction was not so lucky and it was soon lying dead at my feet. It was then that the shoot turned from a hair of the dog, as I was suffering after a long night with the Church Choir, into the tale of the hare and the dog.

Out of the woods scampered a long haired dachshund some time after the hare had met its demise. I presumed it was a case of the hare and the tortoise and like in the fairy tale this short legged hairy anthropomorphic 'amphibian' was undoubtedly the winner on the grounds that the other competitor was somewhat incapacitated. This did not stop the victor from tearing at his spoils and I bent down to prevent him from demolishing my trophy. This was a mistake and 'one in the eye' for the departed spirit of the hare as the dog's teeth bit into the bladder squirting a jet of stinging urine up into my left pupil.

Later we sat around the campfire under the bare bark of the trees in the dusk of a cool autumnal night singing songs. I was asked by my fellow hunters if I would contribute to the merriment. My language inhibitions had been worn down by the wine and I told them that traditionally English hunters told stories rather singing songs.

"Alright Englishman, then tell us a story" said a voice from the darkness.

"Well, I know a good hunting ghost story" I said poking at the embers of the fire with my boot and looking around at the faces that flickered in the firelight.

"I have seen two hunting ghosts in my life. The first was after a long day of stalking in the hills above Loch Tay in Scotland. I finally found a 'lie' near to a herd of deer and the stalker pointed out a stag. I pressed my eye to the telescopic sight and there in my cross hairs was the most beautiful white stag standing so proud like the ghost of the monarch of the glens. Of course, being a gentleman, I did not shoot and the stalker thanked me for my generosity of spirit handing me a hunting trophy that he felt was a suitable reward."

"And the second ghost ?" enquired another voice from the shadow of the night.

"The second occasion was in Norway where they hunt Elk with fine grey elk hounds in the woods. The hounds held a wonderful Elk at bay and again I lifted my rifle, only this time propped against a fir tree. The beast was a magnificent specimen with huge muscular fore legs and he cast one of the hounds on to its back. The hunter that accompanied me instructed me to shoot lest the wounded hound be gored to death so I shot him cleanly through the heart and the hunter finished him off." I paused to kick a log on the dying embers.

My terrible amateur attempt at telling a tale was ably assisted by my host and patient translator Lothar, and I could see the attentive audience imagining the story which was so much better than any television presentation despite the dramatic sound dubbing.

"The moral to my second tale came about as we were driving home that night to Oslo and we were involved in a terrible car crash. The car overtaking us hit another Elk and we all finished up in hospital. In the hospital waiting room the doctor asked me if this had ever happened to me before ? I replied that I had once unfortunately hit a kangaroo in Australia with similar consequences after a hunting trip in the Outback and indeed a sacred cow in India where the taxi driver fled for fear of his life. My moral is simple. There is a ghost in every human and animal on this earth and it is wise to respect it whether you hunt or accidentally take another life on the road. That is why I am impressed with your horn music for the hare that I shot today and your respect for fellow hunters and the hunted."

The story was difficult to translate and I sympathise with those who struggle daily with the spoken word but I hope this transcript record shows another purpose for literature. The spirit of the hare will live far longer on this page and the spirited dachshund ran home to Höchst much to the amusement of the hunters who probably sang on well into the night.

SONNTAGSESSEN, DAMÜLS PROTOCOL, A PET PHYSICIAN AND A NEWSPAPER HEROINE

The telephone never stopped as I struggled with teaching, house building, the opera and being the family taxi driver. Being born into a culture that held Sunday as a day of worship followed by the traditional family gathering around the lunch table it was always a great relief to simply relax and enjoy a Sunday Excursion. This generally followed a customary pattern as we were living in quite cosy conditions and the farmhouse roast was desirable but quite impractical to our circumstances. Accordingly we would leave the church and drive out into the nether reaches of Vorarlberg in search of the exclusive 'Sonntagsessen'.

"We want to go sledging on our 'rodel'" chorused the children in the car.

The slopes of the Bödele marked the entrance to the Bregenzerwald region of Vorarlberg and I had spent some time writing the Opera libretto there looking out over the spectacular valley above Schwarzenberg. The slopes were lower than other mountain resorts but the first slushy snow on the shady side of the Lank afforded good sled runs. There is something to be said for 'Sunday Sledging' as you hurtle down a hill on a wooden toboggan completely without care or control. My children were masters of speed, agility and above all wipe outs and I could quite understand why no self respecting cow wished to remain outside during the winter sports season.

The American farmers mark their livestock with the white painted word 'cow' in the hope that a stupid eejit can read and won't pump his 'fully automated hunting gun' into these harmless grazing herbivores under the pretext that they looked like fair game. Alpine farmers risked their livestock being used as slalom poles by crazy sled slayers. Even the lilac cow from the chocolate bar would not be stupid enough to stand outside in the snow to become a target for wooden suicide sledges as it was far safer standing in the middle of an Autobahn.

"It's time for lunch and I want to take you to one of the last villages to be connected by road where they used to ride to town in a horse driven sleigh" announced our family expert and guide.

So we drove on through the Bregenzerwald following the Bregenzer Ach river through Schwarzenberg and on past Bezau, Mellau, Schnepfau, and then turned up towards the Walsertal Valley at the small town of Au. The steep and pretty road that we followed up to Damüls was in fact of relatively recent construction in that it was only until the nineteen fifties that cars and buses could pass safely along it. Prior to that point this village had remained untouched by the pressures of skiing and tourism although it was clear when we arrived that commercial tourism influences had completely changed the original settlement. It was now a fully mature ski resort and the snow was almost ready to welcome the onslaught of skiers that had inexorably changed the fortunes of this whole region.

None of the ski resort hotels bother to open during November which is a point worth remembering if you are seeking off-season holiday accommodation during this period. However, most villages have a local guest house that never really closes as I have yet to find a Bürgermeister who eats sandwiches in his office during 'mittagspause' and Damüls was no exception to this unwritten Gemeinde rule. It was a rule of thumb that I had learnt whilst writing in the Bregenzerwald and it could always be relied upon to act in your favour if you required an audience with the key figure of an alpine village especially if you were liberal with your purse. Politics had certain protocols and it was a wise man who followed them even if sometimes it involved seeking the guiding hand of a very sloshed sage.

"Welcome to Damüls and we have hirsch on the menu today" said our hostess.

We sat down in the pleasant restaurant of the small but snug Gasthof Lucia and enjoyed a hot local lunch looking out on a cold snowy and remote landscape. After lunch whilst the children played snow 'bawling' outside we retired to the older 'stammtisch' room carefully avoiding the Bürgermeister's table as he was 'holding audience' over lunch. We were joined by the elderly invalid innkeeper, Fridolin Bischof, whose hospitality was renowned in the village as was his ancestry from the original twelve Walser families who first settled in Damüls in the middle ages in the hunting area of the Fürst von Wallis from Valise in the Grissons. This was not an easy time as many settlers simply starved and they had to promise never to return to their 'Heimat'. It was also quite a struggle with all supplies being carried up into the mountains on horseback or by backpack.

The name of Bischof had remained predominant in the village for several centuries and still was the surname of sixty percent of the inhabitants despite the influx of tourism (as many families had since intermarried). The actual name was nothing to do with bishops but originated from the words 'Bei-schöffen' or By-the-magistrate. It was however quite common in this region to find such large concentrations of one family name and he explained that everybody was identified by their house name or first name. I laughed at the similarities to my mother's family in Ireland where families were identified by their profession so that you could not confuse the butcher with the undertaker.

There was no doubt that Damüls was one of the most inaccessible parts of Vorarlberg at the junction of three mountain passes to Grosses Walsertal in the south, the town of Feldkirch to the west and the village of Au in the north. This latter village still retained the strongest connections with this community and he told us that every St.Katherinatag (which happened to be the next day) they would walk or sled down to Au to settle up their debts and buy stores for winter. The 'Tourengeher' ski tourists only really started to arrive in Damüls in the spring of 1943/44 walking on skis with furs on the 'Firnschnee' after the avalanche season. The first ski lifts arrived in 1952 and the village soon began to prosper after many years of poverty where everyone barely survived on bread and cheese sharing hand-me-down clothes and shoes until Katherina market.

He could remember his days helping the 'Kutscher' to drive horse drawn sleds from Au to Schwend where his father used to have another inn. The 'Pferdeschlitten' once had a terrible accident in the winter of 1952/53 on the narrow winding pass. There were two sleds full of guests and the first, more experienced horse galloped away at the sound of an avalanche. Unfortunately the second younger horse followed on too late and failed to stop running directly into the path of the snow slide and the sled fell into the ravine tragically killing a French tourist. It was also sad that his tales were being simply forgotten as the village immersed itself in the hospitality industry and now the slay bells were silent and cow bells had all but disappeared from the village.

We drove back over the high pass into the Grosses Walsertal valley through mountain villages cut into the steep sides of the gigantic mountains. It was a distant echo from a time now almost lost in the pages of torn scrap books where familiar faces smiled out from sepia photographs beckoning me to hear their story. The children drank carbonated drinks from carbon plastic cartons and we drummed to the sound of hip-hop and African-American lyrics which reinvented a new vocabulary based on mispronounced vowels. I thought of the languages and dialects which had evolved here untouched by the Western World but purism and sentimentalism can breed anti-social misanthropy. Just some appropriate words that would be only jungle sounds to those primeval rap artistes. Perhaps that was how the yodel was born here and my chronicles finally had a purpose to record the rapping yarns of the past.

****

The world of politics had been a part of my life in England as serving on Parish Councils, County Councils and the Westminster Parliament were responsibilities that were inbred into my sense of public duty. I had had a fairly typical political career being associated with the old style of Tory landed gentry losing my last fairly remote chance of a Westminister seat in Scunthorpe on an exciting second ballot just one year before I had left for Austria. The old guard of the party were now all being guillotined by the Blair Republic and the House of Lords where I had attended my interview as a 'bright young candidate' was being gradually eroded in favour of the professional, rather than duty bound hereditary, peers of the realm.

My father had loyally volunteered to serve his Queen and Country as an Army SOE Captain, and later as a High Sheriff, Deputy Lieutenant and Vice Lord Lieutenant and local Royal Escort. He had even founded an Association for Sheriffs which I had grown up with as we had shared an office for over seventeen years. It was a role that I admired and to a certain extent had emulated on a more political path with his encouragement. Sadly he had a heart attack in his seventies and I could see that those golden days were over as my artist brother was much more of a reclusive personality with different sense of public duty.

It often happened this way on the great English Estates based on large often crumbling historic houses built in a bygone era of life long butlers, gifted landscape gardeners and in our case also a wonderful zoo too. I had loved working with all kinds of animals over my seventeen years in the zoo becoming a capable falconer, natural history teacher and indeed a self taught animal carer. Like Gerald Durrell, my great childhood hero, I had taken an active role in local ecology, natural history clubs and studies, and Farm Park and Zoo projects. So much so that I would travel the length and breadth of Lincolnshire and Yorkshire in the voluntary service of the regional Tourist Boards, Museums Associations, Historic Houses Associations, English Nature, the Royal Forestry Society and more recently advising on Farm Diversification and Rural Tourism Strategy.

Vorarlberg was a strange place to land after a life of meetings, committees and public speaking in the service of tourism and the countryside. I was at that point of my midlife crisis where you take stock of your life for the first time. I had a chance to enjoy a bit of personal freedom to write an opera and indeed this chocolate mountain chronicle. But there was no doubt that I missed my animals and so who better to console me but the local self styled version of a great Yorkshire vet who invited me to his evening surgery.

"Do you live near Harrogate as I am a great fan of James Herriot ?" he had asked.

I met the cheering, jovial and ever so slightly corpulent, Dr. Bruno Fink for the first time at a rather uninteresting public meeting of the Höchst Gemeinde in the Fire Station. I had attended in the public seating upon the invitation of the legendary 'Twenty Four Hour Bürgemiester'. He had instinctively detected that somehow I was missing my previous public duties and needed some 'boring meeting therapy' to help me to realise just how lucky I was to have my freedom again in Vorarlberg. It had certainly done the trick and I was about to run back to my line dancing class but his black T-shirt with interesting animal footprints and his rounded winning smile was enough to rekindle my flagging attention.

"I am hoping to build a small animal park here along the edge of the old Rhine. I am involved in the 'Freizeittierhalter Club'. We hold an animal show with over six hundred 'Tiere' at Luise's Farm on the Sunday after Mother's Day. Please come and visit my small animal surgery if you are interested" he said as the meeting closed for a statutory drink.

This was an invitation that I was not going to miss as seventeen years of working with zoo animals was beginning to give me a certain longing for the company of like minded creature carers. It was not long before I was walking up the pretty candle lit pathway to his modern peculiarly hexagonal surgery extension of his modernised house in the centre of Höchst. We chatted and reminisced about his Vorarlberg version of the James Herriot stories whilst he spayed an unconscious multicoloured cat.

"Only female cats have three colours or more as their chromosomes and genetics permit them to be more colourful than the males" he said as I winced at his scalpel swipe.

He was certainly an exception to this rule as I discovered after the surgery was completed. We strolled out with his young son, Ferdinand, to see his pet South African lop eared Boer Goats in their four star accommodation complete with adventure playground facilities and pine cabin sleeping quarters. We laughed as he told me about life as a local vet in Vorarlberg where you could be asked to fix up humans as well as animals and you never put your hand inside a sack in case it really was one of the most poisonous snakes in the world. He agreed that often the pet suited the owner except in the case of the 'cockerel crown haircuts' of Punk Rockers where he often had to operate on their pet pocket ferrets lest their gland scent secretions be misinterpreted as their human body odour.

We sat down to drink wine from the 'Burgenländer Heimat' of his loving and lovely wife whom he had met over twenty-five years earlier during his veterinary studies. She pinched his chubby jowls when he was being naughty about his version of the midlife crisis and our cheeks reddened as the crimson sunset drew in and the stars twinkled in our eyes. We pawed over old photograph books of his animal shows which always seemed to show him with the same impish and contented smile. When we began to delve into the books on anatomy and early farming practices in search of the original Montafoner Brown Alpine Cow that had been the dominant alpine bovine during his long and varied veterinary career, I knew that it was time to return to the fold. I was completely cured and slightly pickled too.

****

The First of Four Sundays in Advent was always used as an excuse to indulge in the Vorarlberg version of pre-Christmas retail therapy with a 'Christkindelmarkt' in virtually every city, town and village. We were lucky enough to visit one of the greatest examples of these festive markets in Stuttgart in Germany where the long lines of wooden huts were richly decorated with mythical, religious and even forest creatures. The giant red soldier from the Nutcracker Ballet greeted us as we entered a fantasy world of hundreds of Christmas stalls selling anything from honey candles to shiny baubles; traditional or contemporary ceramic pots and pans; new age and antique jewellery; and every kind of food and drink from smoked fish on sticks to strange herbal teas. The smells of lavender blended with soused herrings and the sounds of organ grinders wafted over the chatter of thousands of Sunday Shoppers.

The Höchst interpretation of an Advent Market was centred upon the church square with a selection of covered wooden market stalls merchandising mostly food products for a seemingly underfed local community although few of the customers could not see their toes due to their well rounded girdles. Likewise a smaller more concentrated market concern next to the Convent in Gaissau attempted to quench the village thirst in the form of 'Glühwein' or convent coffee and massive cream cakes for those inclined towards the holy missive of abstinence. I partook of the warm spiced wine and watched as the priest demonstrated the different types of incense until I was pigeon holed by a smiling dove in the shape of a nun. Her hallowed apparition in a cloud of oriental smells appealed to my sense of humour.

"We are selling some old English books ? "she beckoned with a sacred selling smile.

The nuns were very active in the village as the sentinels of the bible spreading the word of Catholicism. I was persuaded by her wonderful dialect and my sentimentalism to also indulge a little in the service of convent fund raising, carefully avoiding the spume from the beer and cream 'kuchen' which tempted me towards the sin of gluttony. I leafed through the wonderful old exquisitely bound tomes that were being jumbled in the name of a library clearance and to my astonishment found myself hastily purchasing a small library.

"Darling, don't you think that you have enough words to think about without adding a bygone ancient German library to our lives" said my hypocritical academic book hoarder.

"But this is different just look what they are throwing away. You can't expect an author to stand by as they discard great English literature" I retorted defensively.

The truth of the matter was that the library had simply adapted to the age of the Internet, CD and DVD hire. It had left the boring art of reading behind, consigning literature to the antiquated world of the silent written word. The smell of leather bindings by the warmth of a log burning on the hearth and the feeling of discovery as you leafed through water marked pages seemed to have been overtaken by the modern multi-media. Even the travel book writers had forgotten this library paradise as they competed for the last literate travellers in transit or their bored spouses sun bathing on the beach. Reading was simply a means to an end. Books were now scrawled in a time of turmoil or rather in no sensible time at all.

The books I had purchased were from another dimension and my tools of the trade as many travel writers relied on the source material of other more specialised and learned authors from the locality. Although the plagiarism and the poor use of gossipy, uninspiring vocabulary of recent travel books on Ireland had annoyed me intensely. Being half Irish I had sympathy with fellow comic authors who simply wrote as they spoke without a thought for grammar, diction or the slightest inclination of what the words actually meant to the reader or indeed themselves. This verbal diatribe was akin to a cheeky cholera but it splattered out from both orifices simultaneously over the pages of a quite mundane mixture of dialogue and regurgitated words best swallowed again. However such hilarious travel books sell in large quantities to a readership used to personal columns in magazines and possibly the odd well chosen word between the pictures. Just as Thackery had commanded a huge and loyal following with his diaries, so too were the new twenty-first century hacks carving new ground against the factual well researched travel books for practical pompous prigs like myself. Where was my spirit of adventure but then perhaps that was my problem.

"Look, here is a first edition of Kingslake's Eothen. Now that's real travel writing on horseback, buying slave girls without fear of the plague and hiring magicians to conjure up devils in the Pyramids" I said flicking through the leather bound diary secure in my bed.

We had first met in a tomb in the Valley of the Kings and I could see Marina's face as her eyes lids rolled back to those fond memories. The heat and the sand had brought us together at a time when we were both ready to commit to family life. The adventures we had shared in Sharm-el-Sheik in search of elusive camel's condoms and in the romantic sauna in the sulphur caves amidst the minefields. Egypt was not the same as in the wild public school adventures of Kingslake's Travel Tale of 1845, but we had still found something magical besides the pyramids and the echoes of the piano in the empty, crumbling imperial bygone hotel in Alexandria still played on in our hearts. The refreshing evening breeze as we rode in an open Landau carriage to the temple of Karnak still cooled my tingling skin as I untied the mythological red ribbon of passion that had hidden that lost parchment of those happier times.

"Do you remember those three uncouth Arab boys who peeped through the ties of our beach tent? Their faces turned white when you swore at them in their mother tongue but they wouldn't leave until they had retrieved their lost gym shoe from under your pillow. I still wonder what it was doing there to this day" I said staring at the cobwebs on the ceiling.

"And the red face of the check-out girl in the supermarket when I brought those ten packets condoms was embarrassing enough, especially when I read later each packet contained twenty latex sheaves fit for camels ! She must have a shocking view of western culture, never mind what old Kingslake got up to with his slave girls in Cairo."

The ancient, well travelled English book with its musty smell had found a new happy owner and I noted that it's previous owner was also called Robert and of some impressive standing in exploration clubs. The gilded spine was from a time when travel stories were either preached to a cold church congregation from the great bible or gleaned from the diaries of these great horseback adventurers from the magnificent days of the Royal Statistical Society. As I digested the 'gung-ho' diction I longed to turn back the clock to my youthful motorcycle tours of America and Australia. Those great Imperial Institutions of Exploration Club Smoking Rooms had now become Snooker Rooms but middle aged men with middle age spread still bragged about their global adventures and female conquests. But nowadays the discoveries of the diarist hand written in italics whilst astride a beast of burden had been replaced by miniature cameras strapped to a camel's buttocks.

"I met a local newspaper editor who wants to read my diary. Maybe she will encourage me and give them a wider readership too" I said optimistically switching off the light. "I don't suppose I could interest you in an illustration of Egyptian Exploration."

****

The newspaper image of the local Vorarlberger Nachrichten newspaper was as transparent as the great glass cathedral in which it was housed outside Schwarzach. If the building failed to impress visitors as to the openness of the only paper of substance in the region, then the frank and friendly staff were bound to captivate you in their sheer enthusiasm for the future of the written word. The days of lead typesetters and inky fingers from broad sheets were not altogether lost in this 'brave new world' of environmentally friendly and technologically superior internet interactive newspapers. Aldous Huxley would still be able to find some individualist agnostics in a media monopoly that had spanned three generations since the War under the leadership of the same local Russ family proprietor. This new modern church of the multi-media was careful not to be dogmatic or to categorise local readers, and to wisely fend off other international tycoons that might prey upon its unusual independence.

"Thank you for giving up some time to help a struggling writer" I said nervously.

"It was a pleasure to meet you in my only off duty activity these days where they can't get hold of me on the telephone" she replied with a steadying handshake.

Marianne Mathis was referring to our first acquaintance by the fireside during the hunt in Gaissau where she was trying to relax as well as record the event for one of her many columns and magazines. She had a totally different perspective on hunting with which I sympathised as for her it was a chance to download in the silence of nature and to switch off her mental computer. Judging by the number of calls we received during our time together it was a wonder that she did not simply short circuit and implode.

Her business card gave her the fascinating, but totally understated bizarre title of 'Stellvertretende Chefredakteurin' as she had an independent and astute presence of mind and over twenty five years of newspaper journalism under her belt. She ran unintentional smoke rings around me as we delved deep into the data driven new media age in search of the meaning of the written word. It was clear that this newspaper still believed in being inclusive whilst also being relevant to an increasingly mixed and migrant population often only able to read basic deutsch. Literature had its place, but author's like Goethe were not an overriding influence on the contemporary communication sphere of modern internet led newspapers.

"The paper has survived virtually unchallenged in Vorarlberg because everybody from the mountains to the mosques can find themselves in the paper. The cardinal rule of good journalism is that everybody is important" she said puffing on another cigarette.

This made me feel better too as I was quite nervous about being inside a glass membrane which was nurturing the ever growing and all consuming multi-media age. It was clear that such architectural transparency of the media womb left little room for privacy as every heartbeat was being monitored by technology. The King Bee of this gigantic hive might one day simply discard these worker bees in favour of a synthetic newsprint nectar just as the thousands of newspapers printed in the adjoining fully automated computerised plant were now published virtually without a human presence.

There were certain advantages to this mechanical cyber world notably for the 'Umwelt' as the process was greener and cleaner although the amount of waste to be recycled after the readers had discarded their daily paper would probably remain the same. The plant produced several different papers for Austria and Switzerland and could produce 100,000 copies of the Vorarlberger Nachrichten in less than three hours at the simple touch of a computer button. The internet was an exciting new alternative to newsprint with a growing instant interactive readership and the spoken word of the radio was now so advanced that the audible vocabulary included many different languages. But deep inside I still held a secret hope that my chronicles might survive this brave new world, if only to record the momentous changes to literature and possibly the beginning of the end of literacy itself.

"For me everyday is a challenge. Change is the only constant in life" she quoted.

She was right. Pictures and sounds were becoming words in this perpetually inconsistent silicon biosphere built on the reality of instant world and local news events at its foundation. Yet it was blurred between the lines by the unreality of repetitious digital rather than thought technology, so much so that I wondered if the lines ever ended. As I left the building I was brought back to Planet Earth by a receptionist whose attire and hair colouring reminded me of a calendar girl version of Krampus. She was one individual that would never be constant, although the thought of the white bearded Saint Nicholas spanking her for being so non conformist did cross my mind. In fact later that evening I was presented with a Line Dancing Award and co-incidentally the men in the group were also given a 'pin up' calendar. The adult literacy required to read the numbers under the photographs was more a case controlling your natural instincts and blood pressure rather than any literary deficiency.

The power of words cannot take away the physical presence of pictures and naked images and numbers on a calendar without any captions could still say a thousand words. Imagination requires only stimulation and after all is said and sometimes done the reality is that humans have managed far longer without written words. The prehistoric cave drawings found in French caves used pictures before pictograms and indeed the reconstructed thatched houses on stilts in the famous Bodensee Museum of Unteruhldingen showed little evidence that writing had developed much beyond symbolism until the invasion of the Romans. The Latin interpretation of the pre-existing verbal language of the native population remains an integral part of Germanian 'deutsch' today although this is always open to conjecture, especially with localised dialects. The newspaper I had visited now supplied information to several different dialect speaking regions in Vorarlberg and indeed was 'read' by many German illiterates and itinerant visitors. Was the written word essential within this framework of traditional spoken dialects and such pleasurable pictorial aids to communication?

"You'll catch Aids if you look too long at that calendar" smirked my wife.

"But darling, I'm studying the local communication media" I replied with a kiss.

Here are just a few of the Chocolate Mountain Characters that star in this snowy satire ... Thank you for reading our story.

Lothar the Jäger
on another Mission

Family Blum the Butcher
& the butcher's daughter

Alfons the Baker
with his pipe

Armin the friendly
Feurwehr Chief

Angelica Kauffmann
Painting

Dr. Willi Meusburger as a
Chocolate Mountain Santa

Some Clinical Clowns with
Dr. Schusel & Dr. SoDaLa

Dr. Sausgruber as the
Starship Landeshauptmann

Dr. Bruno the
Pet Physician

Marianne the Editor
& my only Fan

Werner the Twenty-four
hour Bürgermeister, Höchst

Manuel the Snooker Hustler
with Robert the Cool Cat

In the shadow of the
Phantom Plumber.

The Nice Border Guard
from Gaissau

Egon as the Vorarlberg
Pro-Western Cowboy

The Priest & his
Secret Angels.

Cousin Gerhard as
the Singing Baumeister

Franz Vornier as the
Rolls Royce Wild Man

Bezirksinspektor Bernie
and the Blue Light

Ghost Train Spotter
James Joyce

The Lilac Milka Cow
as Milki My Man

Andy the Ski Jumper
& Cool Snowborder

A Haflinger in the
snow just for Emily

Hemingway's Black Bearded
Kirsch Drinking Ghost

Plastic Santa as
Sankt Nikolaus

PS: We apologise to the Fürsten von Liechtenstein & Queen of Holland whose stamps could not be reproduced for this chronicle but their royal images are in many other publications.

NB: If you would like to learn a bit more about us, visit **www.vorarlberg.at**

The Great Floating Stage of the Bregenzer Festspiele during La Boheme. The Author's First Assignment

Opera with a Midlife Message   A wonderful Open Air Opera looking out at Lindau   Three Stage Choreography

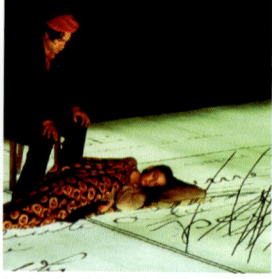

The sublime swan songs at sunset on the Bodensee   Inspired to write by the death of a heroine

Photographs loaned courtesy of the Bregenzer Festspieple. (www.bregenzerfestspiele.com)

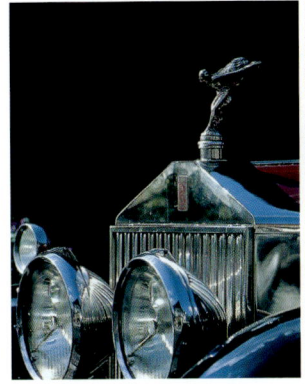

The Rolls Royce Museum in Dornbirn

The Author explores the Phantom Rolls Royce Hall of Fame with fellow Wild Man, Franz Vornier

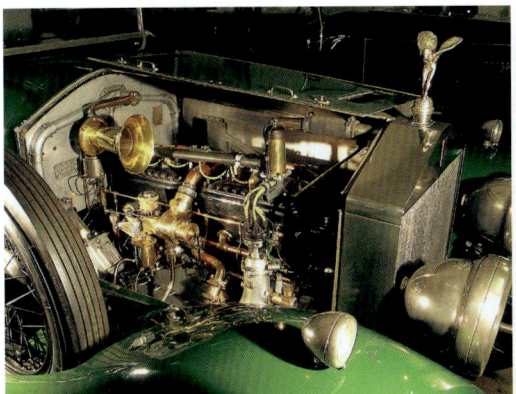

The Engine of the infamous Silver Ghost but a Phantom One is much more reliable

The Author is invited to lunch

The Original Engineering Workshop of Charles Stewart Rolls in Action

Inside the Cockpit of the Phantom One. An alpine addiction other than Cows

The Beautiful Emily

Photographs courtesy of Rolls Royce Museum. Franz Vornier GmbH. www.rolls-royce-museum.at

The Chocolate Mountains. Appenzellerland. Switzerland

Appenzellerland from the Bodensee

Cowmen in Tracht at a Cattle Show in Appenzellerland

Judging the Best Udder!

Gathering to bring down the cattle in Appenzellerland

Appenzeller Cowman's Alpine Garland

Painted Pail

Appenzellerland Wood Carving

Silvesterklaus

Appenzellerland Assembly to Vote

Santis Mountain above the clouds

All Photographs loaned for this Diary.

Appenzellerland.
Vom Bodensee bis zum Säntis.

For further information please contact
Appenzellerland Tourism (www.appenzell.ch).

Urnäsch Silvesterklaus

Schöne Schuppel with Nachtrolli in Appenzellerland

Zaure in a Schöne Schuppel

A Schöne Schuppel Group jodelling a Zaure. Urnäsch. Appenzellerland. (Note Vorrolli & Nachtrolli in Skirts)

Appenzeller Belts, Buckles & Braces

Forester's Schuppel Mask

All Photographs loaned for this Diary.

Appenzellerland.
Vom Bodensee bis zum Säntis.

For further information please contact
Appenzellerland Tourism (www.appenzell.ch).

Bringing down the cows from the High Pastures

Alptag in the centre of Schwarzenberg

Schwarzenberg. Bregenzerwald. The Author's favourite village & Heimat of Angelica Kauffmann

Writing the Opera in the Hirschen Hotel

The Author's wonderful Stammtisch.
Inspired by a fake Hemmingway Ghost

Photographs by kind permission of Schwarzenberg Tourism Office. Bregenzerwald. (www.schwarzenberg.at)

The Angelica Kauffmann Halle during the Schubertiade. A Revelation for an Opera Libretto Writer

Church with Angelica Kauffmann's Painting

The Special Ladies Tracht & Bregenzerwald Beauties

The helpful village Heimat Museum

An Angel in the Cemetery

Bregenzerwald Alpine Cheese. An Andelsbuch Experience!

Photographs by kind permission of Schwarzenberg Tourism Office. Bregenzerwald. (www.schwarzenberg.at)

Fasching & The Schalmeienzug Höchst
with strange Schalmein Instruments

Voralberg Clowns awarded Author a Medal & Blue Nose

Egon's Pro Western Bar and Vorarlberg Cowboys on motorbikes

The Gaissau Kirchenchor. Don't believe everything you see

Gaissau Church

www.hoechst.at – www.gaissau.at

Cool Chris. The Skateboard King

Chris in Action after his Crown

While other's take Flights of Fancy

Getting some Fresh Air in Halle 8a Dornbirn

"We go Snowbording on Sundays too"

Photos courtesy of Dornbirn
elmar.luger@dorbirn.at

Author often spots spotty Snowborder's getting some Air
Photograph courtesy of Vorarlberg. (www.vorarlberg-tourism.at)

The Bregenzerwald. A wild and wonderful paradise

From the Pfänder to the Bodensee and Höchst

Author goes in search of another Fantasy in Schoppernau in the Bregenzerwald

In search of Schoppenau Schriftsteller Freedom Writer Franz Michael Felder

Similar Schoppenau Surnames, Bregenzerwald breeds Beauties!

Photographs courtesy of Schoppernau Tourism & Vorarlberg Tourism (www.voralberg-tourism.at)

Castle Vaduz Liechtenstein and Walser Museum

Haflingers in the snow in Brand

Montafoner Tracht at the Partenenhof as Author follows
in the Phantom Footsteps of Hemingway

Schattenburg Castle in Feldkirch as Author goes
Ghost Train Spotting with James Joyce's Ghost

Klein Walstertal and the Ketchup Border

Hemingway & Three Towers in the Montafon Valley

Pictures loaned for Chocolate Mountain Chronciles by Vorarlberg Tourism and Liechtenstein.
www.vorarlberg-tourism.at – www.liechtenstein.li

Lindau Insel looking across the Bodensee to the Chocolate Mountains.
Panoramic Photo courtesy of Lindau Tourism (www.lindau-tourismus.de)

Bodensee at Sunset. Courtesy of Kontanz Tourism.(www.kontanz.de/tourismus)
The Author plans to circumnavigate Lake Constance in the next Chronicle

SAINT NIKOLAUS, THE TWENTY-FOUR HOUR BÜRGERMEISTER AND JASSEN JOKES

There is one special religious festival that is not really celebrated in England or indeed most English speaking countries, not because the saint's name is difficult to pronounce but mainly because Catholicism is not so ingrained in popular culture as it is in Vorarlberg. After some unsuccessful research and much hearsay bordering on horrifying heresy, I eventually gleaned the official story of Saint Nikolaus from the very professional and efficient priest of Höchst. According to his encyclopaedia of holy saints, and other early documentary evidence, all that is actually written from that time is that Nikolaus was the Bishop of Myra (now in Turkey); he attended the Council of Nicea in 325 AD; and he died in 350 AD.

He was venerated as a saint by the Eastern church around 600 AD and became a figurehead much later in the 10th Century in German speaking countries. His bones still rest in Bari in Italy where they were brought for safe keeping by pilgrims in 1087. He was one of those saints that has a ghoulish repertoire of legends where he undoubtedly shines out as the only sane person amongst a deranged local population. He apparently started his holy work by throwing coins through a destitute nobleman's window so that the rather desperate impoverished gentleman would not sell his three daughters into prostitution. This was something of a temptation for impoverished writers like myself too with tiresome teenage daughters to contend with sprawled on the sofa, but my daughter would only fetch a couple of camels and maybe that pony she was demanding for Christmas. However money would probably fly out of the window on her behalf but I remained hopeful of a passing patron saint with a golden book, long red cope, white beard, bishops mitre and that admirable crook.

I spotted several version's of him in a street identity parade but the police might have great difficulty identifying them by their crooked crooks. I did notice that the one that knocked on our door sounded a bit suspicious. St. Nickolaus visited children in the village to tell them if they were good enough to get sweets and treats or conversely too naughty meriting only a spank from a birch bundle or, in times past, being put in a sack by a bearded Krampus. This latter act of child kidnapping was now discouraged by the church in favour of a couple of black faced girls in stripy black and white shirts looking like gangsters with a swag bag.

They all certainly alarmed our children, especially as the golden book was pre-primed with a little parental guidance to contain some interesting misdeeds. The visit is actually more worrying when you know that the person with the beard represents a sacred bishop that saved three dismembered children from being eaten by a cannibalistic innkeeper. But it wasn't only this that made me concerned. It was the fact that our St. Nikolaus had quite a high soprano voice and a very unusual bulge around the chest area. It was only then that I realised that my previous midlife fascination with the spanking of a flirting calendar girl version of Krampus could also be extended to what appeared to be an effeminate 'Nickerlass' under that fake white woolly beard. It wasn't until our exhausted chocolate stuffed children were tucked up in bed that I raised my suspicions to my wife about our rather unusual evening visitor.

"Darling, it was fun eating chocolates with the children but there was something really peculiar about that Nikolaus" I said waving a birch bundle.

"I was wondering when you were going to mention that little bit of local spice to Sankt Nikolaus Tag. You don't need your calendar to spot the girl guide in the kinky clerics costume. All the charities have their particular fund raising day and somehow the Pfadfinder have a monopoly on Nikolaus costumes. They get a bit short of men with deep voices."

"I just can't wait to go for a grope in Santa's Grotto" I joked with a lecherous grin.

There were several male appearances of the white whiskered bishop notably at the tap dance school of my cutest son, Leopold, who was the only male dancer to dance for Nikolaus amidst eighty girls. He didn't care at all sitting with his slightly tilted Santa hat and a pair of red wings on his back. Maybe being an over sexed voyeur was my problem and the route of my male menopause and only by taking things on face value like a child could I recover from this mental derangement. This terrible anxiety about ageing that had been ruining my life was just like a childhood phobia of what Nikolaus might say or about Krampus spanking me. I had seen the light and promised to learn more from my children but then I had caught a slight glimpse of silk stocking too. Surely I was just being perfectly natural for my age.

The original Saint Nikolaus also held a mind blowing list of other holy duties besides being the Patron Saint of Children as he was also the Patron of Apothecaries, Bakers, Grocers, Corn-Measurers and Merchants, Seed 'Händlers', Weavers, Embroidery and Cloth Makers, Lawyers, Butchers, Seafarers, Brewers, Fishermen, Pilgrims and Travellers. Only the Bürgermeister of Höchst had more duties, but he didn't have the halo although I thought that he might be a shinning example to me to mend my wayward thoughts. Who better than him to give me a new direction as he was wise, bearded, and a fellow man of the world; so I booked an appointment to see him. He was always reliable, dependable and indeed held the nickname of the 'Twenty-Four Hour Bürgermeister' and maybe he could bring my sanity back again.

His little corner office in the Gemeinde was meagre but comfortable as he was a suprisingly modest person. He peered over his half rimmed reading glasses as I entered the room and put his fountain pen down sparing me some time from the busy task of writing Christmas Cards to all of his 7096 'Bürger'. The post of Mayor did not include a chauffeur driven Rolls Royce; a red fur lined cloak and three pointed hat; a gold badge of state that reminded citizens of a lavatory chain of office before they flushed red with embarrassment; or indeed even a key to the village gates as it might have done in traditional good old pompous England. His private secretary was more akin to the receptionist in a business bureau emailing his missives rather than sending for the Town Crier to ring his bell and yell out his decrees from a parchment scroll . This Gemeinde was a place of local administration not ostentation. Werner Schneider was the longest serving Bürgermeister since the War with fifteen years of indispensable sagacity, administrative admonition and doubtless political oration skills to keep him so long at the helm of a very tight ship in Höchst.

As we chatted about religion, politics, statistics, demographics, roads, sewage, social care and schools it became clear to me that he had made something of his life. He confessed that he hated dancing and sport was a luxury of youth, but he had basically devoted his life to the seven thousand odd souls of Höchst. In fact it turned out that he had taken the post after Franz Grabher in 1987 and he was very proud of his family, especially his wife, Ursula, and son, Tobias. He was also always able to escape on holiday sailing on his boat on the Bodensee to switch off from the job too. I asked him politely if I could use his nickname as the 'Twenty Four Hour Bürgermeister of Höchst' that somehow had stuck in my mind. He laughed, saying he was used to it as in fact he had been an engineer responsible for the mountain tunnel near Bregenz known as the 'Pfändertunnel' before he took on the mantle of mayor. He had once literally spent twenty-four hours on Christmas Day at work due to an accident with a spilled load of textiles that had blocked the tunnel entrance.

"Do you regard yourself as being like the Doctor or the Priest?" I enquired.

He smiled and a knowing, well-rehearsed, mindful and ever tactful reply seemed to flow from his lips as though he was facing a television interview for the job of the next Prime Minister of England. Come to think of it, he would do a better job with the firemen and with a lot more sincere 'sincerity' than our current media led incumbent.

"I suppose I am a bit of both, but I can't help everybody" he replied with a grin.

There was a certain realism in his honest reflection that you simply could not please all of the people all of the time and he had learnt that it was a totally pointless waste of time aspiring to this principle. When I inquired whether he felt an affinity to Saint Nicholas he roared with laughter again replying that he was more like the 'Good Ghost of Höchst' which showed his great political ability to make sound bites in English too.

"I have learnt a lot from my children today. What do you think you would carve for the children of Höchst if I gave you a stone tablet ?" I said with my tongue in my cheek.

He sat forward in his chair and turned over a clean page in my book of scribbles. He wrote carefully, slowly and with the deliberation of a stonemason. I joked that it would have to be a huge boulder if it was going to be as long as one of his speeches. He was a patient man of the world with a wonderful ability to see beyond his term of office. He wrote:

'A child should make wishes and follow them as they can become true. I wanted to become a Captain and now I am the Captain of Höchst.'

As I was leaving he presented me with some wonderful books on Höchst which he signed with his fine italic ink fountain pen:

'Dies vom Höchster Kapitän'.

****

Our farmhouse had now suddenly become a hive of industry although I missed the British builders with their cheeky whistles and sagging trouser cracks. It was too cold to show a builder's bum and too dangerous to wolf whistle at a passing nun. However, the old roof came off and the new roof was put back on with better insulation at lightening speed in between bouts of equally sudden terrifying thunder and torrential rainfall. It was at last beginning to look like a new home from home and surprisingly even from the top of the highest chimney the wind speed was considerably less than at our home in Lincolnshire.

The main dwelling house was being divided to accommodate ourselves, guests and our increasingly worried Chinese tenants as the disruption was rather like knocking down the Great Wall of China when they were still walking along it. I deeply sympathised with them as sledge hammers crashed through walls, drills started before cockerels had even thought about crowing, and builders yelled as their swinging cranes smashed through windows. It was like a perpetual Chinese New Year, only the firecrackers continued to play havoc with their slumber creating several weeks of sheer hell. We carefully avoided too much contact as the waiters looked like Triads about to murder us and we chose site visits to coincide with the restaurant opening hours to avoid any chance of a noodle massacre at dawn. However, there were some difficult moments especially after singing practice when the Church Choir traditionally retired to play 'Jassen' in the floating Chinese Restaurant.

'Jassen' was a peculiar national game of cards that intrigued me as a pretty average Poker player and a terrible Bridge player. It involved some uncommonly confusing rules and a set of cards that were designed by sixteenth century artists on hallucinogenic drugs rather than by card players. Most normal card packs have thirteen sequential and clearly defined cards in four suits but not this game. It had yellow stripy Christmas globes, leaves of some sort of lime tree, yellow acorns that resembled peeled lemon suppositories, and distinctly crimson blood red hearts. There were even cards with several of these symbols on, just to make sure that you were so bewildered that the rules, which also changed depending on which region you were in or perhaps by the moon, just didn't really make any sense at all. Whoever invented the original variation of the variation of the variation we attempted to play must have lived in a state of constant astrological flux. The unnamed weirdo with an opium addiction also probably ended life and an existential interplanetary existence very suddenly after some paranoid schizophrenic lunatic shot him for cheating (or not cheating depending on which side of his crazed and confused character was pulling the trigger).

"You can play 'Arschloch' with us if you like, Englishman" said the choir leader.

"Okay, but not for money and it's not strip Jassen either" I genially replied.

Anything was preferable than being made into chop suey as I could easily become an additional menu item judging by the look of the cook. The idea of innkeepers in Turkey preparing to serve children played on my mind, especially as every town and village had a Chinese restaurant that had been there since before anyone could remember. The Turkish are more famous for kebabs but I wouldn't be at all surprised if there was also a 'noodle and poodle' joint in Myra around 300 AD. The resident Chinese waiters also had a sense of humour to laugh at obese English guests joking about who might be served up with black bean sauce. I opted for a slow suicide by cards playing a strange game called 'Arsehole'.

This card game variation is designed for idiots like me who know an under from an over and that the odd stray card can send you spinning into touch. I suppose cricket might have a rather similar soporific effect on confused bystanders, but at least you could whack the ball for a six past silly mid off and over the extra cover. Leg before wicket in this game was more a case of cards disappearing under the table and out for a duck was reserved for those who lost, only the expletives would also be too offensive to British umpires. At least the beer replaced the milky tea in the pavilion and you didn't have to stand around waiting for your innings. Everybody got to play at whacking their cards on the table and occasionally slapping and abusing other players too as that was all in the spirit of friendly table banter.

The only advice that I can impart on this game is don't forget to play your over before your under, watch out for strange flying cards with pigs on them, and if you are stuck, stick your cards under the table. I was thankful that they did not drink Schnaps as the blurring of the already perplexing cards would have made any such a trick trickier, if not impossible.

****

The festivities related to Saint Nikolaus often span over the weekend as many other dance clubs and indeed the Feuerwehr used the opportunity to entertain parents for a social occasion. We were parents and expected to be concerned about the activities of our ecstatic if perhaps over stimulated brood. Halls and function rooms were filled with the throng of hyperactive children and exhausted fathers, mothers, aunts, uncles, grandparents and the odd estranged spectator. Our daughter Emily, like her younger brother, had practised her jazz dancing routine until she could emulate if not better the great choreographic video masterpieces of the great pale skinned pop star her class were bent on imitating.

The giant gym in Lustenau was filled to capacity so much so that we were left standing at the 'Standtisch' rather like in the packed Opera Houses of the great cities of Europe only without having to overdress for the performance. We whooped and whistled as she finally strutted her stuff after a endless theatrical bill of teeny gymnastic performers most of whom flew across the stage as though they had been fired from a backstage battery. The really civilised thing in Austria about all these parental gatherings was that most of the parents got to sit at long tables eating, drinking and being merry whilst their progeny tried hard to impress them as flying cannon balls. In all my many days as a star struck thespian I could never drum up as much enthusiasm and athleticism with fellow performers but then it was so much more motivational when you knew that half of the audience were your relatives.

One of the best Nikolaus visitations was in the unusual setting of the Feuerwehr in Höchst for which I had grown a soft spot since my enrolment of as an honorary fire fighter. The Fire Phoenix had yet to raise it's fiery plumage in the village but the station still firmly believed that morale was important and that they should resurrect their 'Nikolaus Nachmittag' for firemen's children. The format was akin to other such festivities with long tables with baskets brimming with walnuts, peanuts and tangerines and pretty little candles which really softened the otherwise quite functional seventies seminar room architecture.

My son, Max, being more of a sporting personality felt somewhat out of place with his little brother and a room full of toddlers. However, he took to this responsibility by house training and then feeding nuts to his over excited smaller dependent until he was heartily sick into the ashtray. This brotherly amusement to an otherwise boring 'Kinderspass' was only surpassed by the knock on the door and the dimming of the overhead lights. All eyes widened and focused upon the arrival of one of the best dressed Nikolaus I had ever witnessed with all the correct attire and indeed the right Feuerwehr 'attachment'.

His 'attachment' was the official church replacement for the alarming 'Krampus' known simply as 'Knecht Ruprecht' and he supported a remarkable black hooded costume complete with animal skins, a hessian sack, a long grey beard and dangling chains. He accompanied the extremely credible Bishop from Myra complete with his gold painted fisherman's staff, a gilded book of children's good and naughty deeds, a long red embroidered cope, a pair of shiny white gloves and a slightly bent gold lacquered mitre. The procession moved with the captivated gaze of the enchanted children to the end of the room where Sankt Nikolaus proceeded to sing traditional songs and tell some of his censored adventure stories.

"So my child, are you wishing for any presents ?" he mumbled through his beard.

"Well...I would like a Rettungswagen" piped up one of the toddlers.

This was a rather appropriate but nevertheless completely sincere request for an Emergency Vehicle from an over enthusiastic tiny voice in the crowd of children seated around him. The candles burnt down to their wicks as all the eligible urchins enunciated their requests to a well trained and well drilled white bearded figment of their childhood fantasy.

For the first time I found myself being drawn back into my childhood by this experience to the days when my father used to dress up as 'Santa' and entertain us all in the library by the fireside at home whilst my mother struggled to clear the detritus spread all over the carpet as we tore open his presents. He was a great inspiration for my theatrical career later attending many of my performances, but his greatest moment was when he decided that Father Christmas costumes were hot, stuffy and boring and he donned a tiger costume instead.

"I've never had that response before" he said anxiously to my mother after leaving a room full of shrieking and wailing children for a hasty costume change.

"Oh darling, you are silly! They think you've eaten Father Christmas!" she laughed.

"FATHER & SON"

SCHMUGGELN, PUMPEULUSISCH, RED MARY AND THE FIRST SNOW IN DAMÜLS

The villages of Höchst and Gaissau had some oral annals that were not documented due to the fact that they bordered on criminality or to be more precise they involved stories of smuggling over the border. I heard several tall tales of 'Schmuggeln' that rivalled the great farcical northern yarns like 'Whisky Galore' where some Scottish Islanders pillaged a cargo of whisky from a shipwreck on a remote island under the noses of the Customs Officers. Some tales were so hilarious that there was many an occasion when I literally cried over spilt milk or rather the smuggled butter and cream that had escaped from its container down the Lederhosen of the unfortunate slippery smuggler.

It was a fact of life for many families for many centuries and quite well recorded in the wonderful books that the Bürgermeister had presented to me to encourage me to write more about his beloved Höchst. The archives mentioned the practice as far back as the 1700's and contraband included textiles, salt, sugar, saccharine, cigarettes, gold, coffee, chocolate, nylon stockings, chewing gum, and even cream and butter despite being a mainly dairy based economy. There were several local folk fables of families becoming rich on the proceeds and even more tales about immigrants and refugees especially during frequent periods of European hostilities and during the World Wars.

Some of the smugglers songs and slang words had been adapted into dialects, notably a strange type of multi-lingual cockney called 'Pumpeulusisch' which, despite many interviews, seemed to have almost completely died out. Many stories were passed down by word of mouth. The local media had an extensive archive including interviews with wartime smugglers and with some still active gangs although these were generally unavailable for comment due the risky nature of their business. It felt like being Sherlock Holmes as I interviewed customs officers, known smugglers and indeed much of the local population who had at least a couple of unconfirmed and naturally not corroborated childhood stories. It was like walking around in circles with a large magnifying glass expecting some street urchin or pick pocket to jump out and say 'Follow me, Guv' except in short leather trousers.

The local bars were full of tattooed characters, some with artificial limbs, that also might be discovered in English pirate inns and there were plenty of little creeks along the Old Rhine to hide booty too. The wilder, more exaggerated stories included rumours about families financing their 'Stickerei' or lace weaving workshops on the proceeds of the illegal trade. It was certainly true that 'Stickerei' production had experienced periods where customs tariffs caused extreme depravity and in recent years the closure of many small family businesses had been blamed on such inconsistent duties on lace. However, much of the fortune of this industry was more dependent on wider world production. The one hundred or more 'cottage industry' sewing machines that were still in production were still flourishing making fine lace for Petticoat Lane and the Jewish and African shops around the Old Kent Road in London for export to Africa (notably for Buba and Wraper wedding costumes in Nigeria). In fact I had met a charming Nigerian buyer on a train who said that she only bought Austrian lace from Höchst and Lustenau because it was simply the best in the world.

The calumny and dangerous defamation of the character of certain respected farming and fishing families was to a large part also unfounded as smuggling had been a relativity small proportion of their main income. Farmers had become rich on the development of their pastures; as a crop of houses far outstripped any reward from the soil or smuggling. I was not sure which was the worst evil as frankly smuggling seemed preferable to vast fields of concrete. The population of Höchst had risen nearly fourfold since the census of 1869 which recorded 1,982 citizens of which probably some were part time smugglers. Few people had entered smuggling as their profession in the recent census of 2001 which recorded 7,096 people noticeably with only just over 1000 or more Ausländer. It failed to record any illegal immigrants in transit which was the preferred merchandise for the modern criminals.

However, the trade in humans was generally abhorred by most people that helped me to compile this book especially amongst the Turkish, Kurdish, Croatian, Serbian and Bosnian communities. This was understandable as smuggling was often used to chastise these communities who incidentally had several amusing anecdotes about bootleg booze.

My favourite smuggling story was actually substantiated by several individuals and had become quite a recognised tall tale of village gossip. It was of very doubtful origin and none of the characters can be attributed to any individuals who are living or indeed deceased as the names and incidents are purely fictional for the purposes of the protection of the author.

It was a yarn that many who related it to me dubbed as 'The Murder of Red Mary' and it was set around the end of the Second World War (or possibly later) when refugees and deserters were fleeing from certain death and a trade of desperate people flourished in desperate times.

"Everybody can tell you about Red Mary as she was the Queen of the Smugglers and more ruthless than that Mafia Godmother in Italy" said my source sipping 'duty free' wine.

Having been to Italy I could readily understand that my anonymous source was referring to the legendary Mafia wedding where a 'Godmother' machine gunned down the principal guests in revenge for her son's assassination. Often grudges could be kept for many years until one day vengeance was served up with a lot of tomato sauce splattered over the wedding cake. It would be difficult to enjoy the reception after the massacre or the tomatosauce tainted 'kuchen' but knowing Italian hospitality that would not stop a good reception.

"She was involved in 'Schmugglen'. At least, her house was full of carpets" he said.

Several sources joked about this sort of smugglers identity tag which was based on the principle that 'guests' unable to pay in monetary terms paid in kind by leaving their worldly goods as a parting gift. The opposing theory was that the fishing boats ran a two way traffic to double their profits. Some sceptics suggested some gangs didn't bother making the trip at all as disposing of invisible people was a fairly easy matter in the Bodensee or indeed in some of the river reed beds and deep lakes near Höchst and Gaissau.

"Anyway, she ran a ruthless gang including members of her family" he continued.

The witticisms that followed were generally centred upon the fact that in many families not everybody was aware that other members of their household might be involved in smuggling. Often this was simply a practical psychological barrier against the police and customs as although innocence is not a defence that could be used in court (or indeed prior to execution in these times) it could put them off the scent for a while. Anyway for fear of interrupting a good yarn the remainder of the 'tall tale' is recorded below.

"They were doing pretty well using the shallower parts of the river and sometimes using fishing boats which had canvas covers to hide their 'cargo' from prying eyes. It was a dangerous time if you were caught as the authorities were often bored troops who were a bit trigger happy especially if the 'cargo' was... well probably due for discreet disposal courtesy of the Third Reich. It paid much better than farming and fishing but it required stealth and a large network too. Probably as far away as parts of Germany to bring in the 'cargo'. In fact one member of this particular gang often went on long journeys."

As it is a purely fictional account the teller might perhaps pause for a homemade possibly illegal sip of local Schnaps and a long slow drag on an illicit tobacco commodity remarkably similar to expensive cigar products normally subject to heavy import taxes.

"Well, one day Red Mary failed to turn up to pick up her shopping which was pretty noticeable to the shop keeper. She was a very good customer especially during rationing where such shops needed some additional under the counter sales and indeed supplies too. The proprietor enquired later of another member of the family where she was, only to receive an ambiguous reply that 'she was worried'. Anyway, that was the last they ever heard of Red Mary. She just disappeared. Some say that one of the gang murdered her in a smugglers argument and that another gang member died mysteriously some weeks later in a motor cycle accident with an unidentified vehicle."

My contributor winked and puffed a smoke ring.

I could see the movie credits spelling out my name as I sold the story for millions to some sucker in Hollywood. (If they do happen to read this story the script is in the post). These anecdotes abounded and my chronicles were overwhelmed with classic black and white blockbusters like the great cult film, 'Casablanca'. I had actually found Marrakesh more exciting on my month long stay in Morocco and that was the only time I was apprehended for smuggling. I unwisely joked with a customs officer who had asked me if I had any 'hash' in my rucksack that it was available just along the quayside, but some wise guy had placed the illicit substance in my baggage. Rifle bolts clicked. I surrendered. Okay, it was a bad joke!

****

"You spend too long at that desk. I'm going to the Linde" said Gerhard grinning.

There are writers that spend many hours seeking stimuli and sometimes stimulants to create the great tomes of our musical language. Gerhard often caught me 'under the bonnet of my computer' verbally fine tuning my midlife composition in a corner of his busy architect's office that he had kindly lent me whilst he reconstructed our house in Gaissau. I had an additional struggle with severe dyslexia which meant everything had to be read aloud until I was absolutely satisfied that the words were in the right sequence like my librettos. Much of my early poetry and work with the radio and theatre was also sharpened and refined on the rhythm, rhyme, rhetoric and rhapsody of the harmony and melody of the English language. No writer could ever hope to win a noble prize for literature from writing travel books except perhaps Hemingway. However, judging by the number of invitations for live readings of the chronicles that were flooding in, my hobbyist scrawling now required a much more focused attention to every phonetic minute or 'spoken minuet'.

There have been many famous composers, opera divas and indeed 'Schriftstellers' that have contended with similar dyslexia problems having to basically read everything in the mirror backwards. There were stories about Albert Einstein of relativity fame; Friedrich Schiller, the revolutionary playwright; Hans Christian Andersen, my favourite fairytale writer; William Butler Yates, my second beloved and adored poet after Byron; and my favourite inventors, Thomas Edison, whose light bulbs lit up my little alcove of inspiration and Michael Faraday, who 'empowered' my writing with electricity.

"Thank you, Gerhard, let's go and play Hemingway" I said with my fingers crossed.

With this positive response we both downed our tools leaving our respective desks strewn with unfinished manuscripts and half drawn building plans. The Linde's invisible bell tolled as we strode across the church square to Gerhard's second home from home where our stresses could be washed away and heart warming wenches could peal at our egocentricity and chime to our Falstaff comedy in celebration of drunken frivolity and manly effulgence. It was like being on stage in a Shakespeare play engaged in the raucous ribaldry of a sub plot about the formation of a great king or perhaps playing a naughty prank on a pompous servant although you could just as easily receive a clenched fist as clasp hold of a fresh cleavage.

The Linde Keller was a place of traditional victuals and vociferous traditionalists whose scabrous japes jostled for the attentions of the singularly attractive and single landlady. She in turn revelled in the attentions caused by her refreshing and enlightened policy towards drunken lechery and debauchery. Instead of ejecting the perpetrators of the odd pinch or peck she chose wisely to amuse them and in turn they tried even harder to entertain her engaging in all kinds of mischievous machinations to catch her attention. She was what one might describe as a 'Director of Drunks' and if she had been in the theatre the results of her endeavours would have impressed the most fastidious of critics.

The cellar of the hotel was a haven for passing travellers and a heaven for not quite passed out drunks creating an atmosphere similar to an Irish 'craic' or a Scottish 'ceilidh' but with Austrian musicians. The euphony and musicology was provided by a shrewd Viennese accordion player known as a 'Schrammeler' whose songs catered for the lubricious locals. He played up to his customers and sometimes took advantage of the language barrier in his lyrics to castigate ignorant foreigners and still receive a rapturous applause from both audiences. His wide musical repertoire was from the customary wine cellar songs of Wien and his intimate style also leant itself to quips, ditties and raunchy dialogue in between songs about romance, rivalry and friendly ribaldry about the transient tourists.

My smoke filled eyes wandered around the roisterers and revellers in the boisterous basement and settled upon a long table where there was a birthday party in progress. It attracted my gaze as two beautiful blondes wearing long satin dresses and large gold and silver fan shaped head-dresses were standing singing a serenade to the birthday boy. I could just catch some of the words which were in a dialect that I thought had become almost defunct in this region. Being dyslexic the words in songs were more powerful often than the music and I was sure that I had heard these lyrics whilst standing in the pouring rain in Dornbirn. They gave a spirited rendition of a unique local song to the accompaniment of a cat stringed guitar and the accordion player courteously supported them.

"You're back early from your shindig with Gerhard" said my sleepy spouse.

My wife was surprised that I had returned before the bewitching hour especially after an outing with her infamous cousin. I remembered returning from another such evening soon after our engagement some years past to find myself locked out with a note stuck to the door in the local dialect spelling which she knew I would not understand. Gerhard had read it and roared with laughter slapping me on the back and complimenting me on my future wife. It was only later after tapping on the bedroom window that I was permitted to sleep off my Schnaps stupor and my stupidity. The translation read that I could sleep in the dog house but the significance gave me some local credibility as a man of the world and my wife gained a correspondingly celebrated reputation as the best wife for such a wayward man. I related what I could recollect of the office outing to her including an impression of Gerhard's trademark side-splitting belly dance which reminded me of Santa doing a striptease.

"It was as fun as it always was with Gerhard and the birthday strip-o-grams have so much more subtlety and finesse here" I slurred in a semi-conscious stupor.

"Go to bed as the wine has got to your head. Du Sauhund, du elendiger! You are going to ski the first snow in Damüls tomorrow and I'm going to kick you out of bed at the crack of dawn. Don't you dare snore!" she said as I fell over a skateboard.

I lay in bed trying not to fall asleep as I knew that this was a fatal move liable to incur bruises from flying pillows. The evening entertainment in the Linde had changed little over the passage of time. That infinite past, present and future corridor of life had a certain cosy continuity but it had become a little wider to accommodate our midlife paunches.

****

The first frozen fresh snow lay twinkling like a valley of white diamonds all around us as the chair lift climbed ever upwards. Leopold grinned anxiously with his deep blue eyes peaking out at the daunting panorama from under his Santa hat. It was in fact the second day of skiing in Damüls and judging by the sullen faces of the lift operators the first day had ended as always with a big party bang and an early morning whimper.

There is not the same mountainous silence during the ski season and the idle chatter from the hundreds of other brightly clad passengers was drowned by the din of a radio station from Germany that had taken up residence in the mountain restaurant. I half expected the noisy nonentities to throw out their beach towels over the recent snow just to show us all that there was nowhere that this great Germanic race of travellers could not invade. I was sorely tempted to vilify my disgust upon the unwitting disc-jockey who asked me to comment as the first and only English tourist in Damüls this season. Luckily I was vindicated when my son asked them to play some patriotic rock music by Queen which was so much more satisfying than burning all their bath towels. I could have made a better barbecue than the Council of Konstanz and with a lot more hedonists than heretics to burn at the stake.

There is a saying in England that farmers should make hay whilst the sun shines and it was a great pity that here the old phrase about gathering in the harvest now only applied to reaping in the unwitting tourists. The price of a drink was more than the price of an alpine cow less than one hundred years ago and the people of Damüls were now milking the boring bovines of Deutschland. The hotel at the bottom of the lift which claimed some stars also won my shooting star prize for serving an Austrian wheat beer in a Bavarian beer glass.

The word 'tourist' meant torture in this resort of living hell but we adored it. We did not want to miss out on the automated fashion queues of spotty teenagers clamped to their 'neat' snowboards even if it was rather akin to the alpine version of a chain gang. I soon realised that my life like many other parents was about to change from teaching the English language to learning teenage bad language as my children struggled with the new complexities of the computerised chair lift. The swish of the first ski of winter was still something that made my heart pump even if it meant sweating blood to reach the slopes. Vorarlberg was about to be smothered with snow and millions of tourists.

As a skiing resort it is probably one of the best family resorts in Vorarlberg with the nicest people apart from perhaps the occasional 'flatlander' invasion in the peak season.

The culture of skiing was something of a phenomenon in Vorarlberg. No self-righteous chronicler could really avoid this sport that consumed vast amounts of uplift energy to then expend it in the purely self-satisfying pleasure of plunging down a snow carpeted valley in a perilous preoccupation with death or injury to one's person. The feeling of arriving at the top could be prolonged by cleaning stylish sunglasses and perhaps a glance at the spectacular view from a vantage point that might have taken a whole day of hot sweaty hiking to achieve in the summertime. The indulgence was not in planting a pole at the summit but in how stealthily, smoothly and speedily you could reach the bottom of the slope again.

Researching the original records of the skiing resembles the history of polo and it is easy to see why bored eccentric English gentlemen succeeded in creating two completely pointless sports. The reason polo became a minority sport of kings was not due to prohibitive expense but more to the availability of flat pieces of beautifully manicured grass to tear up with your steed swinging a long stick at a tiny ball. Accordingly the ample supply of steep treacherous alpine terrain to traverse with two pieces of wood attached to your legs led to skiing becoming one of the fastest growing mass sports (apart from simply kicking a ball).

The reason that skiing has caught the imagination of tourists all over the world seems to be that it is an all-inclusive sport and once you have survived the bruises and bumps of the learning process, the gratification of that achievement is so utterly consuming that it becomes a completely addictive recreation. Few other sports apart from possibly English Rugby and American Football have the same amount of impact injuries. If safety was the only priority then parachuting still remains a far less dangerous pastime with the same feeling of breathless insecurity as you hurtle towards your fate at an alarming speed.

After living and breathing this elixir of a snow life for so long it became tempting to categorise the characters to be found charting out their destinies on the slopes. This sport, which I nicknamed 'Snow-Bum Watching', originated from a natural midlife desire to flesh out the cheeks of the birds that migrate to the ski resorts during the snow season. Gradually it expanded from ornithological observation to incorporate other interesting species of Spotty Snowboarders and Skiing Stags following on close behind their Sporty Hinds. I became a stalker with a black cape of invisibility behind my dark sunglasses gathering up pointless and fatuous character material for a skiing script I knew that I would never write, but, like all 'twitchers' and 'train spotters', it was fun collecting the probably now quite dated data.

The challenge was to quantify the shape, weight, height and facial features of the subject matter without being indiscreet or being mistaken for a perverted dirty old man. The art of physiognomy is now a recognised science and the structural characteristics of skulls are reconstructed to help palaeontologists and archaeologists. For fear of having my face rearranged by my wife who falls into this latter category of study of our illustrious past, this study was a purely scientific experiment for which statistics and results were carefully produced on the back of an old ski map to be compared with future studies on critical mass.

If some statistician of a scientific bent were to take the study further the rewards might include winning a prize for the most ineffectual paper in a long history of feeble numerical facts, but analysis of that warped individual might be more appropriate. However, it would seem that the prognosis of the precise polarity of the rear anatomical buttocks is directly related to the protruding clevage in the case of female subjects and accordingly their skiing ability depended on the axis of these polarities. In the case of male subjects the nasal proboscis played a cognate polarity in this experiment although with the secondary polarity being between their legs and their skiing ability could be calculated on a graph with a proportional axis between these two delicate points.

For those who have no patience for such papers or who might wish to check the accuracy of this investigation in a mirror in the privacy of the bathroom rather than as my subject on the piste; look carefully at your ski pose. If you do try this experiment at home, please remember that cosmetic surgery is not an option worth the expensive investment as there are plenty of padded ski suits to suit all subjects. If you are female and have a big bum and a large chest there is still hope, but watch out behind you. Conversely if you are male with a big nose and a small penis then it is too late to change.

Please just stay as uptight and upright as you are 'Dickhead' because I am not going to ski anywhere near you!

THE PHANTOM PLUMBER, THE SECRETS OF THE PRIEST AND SMELLY SWISS CHEESE

Our building project faltered as we awaited the appearance of the invisible plumber with a broken hand and worse still, my son Max returned to Mehrerau but this time to have his adenoids removed in the old historic and slightly decaying monastery hospital. My wife joined him as the wonderful custom of permitting mothers to sleep in the hospital with their children to ease family stress prior to operations was encouraged throughout Vorarlberg.

"Remember to get the children to school on time and don't forget your dairy appointment to see the priest tomorrow" she said testing the remote control bed.

"Don't worry, darling, it will give me a chance to prove I'm a good mummy."

"That's just what worries me but perhaps the priest will sort you out."

The morning ran fairly smoothly after the children had raised their new 'mummy' from the sleeping to the walking dead and the routine worked quite well after we had found the missing sock and pencil case. Once the children were safely in other more experienced hands beyond the school gates I went to prepare for my long awaited appointment with the priest of Höchst which was quite an achievement as he was a very busy man. I sat quietly in the magnificent church of St.Johann besotted by its neo-baroque beauty and I contemplated the next stages of my inexorable and inevitable journey into the next life.

The foundation stone was laid on the 17th May 1908 although there had been previous Kapelle in Höchst since 1403. The church featured in many guide books as one of the finest in Vorarlberg. The growing congregation had assured that no expense was spared with fine plasterwork ceiling paintings. There were three marvellous gilded altar pieces lovingly restored in the 1980's and a wonderful wooden crucifix from 1740 celebrating the church's ancient links with Mehrerau. The great sweeping balcony housed an imposing organ with gilded floral fretwork and I looked out upon a magnificent vista which was enough to inspire the choir to sing like angels before this pearly pavilion of heaven.

It was such a contrast to walk over to the twenty first century 'Pfarrheim' which had been erected on the site of the old priests house barely a year ago. The new complex housed a charity shop, a state of the art church hall with a gleaming steel kitchen, several church offices for various local visionaries and functionaries, and indeed the very latest computer heated apartments for the man of the most contemporary cloth. I entered the door of the trendy new priest's office and flung my hat unsuccessfully at the hat stand.

"Miss Moneypenny, is the Priest ready for our appointment?" I enquired in English.

"I don't like James Bond or that Secretary in the films. It has too much action."

The priest's secretary had a certain charm and a wonderful wit befitting her previous job of teaching the young adolescents of Höchst something of the

English language. The office never seemed short of action as it was most definitely the hub of a huge ecclesiastical exchange which she was co-ordinating as a less stressful occupation than teaching. She buzzed the priest unsuccessfully and knowing his 'habits' she did not bother to ring his mobile telephone asking me to wait as I was rather unusually punctual.

The priest glided in to his parking spot outside the huge new tinted glass windows like a holy man on a mission. His car number plate did not have that infamous number 007 and he did not look like the Irish type of priest who might want a license to kill. His arrival had the semblance of a professional who perhaps wished for a preaching permit to thrill his ever growing flock of seven thousand souls. He shook my hand and invited me up to his swish boardroom as though he was a special operative in the world of commerce as well as the church. It turned out that he was a very astute and capable priest originally from Schruns. He had somewhat modestly helped to pilot the complicated funding, commissioning and construction of the modern building in which we now sat overlooking his progressive parish.

We struck up an instant rapport which was rare amongst the many tyrannical fire and brimstone Irish parish priests that I had met in England. Admittedly those old fashioned grey haired Celtic characters with disgusting dandruff had a quaint curiosity if not a little queer and queasy singularity to their fanatical love of horse racing and peat bog alcoholic beverages. He was a breath of fresh alpine air to my childhood memories of the smell of whisky and pipe tobacco coming out of the grill in the dark confessional box.

"What gave you your vocation to become a Priest ?" I asked expectantly.

"I don't really know but it probably came from when I was a child. I used to often drive to the Italian coast with my uncle who was a priest in Süd-Tyrol" he replied.

"So maybe you got it directly from the Pope in Italy" I said sarcastically.

"The Pope is Polish and the word doesn't just come by a Papal Missive."

Here was a man that might be described as a slim if not sleek paragon of virtue with a wry wit and sense of the personal perspective of the priesthood. We chatted about the book and the opera and he laughed as I recounted a legend about his neighbouring priest in Gaissau that liked to play Bach whilst sailing on the Bodensee. He invited me to come on his 'rounds' and I accepted his suggestion to join him in the 'Old People's Home' which was a much more accurate description than an Anglicised 'Residential Care Home'.

I knelt silently at the back of the small pentagonal chapel adjoining the 'Altersheim'. It was decorated with dark mishmash stained windows. The small aged holy congregation consisted entirely of women and their short 'Anbetung' prayers gently hummed interspersed by the occasional shrieking echoes of joy from the children on the playground outside. It was a chance to reflect upon midlife and I wondered if the architect had intended that the elderly should enjoy the sounds of playful youth whilst awaiting a heavenly reward.

Outside the church and on several other occasions he was approached by an assortment of ladies on bicycles and I noticed particularly that his mannerisms changed as he listened and cared about their miscellaneous dilemmas. Afterwards in the car as we were speeding off on another assignation I mentioned this difference between the Irish priests that you tried your best to hide from in England and also the noticeable absence of menfolk.

"I nickname them my little bicycling angels as they keep me in touch with my ministry. I don't go to the pub to seek out the menfolk after work but it is a good idea."

He was a realist as his parish had grown by five hundred souls since he had taken on the reins from Fr. Held in 1995 and he was a reactive rather than proactive preacher. The old men that used to stampede across the square to the pub after the communion bell were far fewer than when I had first attended church here twelve years ago. It was now all about admonition and administration of holy rites and his favourite duty was funerals which he liked because the congregation were 'natürlich' and true to the atmosphere of the moment. I didn't want to tell him that there were a few funerals in my family duties with my father that were not quite so true to form. There were several occasions where the priest had fallen for some pretty dubious last speeches from skew eyed and often pissed relatives. At one much celebrated sombre but not so sober ceremony the celebrant had nearly joined the deceased being lowered extremely erratically into the grave as the coffin straps slithered around his leg.

We roared through the village like secret agents on a mission from God. I self-consciously fastened my seat belt and checked that he was not going to press the red button on the gear stick that might eject me into the heavens. Our lightening tour included a visit to a farmer's chapel dedicated to Lourdes built from a donation from Barbara Schobel-Kung. He explained about the tradition of May prayers in the chapel and that the church prayer bells always sounded at six, eleven and seven of the clock. The tiny little chapel had a centre piece of volcanic rock in the shape of a grotto with a Madonna and I was suitably impressed by the unusual dedication having been on several pilgrimages to Lourdes with the Knights of Malta.

The village also had several wooden field crosses and we visited a little forgotten shrine to Saint Nepomuk next to the bridge on the banks of the New Rhine. It marked the end of his parish but I could see that he was a person with an open heart and mind not to mention an open throttle. The church needed priests that responded speedily and that thought about the needs of the future. We screeched back to base for a debrief after a fairly exhilarating assignment. I felt like a driving instructor as I asked him to write down ten words that he would carve on a tablet of stone for my book. I quipped that it should be no more words than the ten commandments and that he reminded me of a very special

British agent. I assumed that there was another highway code for holy men. I scribbled in my book: *'Special agents wear bow-ties but clergymen are the real secret agents.'*

Sometime after this successful sortie I took my poorly son to see his idol 'James Bond'. Max wanted to be a secret agent and I knew who might just give him that vocation.

****

It was not easy trying to juggle with all of the diary appointments, opera composers and the long lists of Christmas shopping and 'elementary living items' for our new home. When it comes to shopping for the stockings or 'essential household products' there are certain fundamental differences and historical mysteries between a man and a woman that are best left undisturbed. After loosing a wounding encounter in the local Media Markt electrical store I decided to flee to a safer haven of tranquillity with the two other supportive males in the family to Appenzellerland across the border in Switzerland.

I drove up into the green velvet hills which were just at that wonderful autumnal in-between stage which made them look like someone had dusted them with snow. I mentally licked my wounded pride and laughed about the shop's extraordinarily apt catch phrase which said 'Ich bin doch nicht blöd'. I wondered if the shop assistants had composed this phrase as we must have seemed pretty stupid arguing over the 'fundamental' principle of a fridge freezer with iced water as opposed to a state of the art computer with twenty other 'rudimentary' gadgets including the latest sound board and games console. Needless to say the sales assistant was well rehearsed in marriage guidance and whelping and whooping offspring with extraordinary pester power. However, he probably went home to his loving wife who consoled him with a cold beer and the shop's catch phrase: 'I am not that stupid'.

"Where are we going and why couldn't I have that computer game ?" said Max.

"Your poor Daddy has to go and earn some cash for Christmas with his scribbles."

The undulating Protestant Kanton of Switzerland known simply by adoring tourists as Appenzellerland bordered on Vorarlberg and its precipitous and arduous hills rose up from the Bodensee above the two villages where I hoped to live at least for another day. The confusing network of steep winding roads were hard work on our ancient four wheeled 'biscuit tin' and we received a lot of 'welcoming' light flashing and horn sounding from smart faster cars as we crawled up into the heart of cheese country. This 'friendly' province of Appenzell Ausserrhoden that produced more cheese than its mainly rural population of 53,515 inhabitants had courteously invited me to sample its internationally famous staple product and to explore the strange customs and rituals of its rustic heritage. It was a precious invitation to a peaceful country within a country which represented one percent of the seven million odd Swiss nationals and correspondingly only one percent of its land mass. It was united by the Red Flag with a White Cross and had no desire to join the European Union.

Switzerland is known mainly as a chocolate and cheese eating nation with plenty of sugar coated mountains to dash up and down in the pursuit of snow sports. I was however interested in the bizarre pastoral world beyond the standard 'hit the piste pissed, break a leg and run if you still can' ski tourism. My invitation was from a tiny museum society in Urnäsch in the Herisau region below the imposing mountain of Säntis. The telephone call was one of those memorable mobile phone calls to a land line where you could hear the footsteps clumping up the wooden staircase as the volunteers went in search of someone who could understand the strange pigeon 'platt-deutsch' of an English 'schrifteller'. I was looking forward to meeting them, after all it was not often that my linguistic style was described as 'flat German' and my profession as a 'plate writer'.

Before we descended upon them I had some nostalgic visits to make to remind myself why I still loved and adored my selfless wife so we drove off in search of the town where we had first eaten together as a family of three in Switzerland. The square in Trogen that had been thronging with menfolk in their best 'tracht' was now deserted and the pretty painted half timbered hotel had closed due to the decline in tourism. I searched vainly for help to ask what had happened to the pretty town that held so many fond memories of crowds of sylvan and idyllic menfolk raising their hands to vote for the last time for their insular machismo political world at the last outdoor 'hustings'.

The gold painted wrought iron hotel sign still shone against the brightening sky as I searched for some assistance during the infamous 'Mittagspause'. The deserted village square was a sign of the hard times now facing Swiss tourism outside of the mountain resorts which saddened me as the welcoming 'volk' had formed such a marked impression on me. Then I saw a door bell of a public building and with one buzz this hive of offices seemed to smell the tourist nectar. Two women sprung into a flurry giving me a spirited sweet Swiss welcome.

"Gruezi. You look a little sad. Can I help you?" said the first charming lady.

"Where is everybody and what has happened to the hotel?" I asked sadly.

"It's lunchtime and the hotel is for sale" replied the other nonchalant teenager.

She told me the sad tale of Trogen which had fallen off the tourist trail due partly to the impotence of the new paper elected rather than public speaking local hierarchy but mainly because of the new type of tourist. I was the old type of tourist for whom nostalgia meant more than skiing with fashionable sunglasses and her diatribe saddened me as this beautiful forgotten village had once hummed like a potential honey pot but now it was a disintegrating hulk of its former pride. However, for those who seek adventure away from mainstream tourism this is a pretty quiet town with magnificent views and charming hospitality. The new 'paper politicians' would do better to get out of their intangible internet based tourist offices and try to serve the needs of the substantive visitor starting perhaps with a public lynching.

We set forth from the deserted village that once proudly shared the infamous annual outdoor vote only for men with Hundwil and drove through the Autumn sunshine enjoying the mysterious pockets of mist that still hung in the valley bowls around us. I wanted to see the state of the art museum that my wife had dragged me to all those years ago which I feared might have also disappeared. The serpentine and torturous road was dotted with pleasant little dwellings which differed from the plain but pleasing wooden houses of the Bregenzerwald in that the shutters and the shingle walls were bright and colourful which cheered me on my long drive. It was not too long before I arrived at Stein to be greeted by the lilac cow's fibre glass sister and a giant cheese outside an outrageously fantastic tourist trap.

The first rule of a seasoned traveller is to remember that such monstrous museum magnets are in fact designed to serve your every foible and eccentric whim. The second rule is to ignore the first rule and simply explore the bits that suit your interests. With this in mind my children rushed to the giant cheese which turned out to be a slide and I explored the stunning 'Appenzeller Volkskunde Museum' which still impressed me as sadly such successful establishments normally never change. The collection included brass cow bells, figurative belts with brass cows, pretty primitive paintings, and my favourite pocket watches and pipes. The museum was famous for its assorted 'working' sets depicting a mountain hut with a 'käse' demonstration; an empty but colourful 'Schlafkammer' complete with painted chest, bed and wardrobe for a rather small farming couple; a weaving workshop which might normally have been attached to an early 17th century farmhouse; and a later example of a mechanised embroidery and threading machine with an almost unique working pantograph used for marking out from hand embroidery.

The exhibits had changed a little as the museum had expanded into new folk stories about ancient rituals and crafts and the accumulation of paintings had been extremely well interpreted with little information sheets for those with specific interests. I had spent a great deal of time in the Museums Association and this museum was as warm and user friendly as the smallest award winning rural cultural vestiges of the Dales and Moors of Yorkshire. It's dispassionate depictions of agrarian rituals and crafts were well presented to satisfy the new flying bus and motoring tourists and the adjacent cheese factory was ideal to sate their appetites for culinary coach retail therapy.

Both places of rustic appeal had cinemas for those unable or quite simply unwilling to separate the real from the surreal experience and I enjoyed the highly palpable pampering of the film commentator with an American drawl. The paradox of being sold an alpine paradise of cows and cheese on film whilst knowing that it was just outside awaiting my pleasure was eventually too much. I made my escape to the greenery of nature from the steely vats of mechanised cheese production. But not before being enraptured by the round cheeky cheesy smile of the shop assistant who persuaded me to partake in the delights of this unique Appenzeller dairy product which I had witnessed being created and curdled on film and through the factory balcony window. She spoke to me in English across the counter.

"This is the Classic and here is the Extra but you might like the Russ."

"Do you eat cheese at home ?" I asked assuming she was weaned on cheese.

Irma lied through her shining white teeth and I was duped into tasting the fruits of the alpine cow's udder. It was an acquired taste but then I was partial to old farmer's smelly socks.

The time was fast approaching for my special invitation to see the Appenzeller Brauchtumsmuseum renowned for its 'Silvesterklaus' costumes, so we departed with directions from Stein written out in longhand by two of the friendliest museum staff I have ever met. If customer care courses were a part of their training then the course notes must have contained some items missing from English training programmes. 'How to deal with more children in urgent need of emptying their bladders' and 'what to do if approached for directions by a scruffy travel writer who stinks of cheese' would probably come somewhere before 'how to handle a child abuse situation' and 'the best way to calm frustrated bank robbers'.

The drive to Urnäsch was through some the most spectacular scenery that this Protestant God had created and of course, being male, I can vouch for the helpful directions of the local inhabitants. If this Great Creator had intended men to navigate, then he would still have protested at letting women drive. It was not true that all men had blinkered vision but driving blind without blinkers or indicators was probably a more acceptable description of our journey. However it was amusing for the children to pull faces and stick out their tongues at the frustrated drivers trying to guess which way I was heading.

"Gruezi. We were expecting you a little later but I'm glad that you found us."

There were several enthusiastic volunteers on hand including a charming child who immediately adopted my restless offspring and took them off to play with him. I was presented with my guide called Emil although he was more of a shorter more mature version of an Appenzeller man than his passionate classic Parisian namesake. We climbed up the labyrinth of wooden staircases of the four hundred year old village house. I noticed that he still had the supple spring of a mountain sprite and a vast wealth of interesting folk tales which would outdo even the smoothest talking Irish leprechaun.

"Why do you think that Appenzeller men were smaller than Vorarlbergers?"

"They probably worked a lot harder!" smirked Emil as I banged into another beam.

He immediately captured my attention mainly because he was so eager and dedicated to the quite outstanding museum but also because you could see the twinkle in his eye as he explained about his ancestors curious habits and customs. Most Swiss people are renowned for being very insular and somewhat inward looking, so much so that one frustrated parishioner in another Kanton had shot members of the Council over a minor property dispute. However, when this philosophy is applied with due reverence to the past it makes the spoken telling of these tales so much more authentic and meaningful, even if some of the customs were rather dubious, if not, certainly a little parochial and peculiar.

We were able to play with a past full of fascinating alpine tools including a treddle lathe, an 'esel stule' or donkey vice, and my preferred exhibit the 'lediwagen'. It was a much nicer example than the Stein museum as it obviously had see some hard cheese and butter making action high up on the Alpine pastures. The wagon was fully laden with all the equipment required for a one man production including a 'milchtasse', 'milchnapf', 'kasekessi kupfel', 'schutteimer', 'milch stuhl' and a wonderful 'buder' churn. The amusement was not so much in listening to and recording these words but in the way that he deliberately pronounced them with an infinite patience and humbling piety. This was a land that was greener than the Emerald Isle of Ireland but the naivety of his expressions seduced me like an innocent child absorbed in a new encounter with a now lost history.

My impatient and hyperactive son Max was starting to behave like a bored school child but Emil knew instinctively what would also galvanise his attention. He produced a bowl and spun a coin around its circumference so that it didn't rattle but kept up a constant ringing tone. He called it 'Talerschwingen' and it was practiced by the herdsmen to accompany songs and the infamous mountain 'jodelen'. However it took on a whole new significance to a child of the computer age where sounds were created at the touch of a play button. My son embraced the ceramic pudding bowl as though it contained sweet smelling Christmas cookies. It was the resonating sound in his ears and the circling spiralling coin that attracted his widening eyes making him forget briefly his ever empty stomach.

We drove back over the mountain pass around the great Säntis mountain range which was famous for its spectacular views above the clouds but my mind was still echoing from the simple spinning coin and the permeating metallic vibrations of the multi-stringed 'Hackbrett'.

I mentally yodelled all the way home.

ICE-DANCING, ANCIENT CHRONICLES, EISSTOCKS AND CHRISTMAS TRADITIONS

There are several other winter sports that are now considered to be indigenous to the Alps but sometimes, because of their flatter topographical requirements, they can be shared just as enthusiastically by English participants. I was often bored by teenage television and playing the boarding school holiday couch potato so my mother used to take me to a small but popular and practical ice rink in Grimsby to exercise my growing limbs. When my children requested a similar respite from the morning schedule of mindless television I readily accepted the challenge and we bundled everybody into the car to go to the 'Eishalle' in Lustenau.

Almost every large centre of population has an indoor and sometimes outdoor ice arena as it is considered a part of the Austrian sporting cultural identity to participate in sports related to this cold, smooth, hard, flat and extremely slippery surface. Ice sports like Scottish curling or European 'Eisstock Schiessen' were based on the accuracy of sliding an inanimate object. We embarked upon the other recreation and sport of attaching metal blades to our feet and skating around a smooth beautifully manicured amphitheatre of gladiatorial ice combat.

The previous description of snow skiers could be readily applied to rear view of ice skaters and the control factors involved were equally tricky to master especially as it was only the second time that I had taken my children ice slipping, slithering, and bottom sliding. However Vorarlberg has a unique teaching method which might be adapted in English ice rinks based upon the logic of using the conspicuous stripy traffic cone.

Simple ideas are always the best and within minutes my inexperienced and apprehensive children were transformed from insecure two legged Bambi cartoon characters into bombing three legged bastards whom I disowned on the grounds that it had taken me months to learn skating. It was a quite brilliant technique which worked especially well when the cone was stolen from them by other more versatile skaters as they had to chase them on two legs to retrieve their missing third red plastic leg. The principle of clutching a cone in front of you was a stroke of genius as clasping on to a bored unstable parent only resulted in a complete loss of confidence and independence and it risked serious injury to both parties.

The other sensible difference between ice rinks in England was based on the belief that skating on two blades did not constitute driving a vehicle and accordingly licensed adult operators could partake of 'Glühwein' whilst in control of their senses. The associated numbing of all sensitivity and indeed the endurance and gall that this inspired led me in a direction that I would never normally have taken upon bruised sober reflection. My stunning repertoire included my best ever one footed pirouette, animated dance moves worthy of a

Paralytic-Olympic medal and even a one legged interpretation of a circling butterfly.

"Darling where did you learn all those dance moves ?" said my astonished wife.

"It's a secret" I slurred. "You learn something new about your partner everyday."

"I'll give you a medal later" she grinned grimacing at my subsequent wine wobble.

The thought of having such an attractive ecstatic audience spurred me on to be even more ambitious as I tried my version of 'Eis Schuhplatteln' lifting my skates up like a karate kid and becoming even more ostentatious with my dance routine. Other wiser skaters began to move further towards the sides as I whizzed past them on one leg with my arms spread eagle like a pickled ice ballet dancer. The jumps grew more daring but like most flashy cars the braking system could not cope with ice. I had probably been watching too many ice action films and had forgotten the cold stark and very hard reality of a injurious fall. Then it was one spin too many and a wrong foot fall and I was flying on my stomach towards the barrier and a very nasty recall to reality. The ego bruising experience reminded me that I was no longer a young supple irresponsible bachelor but in fact a stiff forty something who was going to be even stiffer tomorrow morning not to mention the foot sores.

"That's my dad" said a little voice to his new found mates as I hobbled back to the bench. At least I had got some street credibility with Max as I winced with pain.

"That looked a bit unplanned but it was a good climax" joked my ambivalent wife.

There was no time to laugh at her sensual inference as I could see Leopold by the barrier. I gulped down a glass of water as the ice machine cleaned the ice. I looked with hurt pride across the ice to see another skating Santa and quietly thanked him for stealing my limelight.

****

The week before Christmas is normally a time for baking and shopping and neither of these activities had much macho appeal to a hunter and gatherer like myself. As Max was still recovering I decided to take him with me as I searched for writer's inspiration amongst the hidden jewels of Switzerland. Once again we embarked on a voyage of discovery as, despite much encouragement, I was still searching for a midlife purpose to my penmanship.

"If you want to be a chronicler then who better to learn from than the monks of St.Gallen who have one of the most famous library collections in Europe" said my academic and learned wife.

"Darling, your wisdom from all those years at Heidelberg hides your true attraction to me. Not just beauty but brains to spur me on" I responded with a certain cynical insincerity.

"Don't be silly. Men only really think of one thing if they think at all. Besides Heidelberg University has an equally inspirational antiquarian library but you'll like the Stiftsbibliothek and the monks kept meticulous travel books too" she replied knowledgeably.

The ancient town of the Prince Bishops is set back from the shores of the Bodensee although with 71.000 inhabitants it forms another contrasting Swiss Canton adjacent to rural Appenzellerland. It is much more of a town state and its history since the original wandering monk, Gallus, settled there in 612 has been one of momentous religious upheaval and peaceful cloth trading prosperity. Despite the UNESCO world heritage landmark of the Monastery, School Library and Palace originally founded by Prince Bishops who gave the town a free imperial city status in 1212, the religious allegiance of the townsfolk swayed radically towards humanism during the Reformation. The great zealot "Vadian" or Joachim von Watt followed his friends Zwingli and Luther in 1526 helping them to tear the Christian faith apart. Fortunately Swiss religious strife was so dull that they avoided open warfare and the destruction of the past. The townsfolk were calm and placid traders with a wider vision of commercial enlightenment. They chose peaceful monetary protest and the building of another alternative "Vadiana" library. Perhaps the world could learn from this peculiar pecuniary toleration of other religious beliefs. This was however not an easy scholarly and political cohabitation. It took some monastic sacrifice especially during the dissolution in 1805 but the Abbey Library of St.Gall has an apt Greek inscription above the door which translates as:

'The Medicine Chest of the Soul.'

The tiny ornate temple of books is not much longer than twenty eight metres and not much wider than around ten metres with a pink plaster stucco bordering around a dark painted ceiling depicting the first four Oecumenical Councils of Nicea (325), Constantinople (381), Ephesus (431) and Chalcedon (451). It was such a beautiful thought provoking library of over 100,000 tomes with an incalculable wealth of knowledge representing Classical Antiquity, Christianity and the Alemanic Culture and it was probably this determinant that saved it from destruction. We wandered in wonder in our woolly slippers enjoying the rich Rococo architecture which was completed in 1767 after nearly ten years hard work by famous craftsmen like Peter Thumb from Vorarlberg, Friar Gabriel Loser from Lindau and the infamous Joseph Wannenmacher from Ulm. Their surnames were so easy to remember as it was a rule of 'thumb' that I was a 'loser' but I 'wanted to make a' success.

The exposed mummy skeleton in a glass case from Upper Egypt (700B.C.) with its double wooden sarcophagus attracted Max's morbid attention whilst I pawed reverentially over the hand inscribed calligraphy of the antiquarian chronicles in the glass cases dotted around the library. The light from the stained glass windows had been so diffused as to still preserve these unique leather and cloth bound records with enchanting European names like Klingenberger, Frunds and my namesake, the Crusader Chronicler Robert von Reims. All the books displayed represented divergent styles, symbols, and so many other tongues (with one New Testament written in twelve different languages). These learned monks must have been so much more linguistically advanced even for our age of free thinking secular academics. I left with the scent of the ecclesiastical past in my nostrils and my lungs were filled with that musty respect for ancient literature. Needless to say that I coughed myself back from boredom to consciousness in the courtyard as my age old dust allergy caught up with me again.

For those with a tourist inclination I recommend the interior of the late Baroque Collegiate Church with ornate plaster stucco work in strange tropical sea blues and yellow sand colours and the gilded wrought iron altar screen hides a wealth of carved choir stalls.

If you leave this bizarre church which is dedicated to Saint Gall and Saint Otmar and which boasts no less than sixteen of the finest carved confessionals for those of a more sinful nature, and you care to wander around the old town you might notice the lantern shaped windows protruding from otherwise quite ordinary buildings. There are over one hundred of these Oriels preserved as a lasting reminder of the affluence of the townsfolk who boasted with bay-windows to display their riches mainly from the cloth industry. I could think of a few such examples in England which looked just as incongruous in an otherwise uncluttered townscape but I noted that there was probably plenty of cloth for net curtains too.

We ambled around gazing up at these splendid pimples of the past some of which had motifs of camels, stars and bears carved onto the bays and others with oxidised green copper balloon shaped roofs. The semi-pedestrianised part of the old town was not suprisingly full of Swiss shoppers hurrying and scurrying like mice after their Christmas cheese. We finished our business with the town's infamous bookshop which was appropriately full of other bored authors absorbed in the written word and peeking at the sexy sales assistants. Soon we were heading out of the quite pleasant but depressing glass and concrete jungle of the modern city past the wild and wobbly architecture of the Rudolf Steiner School towards the Bodensee.

"Where are we going now ?" asked my irksome and annoyed son.

"Here we are and just look at that pretty Kloster!" I said swerving up the drive.

The red timber entrance doors to the inner sanctum of the Nunnery of St. Scholastika in Tubach were rarely open in times past but traditions had moved on from tugging for attention on the crucifix shaped bell handle which sounded a tiny bell in the climbing bushes above the gateway. It was no longer necessary to give my son a leg up to scramble over the white pan-tiled garden wall that might keep us from the apples of this Garden of Eden in the green hilly heavens overlooking the Bodensee. But we climbed up onto our Landrover roof-rack and checked out the pretty little garden for nuns with pitch forks.

"But Daddy, the gate is open!" observed my alert son.

"I know but just look at that view" I retorted from the roof rack.

The Kloster was set on a small hillock with a view of the Bodensee that had changed as little as the history of this pretty red and white half timbered place of rustic worship. The nuns that remained in this heaven from heaven were dedicated to the life of Saint Francis of Assisi and to producing fruits from the land and exceptionally large vegetables as well as baking hosts in a special 'Hostienbäckerei'. We tentatively trespassed on the holy turf and half expected to be weeded out like a foreign blight or to be mistaken for one of the ever growing population of prosaic pests from the commuter population that surrounded this walled sanctuary of God.

Suprisingly we were welcomed by a lady in pink rubber gloves who was probably mopping up the blood after the last unwanted visitor. It turned out that the Kloster now encouraged guests and long gone were those closeted days of the Sound of Music. I thought perhaps Julie Andrews might have skipped across their green pasture had the Swiss bothered to try to host the production instead of Austria. We were shown into the church of this most contemplative of holy orders to pray and to admire the colourful Byzantine wall paintings notably depicting mural figures of both monks and nuns.

As we left this hidden gem high up above an otherwise increasingly overdeveloped Bodensee coastline I spotted a little stone garden stairway which led down to a Grotto under the entrance steps to the church. There was a painted statue of the Madonna and a smaller porcelain kneeling nun praying by her side. The inscription in her shining halo read 'ICH BIN DIE UNBEFLECKTE EMPFÄNGNIS'. Max lit a candle to cheer us up and we climbed back into our vehicle to head for home. Just as I was winding up my window I heard the hollow clang of the Kloster bell and then the great grey heavens above opened up as though this was a cue to pour down scorn upon us for disturbing this silent and secret holy haven.

When we returned for a hearty meal to revive our flagging spirit of adventure I thought it prudent to ask my wife to translate the words on the Madonna's halo in the Grotto.

"I had this strange experience in Switzerland" I said showing her my notes.

"Whose garden were you nosing about in ? Was it a Kloster by any chance ?"

The inscription translated as *'I am the Immaculate Conception'*. You can't hide anything from a woman who clothes and feeds you and who helped to conceive your children.

"It's Christmas and you're becoming a saucy old cliché!" she said over my shoulder. "You're ready for a break, not a religious retreat."

It was true that I was beginning to get confused between the manifold and convoluted roles of Chroniclers and Tourist Guide Books. I had digested not only these ancient inspiring tomes from St.Gallen but also several other popular contemporary travel books which merely confused me and lost my sense of direction. I was also losing my diection or perhaps I had somehow had an apparition whilst out apple filching that might give me a new faith. But the facts were still the same as St.Gallen was fascinating but completely lifeless. I hadn't come out of Switzerland with any golden apple. This was mainly because the apple harvest was over and I was, like my exhausted children, ready for Christmas in Germany.

****

"You remember my ice dancing? This short guy with a cherry coloured nose and a silver medal around his neck hung his arm around my shoulder in the bar and gave me an invitation to go 'Eisstock Schiessen'" I said still optimistic of finding a midlife mission.

For those who don't know about this sport, it has definitely nothing to do with sliding stones along the ice as that game is called 'curling' which is only for ginger curly haired Scotsmen in tartan skirts. I have often been mistaken for one of these friendly highlanders and have even been once honoured to be an Honorary Chieftain at a Clan Gathering as the after dinner speaker. Fortunately Scots have a liking for fine whisky and a great ability to laugh at themselves or I might well have been served up with the neaps, tatties and the haggis (or stuffed sheep's intestines as it was known to sagacious Sassenachs like myself). I opened with the old routine about an unfortunate Scotty dog called 'Sex' and the couple who asked for a separate room for 'Sex' because of all the sniffing and baying at night. The audience stuck their lethal looking 'dirks' back into their socks and adjusted their other weapons under their kilts for an English comedy diversion and a great 'ceilidh' with reeling until daybreak.

This was not the Scottish game and it used 'Eisstock' probably because Vorarlbergers were not great hairy highlanders used to hurling pine trunks or strange hammers. The rules had some similarity with three to four players in a team playing three times at each end of a twenty-eight metre long ice rink into a 'Spielfeld' square. This was approximately six metres long and three metres wide which is in fact, like cricket and just to confuse novices, a rectangle. The 'Eisstock' had a long joystick handle attached to a thick round plate. The bottom of this plate had a plastic coloured plate which was readily interchangeable depending on the velocity required. These interchangeable coloured plates were coded in descending 'speed' order from rapid black, to brisk grey, to lethargic yellow and tortoise blue and also confusingly each coloured plate had three speeds too giving the player at least twelve choices.

The rules were that you tried vainly to slide the 'Eisstock' as near to a moveable black rubber disc in the 'Spielfeld' and then the other players tried to get nearer to the disc or to knock you into touch. Finally the scoring was three points if you got your team's Eisstock' nearest the disc, two further points if your second team's 'Eisstock' was also nearer than your opponent's 'Eisstock', and sometimes two further points if all three of your team's 'Eisstock' were in the right place and still in the 'Spielfeld'. There was a remote possibility of all four 'Eisstock' winning a maximum of nine points making a maximum of fifty four possible points in six ends but generally it is around thirty points to secure an outright win. Normally these points are shared between two teams making average scores for better team versus a terrible team around twenty something and more even teams perhaps even less points.

I had once before played this game on the frozen Nymphenburg Canal in München where it was cold enough to freeze 'the nuts off a brass monkey' or in my case to require some strong alcohol just to thaw out and drop my 'walnuts' again. However, there was something naturally instinctive about sliding things accurately along the ice probably to do with snooker tables being relatively long with small 'balls' too. The technique involves swinging the 'Eisstock' like a pendulum through a one hundred and eighty degrees arc and then placing one foot forwards as you release your 'Schuss' in the desired direction.

Desire and direction are only achieved with a technique akin to a romantic preamble to a liaison with a virgin in a tightly locked chastity belt. No matter how hard or swiftly you try to slide it in you will hit the barrier if you try a 'fast one' and simply 'miss out' if you don't get into the field of play. As a monastery educated boy without this practice I was a fast mover and with appropriate direction I was soon slipping it in with this 'rhythm method'.

****

There was a rustling of music sheets then the odd throat clearing cough from those who were not sucking on a potent spearmint 'Fisherman's Friend'. It was the last choir practise in the Cimmerian Gaissau church and I felt lonely sitting below in the dark pews looking up at the shadows of the choir silhouetted around the organ on the balcony. The stark rendering bore a few cracks but otherwise there was little else to distract the eye from passing up the cold grey arches into the heavens above in search of that mythical star of Bethlehem.

Then the organ whirred and the sound of resonating and trilling pipes pierced the still frozen blackness followed by a multitude of emasculated voices. It was the infamous Messiah Hallelujah Chorus by Händel that echoed from a distant pastoral heaven high above me and I sat sadly in solitude quietly wiping away a tear from my icy spiritless cheek. The memories of this magical music being sung in fine mediaeval carved stalls by boys choirs in the lavish cathedrals and abbeys of England came flooding back to drown my tired homesick soul in a torrent of nostalgic memories of Christmas past. The music built up higher and higher and I wept louder and louder until it reached an ear splitting tumultuous climax. Then the soft base vocals began to catch up with the high alto lament bringing back some sense of order and firmament to this enchanting but archaic inter-denominational adoration of God.

"Nobody should be alone on Christmas Day" said one of the choristers afterwards.

The choir sat enjoying their drink after the 'Probe' where the choir master had driven them to distraction to train them for midnight mass and several other festive engagements. The orator was sitting opposite me gossiping with the usual giggling gaggle of girlish geese whilst I flitted between their Christmas cackling and the boisterous honking of the adjacent ganders' table. The two conversations could not have been further apart. The girls tattled about strange Christmas roadside sculptures and cooking Schnitzels whilst consuming wine and foul tea. The boys gobbled about slaughtering chickens and flame grilled bull's balls whilst sating their thirst with weak Austrian ale. Such idle chatter was as pleasing to the ear as was the concert practice as it meant that 'Christkind' was coming. I was going to Stuttgart to eat a transsexual goose together with our family and then moving on to my beloved City of Culture to see more performing fowl at Circus Krone and enjoy some better beers in München.

I was cheered out of my despondency by the knowledge that Christmas was no longer an English festive season of television tantrums and turkey gluttony in splendid but rustic isolation. It was time to travel back into a world of dynamic diversions in beautiful baroque theatres, in sawdust smelling Circus rings and in incense wafting and bishop waffling big city cathedrals. Then there was the blending of two cultures with German presents before midnight under the symbolic 'Schmuck' and bright baubles of the 'Weihnachtsbaum' and futher English presents before dawn in the stockings under the chimney breast followed by fleshy juicy brown goose breast, sweet red cabbage, steamed sprouts and soft oven dripping soaked potato dumplings.

The English Christmas lunch of my childhood was also a very special tradition with lean white turkey breast blended with bread sauce and cranberry jelly, pink steaming ham, batoned carrots, boiled fresh green sprouts, and crunchy golden roast potatoes washed down with a thick brown gravy. The additional blue brandy flaming plum pudding where the holly always caught my father unawares as my mother doused it with a tea towel was something I still missed (along with her secret recipe for brandy butter that always complimented this strange steaming alcohol soaked yet mainly dried fruit cake). There was also the excitement of snapping open long awaited crackers with plastic magic toys and those simpering childish jokes. This was always followed by party games with origami and my father's knotted handkerchief that looked like a pirouetting ballet dancer in Swan Lake. These were fond country memories along with long walks in the drizzly grey weather fortified with knobbly fallen tree branches on a mission to take the empty stilton skin to the very fat pony.

These were two quite different Christmas Day lunches but alpine families sometimes had a boiling soup (rather than a cooking oil based) fondue where you braised raw meat in a communal pot whilst whispering sweet dietary nothings before a sauna and roll in the snow. Thankfully this was as anomalous as a vegetarian slaughter party but everybody had something that made this feast a special cultural tradition. Thousands of Christmas trees are felled to glitter for the glory of Christmas, thousands more gaggling or gobbling fowl fall foul to the oven, and many millions of us fall fatigued and flatulent in front of the television.

"X-MAS"

A CITY CHRISTMAS OF CRIBS, CURIOUS CULTURE AND CIRCUS KRONE

Christmas in a big German City gives a writer time to reflect upon the countryside with a certain longing but also permits everybody to enjoy a chance to breathe in a little culture amongst the exhaust fumes of the home of the automobile industry. Both Stuttgart and München boast not only the Mercedes, Porsche and BMW museums but hundreds of other cultural and uplifting utopia for both the mind and the soul. It is a time for families and friends too as well as religious rituals including walks around the zoo to smile at the crocodiles, grin at the giraffes and of course whoop with the howler monkeys.

Whilst I had enjoyed the botanical blooms in the great glass houses of the Wilhelma Zoo in Stuttgart it became also clear to me that my children were not too far apart from some of the bored species exhibited for their pleasure, education and gratification. They had grown up in this zoo and the Hellabrunn Zoo in München over the past twelve years and so had many of the animals who were now like family friends rather than wild untamed bestial beings. It was not always clear whom I might like them to swap places with as I yanked them away from knocking on the glass of a snoozing Lion or attempting to kiss the 'Rote Piranhas'. I concluded that it did not take a genius to work out why there was a barrier between the vandal voyeurs and the predatory representatives of a lost or dying genus.

"What do you think these kissing fish like for Christmas ?"

My youngest most hyperactive son Leopold was pressing his nose against a large tank of sharks and his drumming fingers must have sounded like sonar sonatas to the rock fish that were rolling over in the deafening pain of his distinctly unpopular pounding music.

"Their relatives have been known to eat children diving for pearls" I replied.

"What kind of pearls, the one's mummy likes to wear on her neck or the invisible know all ones that Emily keeps in her head?" he said compressing his nose on the glass.

"Well, the one's mummy wears come from those shells over there and Emily's pearls of wisdom come from growing up into a teenager" I said enjoying reliving my zoo past.

"This fish has got big girl's lips" he said pursing his lips and trying to kiss it.

"And it can't talk back" added Max knowing his sister was well out of range.

The Wilhelma Zoo was a bigger, bolder and more brazen example of the human ability to exhibit other species as though somehow the human being was intellectually superior. Wiser observers might think the 'captives' more rational and logical as the accommodation was often larger than a zoo keeper's one bedroom flat with more than likely more greenery and charming fairytale scenery. The zoo was a former palace built for King Wilhelm I von Württemberg in the early nineteenth century with a Moorish Spanish architecture in mind from the Tale of 1001 Nights. The later reconstruction of Architect Ludwig von Zanth's masterwork after extensive Allied carpet bombing in the Second World War is a testament to forward thinking and lasting traditional architecture. There were also modern additions to house the sizeable animal collection of over 1000 species including huge domed wire flight aviaries with simulated waves and strange looking sea birds, tall glazed Amazonian rainforest environments with live hooting and hollering monkeys and a steaming jungle with a waterfall, and my personal preferential petting area in the children's animal farm which always had the friendliest of back scratching pigs and horny hungry goats.

I also adored two other zoos nearer to the Bodensee, including the Zürich Zoo which is built on a similar steep incline and my favourite tiny family run 'Tier Park' called Walter Zoo near Saint Gallen named after the eccentric former owner who started with some monkeys in his back garden. Having worked for seventeen years with my father creating a similar, though somewhat under funded zoo project in comparison to these luxurious state of the zoological art collections, I always felt an affinity with the 'guests' being in their home from home. The only other place that made me feel like this was when I was able to witness other animals in the service of the future education of mankind in the Circus.

There are many controversies over the best way to conserve and educate the future human guardians of our environment. Flying them out to see a sleeping lion on a safari in Africa or hoping that they might flick on a long often boring television documentary on copulating elephants in the India may seem natural, but I could not think of a worse scenario.

The former safari was often prohibitively expensive, hot and packed with other stuffed stripy van loads of camera clicking tourists. The latter artificial media answer to everything to do with the environment on your square box in your rectangular living space in the concrete jungle was simply drear, depressing, and deceitful to a natural human instinct for live entertainment. There is nothing quite like the smell of horse urine soaked sawdust as the whip cracks above the feather bridled dancing chargers and the sight of steaming elephant dung being swept up by a uniformed attendant as the massive wrinkled four legged mammoth descendent lifts a scantily clad dancing girl onto his shinning white tusks.

"Daddy, are we going to see the lions at Circus Krone this year ?" cried Leopold.

"We're not just going to see them. We're going to roar and cheer with them."

The greatest circus of all was a Boxing Day event that Marina's sister, Monika had tirelessly treated us all to since we had first produced progeny able to comprehend this spectacle of skill, agility, endeavour and daring which did not disadvantage or discriminate against animals treating them as a human equals. Circus Krone not only kicked the boring bearded 'greens' out of the ring but it showed them that humans should not think that animals should be treated as some inferior ignorant wild untamed preserve of the wilderness. Should any such person be reading this passage then perhaps I might sympathise with the banning of smoking beagles but only in no smoking areas and perhaps if it was because they got a bit singed jumping through a hoop of fire in the Circus ring.

Circus Charles, as it was originally called in the early twentieth century, has a proven track record of popularity through famine, strife and recession. It is still run much as it was over one hundred years ago but not by the legendary Carl Krone but by his caring and still performing granddaughter, Christel Sembach-Krone. She always appeared with her beautiful troupe of black, white and bay stallions and mares snapping her switch as they encompassed her in galloping circles. Her choice of a background look-alike Elvis Presley mumbling to music on a desperately inadequate PA system was a sign of an ageing embodiment of a living entertainer's adoration of a twentieth century celebrity that might be best as a dead day dream. We did not care as it merely proved that humans with gyrating hips were no where near as entertaining as flying felines, elastic two legged elephants, and leaping lions.

Whilst I watched the brilliant musical clowns perform the classic musical instrument routine with a vast array of curious instruments, my mind wandered back to my first English Circus performance in front of my father and honoured local mayors and guests in a marquee in the Park at home. The show received some rave reviews as *'the most skilfully presented comedy circus chaos'* in the local newspaper and I smiled quietly to myself as I watched as the professional Circus Krone veteran ringmaster stepped in to introduce the last act.

My debonair debut in this role had not quite gone according to plan as I had strode into the ring to save the magician who was struggling to remove a sword from a cupboard inside which his assistant was screaming in agony. I raised my microphone to introduce the next act who called herself *'the mounted mirage of the seven veils'* and then just managed to dive for cover over the magician's saw bench as a horse charged past being chased by a hobbling half naked belly dancer. The horses reins caught one of the sword handles sending the cupboard and the now traumatised contents into a nearly fatal spin. However as luck played a higher billing to any artistic skills on this amateurish occasion the magic door flew open depositing the dizzy, dazed but dramatic contents onto the mayor's lap to receive tremendous standing applause and wild hoots of laughter and wolf whistles from the press bench.

My father returned to the tent after dispatching the dignitaries and animal wardens on a ring formation dance to catch the wild horse that had managed to leap into a field of sheep. I was trying to make light of the clearly painful cuts on the left buttock of the magician's gorgeous assistant with a suitably cheeky remark whilst the man of magic was being pinned to his bed of nails and summarily throttled. The scene was one of slapstick chaos normally associated with the clown routine but with clearly murderous intent. Together we managed to prise her off her gasping victim and my father patted me consolingly on the shoulder.

"Well Robert, you were on a knife edge with that last act. We'll have trouble catching the other bounding belly dancer and her bucking bronco for the next performance" he laughed.

****

Christmas cribs are often forgotten as you struggle to stay awake during mass and not to drip candle wax on the unfortunate member of the congregation sitting below you. They can help you to focus your attention without having to insert match sticks under your eyelids as you listen to the incomprehensible sermon on the coming of Christ whilst waiting for him to hurry up as it is actually after midnight. This tradition of late night services is enhanced by singing carols and possibly listening to soloists singing in the true spirit of Christmas.

It is not so much the importance of the choice of venue but more a case of finding a church with a suitably adorned Christmas tree and the supremely important insomniac's crib. The baroque and rococo architecture of the great Catholic Churches of München are only surpassed by the Protestant Mediaeval Cathedrals of England which were confiscated by a dubious deceit from the true faith some five hundred years ago. The Kings of the Schwaben Protestants declined to do this in Stuttgart and the result of their evangelical conversion and the Allied carpet bombing of World War Two has meant that there are few such architectural places of worship left. Hence it is the contents of the church that have become more relevant in these ghastly often popular philanthropic rather than royal patronised places of worship that have sprung up like postulating pimples throughout Swabia.

Christians of an historical rather than modernist bent have been celebrating the birth of Christ since late in the third century and St Francis of Assisi celebrated Christmas Eve in the forest of Grecco with a real honking donkey and lowing ox. The crib replaced this more exciting live nativity scene doubtless because of a similar failed circus act in church although the smell of incense still reminds me of donkey droppings. By about the fifteenth century a fixed reconstruction often with life sized figures was set up in special devotional rooms as an expression of pious desire and partly to promote pictures to a mainly bored and illiterate population. 'Die Weihnachtskrippe' caught on in German speaking countries not only to tell the Christmas story but also to depict other ripping biblical yarns like the Flight from Egypt and the Feast of Cana, as well as celebrating other feast days like Easter with Lenten Cribs.

One of the finest exhibitions of 'Krippen' is at the Bayrisches National-museum in München hidden behind glass in the darkened rooms of its extensive cellar. There are many such treasures to be found away from the normal museum tourist traps and none are more pertinent to the Christmas. English cribs are often found missing or at best are inadequately depicted due to over zealous Victorian Protestants and insufferable Modern Catholics. The figures in this museum are not plaster or plastic replicas but hand carved and beautifully clothed doll-like representations of centuries of devotion to one great biblical fairytale. The difference between a Doll's Play House and a Nativity Scene is at first glance difficult to see as both were lovingly made by adults to tell children a parable that represented their time yet also marked the beginning of time. The nativity story has lasted a lot longer than plastic action dolls and the crib figures represent the beginning of time as we choose to record it.

"Daddy, are you awake ? I am falling asleep" said Leopold slumped on my arm.

"The singer has a lovely voice. Try looking at the crib" I said pointing my candle.

"That donkey looks wonky and where are the three kings ?" he responded.

"They don't put them out until Three Kings Day" I replied watching his eyes open.

The shrill voice of the soloist echoed around the otherwise plain 'Schlosskirche' in Stuttgart and I tried to read the coats of arms on the ceiling roses. The great Kings of Swabia were linked to Lichtenstein, Mailand and Bayern and they had built several other more modern palaces since this 'Altes Schloss' which had clearly suffered quite badly from the bombing. There was the elegant Schloss Ludwigsburg with its fairytale garden depicting other stories from the brothers Grimm and famous porcelain and of course the pretty domed Schloss Monrepos and the Schloss Solitude. Every thirty miles you can find a castle or historic residence in Southern Germany and here I was with three snoozing restless children in a stone sarcophagus patiently and penitently listening to a boring Evangelist preacher on 'Heilig Abend'.

I thought of the beautiful Cathedrals of München and understood why the Swabians were so boring when it came to Christmas. They have an old song known as the 'Lied der Schwaben' and sacrilegiously I hummed the last lines which translated 'When at last he is finished his arsehole closes up. O Schwabenland, lovely land, how wonderful are you.'

Midnight came and the old preacher finally stopped talking out of his arse too.

****

The greatest thing about great cities is the variety of vibrant and vivacious diversions and both cities have much to offer regarding opera, concerts, and the theatre. No sane writer would miss an opportunity to stand in the gods enjoying the finest voices of the opera or to simply sit outside listening to the resounding echoes wafting on the icy wind. There is so much more than drinking in 'Bier Kellers' of München with paralytic paranoid teenage Anzacs who cannot be bothered to learn any language beyond ordering a beer. Some of these haunts combine both beer drinking and drama. Fortunately the New World of alcoholic tourism has not discovered them as Volksmusik remains their only clash with culture apart from perhaps bare arse bonking in flagrante delicto behind a beer tent. This held no appeal to me and many such relationships simply reinforced the colonial clone image that now haunts Australia as *'the land of the free and easy'*. Great romance is built on tradition and tragedy not on *'trousers down and tuck it in mate as we're talking a tall one, mate'*.

The alliteration and adulteration of these ex-colonial dialects has cannibalised English to such an extent that it has succeeded in becoming the second most important spoken communication language in the human world. The Bavarians were not prepared to be raped of their spoken heritage by outsiders. Although judging by my visits to the Octoberfest there were many girls who were prepared to be seduced by the muscular colonial *'corpus delectus'* as opposed to the local figures more akin to a *'corpulent delicatessen'*. However the preservation of the dignity of Bayern dialect is to a large part due to the Volkstheater (and in rural areas the Bauerntheater) in suprisingly raunchy and often rapacious rustic situation comedies and plays. The stars from these long playing folklore theatres were greatly respected by an adoring but ageing local audience and newer dramatic interpretations have been adapted to attract younger viewers with some success over the stayed television versions.

"Tonight you are going to be inspired by the great Wilhemine von Hillern and the alpine tragedy of Geierwally" whispered my wife as we entered the Volkstheater.

I had been to more impressionable theatres in München but the theme was interesting and the writer was also of a theatrical background with later aspirations towards creating her own play too. The play was a runaway success and the modern interpretation still had the original flair, comedy and tragedy of this tale of a head strong woman who had climbed up a mountain to retrieve an vulture fledgling and then proceeded to defy her father's wishes with regard to a prospective groom. The story line was such that it had been on the big screen and had a very charming but complicated opera representation and during the interval my patient wife explained that death eventually befalls her at the hands of her spurned lover.

"Well it's very graphic but I didn't really understand it at all" I had to admit.

"There are several dialects. Bayerisch is quite bewildering" she said sympathetically.

"At least the beer is international" I said trying not to be a brainless bimbo.

"Well, that's why Bavarians have brains and big bellies" she giggled.

The Bavarians were justly proud of their dialect and indeed the history of the Kingdom of the Löwen King but it was easy to see why the rest of the world spoke English rather than Bayern as a second language. The amusement was not so much in the incomprehensible last desperate death of the heroine but in the audience reaction as we seemed to be sitting amongst some country folk. As the curtain fell on the lover and murderer holding her in his arms not one tear trickled down the rosy cheeks of the flatulent farmers in front of us. They cheered and bellowed like male misogynists screaming for blood on a night out watching Christians being devoured at the Roman Collosseum.

"I thought it was supposed to be a tragedy ?" I whispered behind them.

"It is, but they are cheering the Schuhplattler and the band" she laughed.

The curtain call was a curious affair as the standing applause went not to the heroine but to the men who had spent most of their time drinking large quantities of beer on the stage interspersed with the odd group huddle and thigh slapping. They leapt back onto the stage twice to greet the volley of encores with a barrage of brass band instrumentals and proceeded to entertain the clapping a cheering crowd to a miniature concert.

"I'm inspired especially by the uplifting applause" I said clapping loudly.

"Do you think you could write something like that ?" asked my translator.

"I'd have to learn to write in Schuhplatteln" I replied observing the wild row in front.

"THE KING"

DAS SILVESTERKLAUSEN, A HOUSE FIRE AND SILVESTER TRADITIONS IN THE ALPS

We returned from two weeks of frenzied fantasy and left the whimsical enchantment of Christmas city culture to rejoin the possibly pagan but predictably protestant peasants of Switzerland in their performance of an even stranger sylvan Silvester spree. The small village of Urnäsch in Appenzellerland had once again invited us to participate in a biannual festival of St. Sylvester and to witness the 'Mummers' or 'Silvesterklausen' performing a bizarre bell ringing and yodel chanting and howling routine to celebrate the New Year.

The New Year custom is performed twice as the older tradition was to celebrate St. Sylvester's Day according to the Julian Callender on 13th January as part of a long running 16th century dispute in which the Protestants of the Ausserrhoden region made a point of not recognising the new calendar of Pope Gregory. However the needs of the subsequently adopted and the more worldly twentieth century calendar and the passing of past times and rich tourists in the nineteen sixties had resulted in a second date recognising the newer Swiss traditions of fortuitous fortune relying on the milking holiday spectators rather than cows.

We happily joined the new herds of gawking and gaping 'Gäste' to marvel at the costumes silently and respectfully attending the 'Schuppel' rings of Silvesterklausen performing a wordless harmonious dirge or 'Zaure' outside of every principle abode in the village. The remarkable costumes were originally divided into three main fashion categories ranging from plain ugly with frightening horned and painted masks and weird clothes and hats made of dried leaves, tree roots and woodland foliage with associated bells; to less frightening masks made of pine cones with moss beards and matching clothing and hats of platted fresh pine branches and similar assorted cow bells; and finally to the 'Schöne Schuppel' whose costumes quite simply outshone all the rest. We witnessed several 'foresters' fashion shows' of mostly the less alarming second category with some youth and child groups too.

The latter 'Schöne Schuppel' group of six male participants was led around the village by a 'Vorrolli' wearing women's clothing supporting a spectacular fan shaped but heavy wooden head dress with seven stars of coloured beads and a central meticulously hand carved dolls theatre scene representing village celebrations. He also wore a leather yoke over his shoulders and around his waist with up to thirteen 'Rolle' or spherical bells. The central four 'Schelli' wore male costumes supporting flat inlaid beaded wooden wedding cake hats with a square open plan landscape with similar carved figurines on the top describing various scenes from the local village carpentry and timber industry. They also wore two massive cow bells on their stomachs and backs which they clanged and clanked to great effect after each 'zaure' performance as they swirled around in the street. Finally the 'Nachtrolli' always took the last position in the group and he was cross-dressed similarly to the leading 'Vorrolli' but with a blue flower hanging out of the lips of his flesh pink female face mask.

This was a man with a story and so I approached him carefully studying the blacksmith dolls portraying a working farrier and wrought iron blacksmith at his forge. It is embarrassing talking to a man of iron in women's clothing but like many rustic types he had a friendly and approachable nature even if his sexual preferences were not clearly delineated.

"So you must be the Hufschmied ?" I said politely.

He raised his face mask to reveal an upturned pipe with a silver top and carefully pondered on a suitable response to such an obviously stupid question from an Englishman but he saw the Krummer cigar hanging out of the corner of my mouth. He was pleased that at least I had differentiated between the various roles required of his profession although most farriers in England rarely worked at a forge other than to shoe horses.

"Einmal Schmied, immer ein Schmied."

He replied with a little wink before prancing off down the road in pursuit of the rest of his 'Schuppel'. I laughed at the prospect of him performing wedding ceremonies at my local museum forge at Owston Ferry near the Trent River in North Lincolnshire. Then I also remembered that another village called Haxey on the Isle of Axholme nearby had a strange Fool's day and a rugby style maul for a leather hood. However, most of these traditions had disappeared in England due ironically to a purge by the Victorian protestant purists who outlawed such 'pagan' rituals. The Gretna Green forge might consider this costume over klits.

The festivities normally start early in the morning and climax around the fireworks to celebrate the New Year but we were soon cold and hungry. The local 'Gasthaus zum Engel' seemed warm and friendly and we climbed up the stairs to the wooden panelled restaurant. We perhaps got more than we bargained for as it wasn't long before a walking forest conjuration of humming and clanging 'Silvesterklaus' descended upon this small public house. The floors were strew with their debris and I enjoyed the unlikely thought that this might have been witnessed by Shakespeare as his moving Birnam Wood in Macbeth.

The play was always a favourite production for any director and I imagined the challenge of moving such a cast into battle in the final showdown with Macbeth.

'Now darling, do you think you could hold your clapper during the speeches.'

'You, over there in the skirt with the wooden birthday cake, could you look less like you are going to a party and more like you are going into battle?'

'Perhaps we should have used the kilts and those pink masks will have to go.'

'If you must adjust that huge 'donger' darling do it in private not on the stage.'

'I don't mean to criticise you, I like the yodel, it sounds like a war cry but could you howl a bit more fiercely as you sound more like a strangled pussy cat.'

The prospect of controlling this wild bunch of rustics who seemed to be imbibing potent Jagertee in large quantities via straws inserted under their masks was another recipe for disaster. I could see the reviews: *'this great unmentionable Scottish tragedy performed with some unusual sound effects reminiscent of the Sound of Music being played at the wrong speed'* or *'perhaps the Director was on speed when he chose to cannibalise the greatest tragedy of all time with this alpine interpretation of a howling dog's breakfast'*.

"What on earth are you thinking about with that big cheesy grin on your face?"

My wife seemed to read my day dreams as I tucked into an expensive but pleasant local 'Chasspatzli' and the stringy cheese had attached itself to my chin.

"Just imagining how difficult it must be to train up for the role." I grinned.

"They often come from farming families or other professions where they have practised for generations. They have the special sounds and rituals in their blood."

The pub started to liven up with a spontaneous yodel from the men wearing knotted handkerchiefs in the neighbouring bar. The sound resonated around the tiny wooden 'Stube' and we listened to the infinite variety of wordless sounds as though they were the chorus from an alpine opera. My mind struggled with the idea of tabulating and scoring this type of music as some of the notes were so long that a minute might continue for at least four bars. The flat sound interspersed with yelps and wailing was as unique as undersea whale calls but without the echo barrier of the salty sea. I had heard African fireside dances on my travels in South Africa but it was nearer to the Hindu religious music that taxi drivers always played at full volume whilst swerving to avoid gesticulating cyclists in Bombay traffic jams. The songs or wordless dirges were not accompanied by native drums or highly strung sitars and the singular breathless tone reminded me of my days in a monastery school.

For those who might think that Harry Potter features in every magical public school, it is wise not to try to relive such exaggerated dreams in a monastic establishment which is more akin to a correctional establishment run by black gowned Benedictines rather than white coated male nurses. Despite this, the strange thing was that I enjoyed the later years of my 'long stay' in such a place of learning after I had finally conquered my dyslexia and I had discovered that the monks actually had legs under their tobacco smelling habits and some degree of academic knowledge outside of religious instruction which I did not possess. I actually began to attend matins and to enjoy the strange chants that echoed around the modern but acoustically sound abbey in North Yorkshire. There was something communal in the creation of sacred sounds and although these chants had Latin texts they still had the same primeval masculine reverberations associated with the earliest Homo sapiens.

The long history of these Appenzellerland 'zaure' was probably not quite as long as the story of Gregorian Chants but then it did not pretend to be a form of worship or to have any real significance other than men having a great time imitating howling dogs. My environmentally friendly daughter snapped me out of my unholy daydreams.

"Daddy, do you think that they recycle their Christmas trees for those costumes?"

As we drove back along the winding way towards home I looked out onto the icy cold mountains as the dark dusk shadows of nightfall rubbed out the last pink rays of the winter sun and closed in on the brilliant white peaks of the Säntis mountain range. The Appenzeller countrymen were a remote but warm and friendly race bred with a natural sense of the cycle of the moon upon which a foreign pope had tried to scientifically secure a rigid unnatural calendar. They were in touch with the intrinsic rhythm of the seasons and had developed a rare and unrivalled musical intonation in the splendid isolation afforded by the refuge of these massive mountains. It is possible to worship the passing of the seasons but no living creature however segregated and isolated from the developed world can read time itself and the bringing in of the New Year had so much more in store for us.

"I'm going to sing with the choir in Gaissau at the New Year's Eve Mass."

"We've been invited by our neighbour to Serbian Firework Party upstairs."

The churches in Gaissau and Höchst were both exquisitely decorated in celebration of the coming of the infant Jesus with huge Christmas trees decorated with straw stars and fine examples of the art of crib arrangement. The choir had taken up its usual post in the organ gallery and the congregation gathered below led by a larger than usual contingent of nuns and a godly handful of priests and celebrity celebrants. A young man gave a long sermon with great zest and youthful enthusiasm to an assembly more keen to return to their inner sanctums of home and respective pyrotechnic parties. We in turn sang our hearts out with a stimulating selection of songs conducted by our perfectionist choir leader but ever so slightly engulfed by the overzealous but faithful organ accompaniment.

I returned from the service to find myself under attack from a youth group of pyromaniacs with a vast armoury of incendiary devices that squealed, fizzed and popped in the street. The whole of Austria and Switzerland was alight with a dazzling display of fireworks lighting up the night sky like multicoloured shooting stars. Mortar rockets were being launched from the upper reaches of Switzerland and not to be outdone the Austrians responded with missile missives of gargantuan proportions that exploded raining technicolor fantasies over the admiring hoards of star gazers.

"Daddy look out !" said Max throwing a fizzing firework at my feet.

It blew up sending cardboard shrapnel up my trouser leg.

"Ooops, but there's tonnes more" he grinned clasping an assorted handful of mischief. "Your funny peeping thing is making a bit of a racket on your bedroom table."

The device was supplied to all eighty or more fireman to mobilise them in times of disaster and for the first time in three months I had left it in my other trousers in the rush to change for the choir concert. I retrieved the pager and scrambled back to the car like a spitfire pilot preparing to take off in the Battle of Britain. It was heartening to serve a more peaceful fire service but a real call sent adrenaline through my emergency blood system. However I was very careful not to fly off owing to the number of children playing with firecrackers in the street and the recent death of a fireman rushing to the station in Montafon.

I arrived to find the fire engines long since dispatched to the blaze in the appropriately named Blitz Strasse and five of the old timers were sitting upstairs awaiting their return. I knew that I was guilty of the ultimate sin of leaving my pager behind in favour of a trivial musical engagement and enquired as to the extent of the fire and its location. It was easy to find owing to the number of fire engines in attendance from Hard, Lustenau and Höchst and I inspected the ruins long since dampened down for the night. The fire had broken out in the loft of the multiple dwelling probably as a result of an electrical fault and had jumped onto the roof of an adjoining house. I was bitterly disappointed to miss my first action especially as fortunately fires were relatively infrequent occurrences. Nevertheless the blackened charcoal remains of the roof timbers and the smoke damaged interior reminded me of what an important duty it was and how brave the firemen were to risk their lives in this voluntary service to extinguish the mayhem caused by the fiery phoenix.

"Darling how was your first emergency call ? No casualties I hope" my wife asked.

"It was a big blaze but they did a good job" I said despondently.

"Don't look so disappointed and come an join us with the Blei Giessen."

"I've burnt rubber to reach a fire and now you want me to melt lead over a candle."

This was one of several traditions on New Year's Eve that nobody knew quite how or why it had evolved but it was a ritual that everybody practised. The idea was simple in that you took a lead cast shape and melted it down over a candle on a special flat spoon which did not convect the scorching heat. Then you dropped it into a bowl of cold water and tried to interpret the strange shape that resulted from this childish chemistry experiment which adults were permitted annually to participate in under supervision of appropriate minors.

The New Year's Eve celebrations in German speaking countries have some other extraordinary customs which include a sacred but now sparse scheduling of the last black and white television classic know simply as 'Dinner for One' (or The 90th Birthday).The more popular scheduling of the comedies of 'Mr Bean' has overshadowed this earlier exclusively English programme of around eight to twelve minutes duration depending on which edition is screened. The words are embedded into two generations of German childhood first English language experiences and many non-English speaking veterans can still recite the entire script which involves a dinner party for an elderly Miss Sophie and four fictitious male guests all mimicked by an old butler called James who is required to toast her health in four voices between every course. The resulting mayhem includes some perfectly timed heel clicking from a imaginary Admiral Von Schneider, some superb slurring from Mr Winterbottom, Mr Pommeroy and Sir Toby, and a marvellous tripping trick with the head of a tiger rug on the floor. For those television gurus who think a change is healthy I would simply drink to their unhealthy demise as this small dramatic interlude in an otherwise often bland and boring catalogue of star studded cataclysms brings comedy of the past to screens unfamiliar with live beautifully choreographed black and white images.

We were the guests of our Serbian neighbours above us courtesy to a large part to the friendships formed by our children with their equally wild offspring. Whilst they threw a vast array of hand grenades and other explosives over the balcony we sat back talking about the aftermath of the Yugosalvian War. It was something that was considered in terms of their distant homeland but it had still affected long term migrants from the sixties and seventies who could see the widening gap between their relatives and their considerably better living conditions. The irony of this conversation was completely lost on the children who were already lobbing incendiary devices over the cars of the neighbours like young street fighters. The innocence of childhood had been torn away in Yugosalavia and many children still lived to throw stones at tanks in Palestine but somehow these troubles were blown far away with the shooting sparkling rockets celebrating another year of the civilised and uncivilised world.

The glasses of Schnaps toasted to aspirations of prosperity not poverty and the 'Sekt' sparkling wine bubbled up my nose and left a strange taste in my mouth. The President of Austria and the Queen of a divided but still sovereign Great Britain had made the usual speeches looking forward to a future without the terrorism of the Twin Towers. I had surrendered my freedom of speech by leaving the world of politics. That French feeling of freedom, liberty and fraternity might have been restored with a fine Champagne but the bitter sweet taste of German Sparkling Wine somehow left me thinking that politics was the least of my worries on New Year's Eve.

"Time to launch the rockets!" announced our host indifferently waving a lighter.

The assorted projectiles placed strategically in the flower pots resembled a multiple missile launcher and he proceeded to launch himself with them. The flickering lighter and the fizzing fuse lit up his gratified grin and then the fireworks flew erratically in all directions except skywards including towards a neighbour's garage. We gasped in horror as one after another the blasting, buzzing missiles flew out of control through the exploding townscape. I thought of what it must have been like watching the real thing fly past the balcony en route to Iraq. At least cruise missiles were more accurate even if cruising was a distorted description but I was thankful that the military had developed flying by wire with computer controls. The papers were full of another war in Iraq.

The children of the Alps play with fireworks but not with toy machine guns or model soldiers. War is something that has long since disappeared from their thoughts and minds except perhaps as a television nightmare from their grandfather's time.

Half a century of peace and prosperity has put them far ahead of the rest of the world.

"WAR & PEACE"

A SEDUCTIVE SCHRAMMLER, LIECHTENSTEIN WALSERS AND GEORGIAN HANDBALL

The New Year had brought several interesting developments with the composers who were finally producing some musical scores for the Opera and some more distributors were inspired by my Christmas Cards to give the Chocolate Mountain Chronicles a wider audience. Most authors and artists that I have had the pleasure of spending time with would generally roll a large joint, drink a bottle of fine malt whisky and lie prostrate in the gutter admiring the tiny new shining star in the limitless night sky at this news.

Not wishing to spoil this traditional behaviour of a profession where such liberties were not considered to be libertine but more expected social conduct I joined my sympathetic cousin and patient patron Gerhard for another evening at the Höchst equivalent of the Moulin Rouge in the Linde. Admittedly I was too tall to be Toulouse Lautrec and my legs were too hairy to take the lead in a troupe of scantily clad Parisian dancing girls but I knew when it was time to have a good time with some fine French wine and a well formed sex pot from the underskirts of Wien or was it a well informed singer from the outskirts of Wein ?

"So you must be Marion from Wein ?" I slurred splotching my wine over the table.

She was young, talented, beautiful and wearing a traditional red dress with silver edelweiss armlets and with a visibly heaving open topped blouse which left little to the imagination. Her eyes were desirously and dangerously dark and pointedly piercing in my direction. Her contra-guitar with an additional set of bass strings reminded me more of a flirting flaming flamenco artiste than her actual profession as a Viennese Schrammler.

"I come from Wien and maybe you have drunk too much Wein" she replied.

As she fluttered her eyelids I was reminded of a crimson butterfly but I couldn't remember whether it was called a peacock or a painted lady. I was normally a good lepidopterist and took great pride in being involved in several conservation projects in England. But this was more akin to ornithology as I watched her preening her guitar strings and listened to her shrill chorus as she accompanied her father on the harmonica. She was more like a bird of paradise where the female of the species had plain but bright plumage and I was sorely tempted to fan out my male tail feathers and dance around her especially when she tempestuously plucked out my favourite flamenco classic request.

"The history of Schrammlers goes back to the music students of Wien in the 1850's who used to play in the Wein Kellers of Wien. There were normally two violins and a harmonica and the songs developed later from the original marches and waltzes. Each folk song tells a story and they are often passed on by word of mouth" she said quite seriously.

She also pouted her vivacious rosy lips as she spoke in perfect English. I was not so much in love but in lust from the debauched lechery brought on by the healthy thinning of my blood from copious amounts of wine. Worse still, her mother had spent considerable time talking about her daughter's failure to find the right man who needed to be a composer or writer with stature and strength of mind to match her desires which included grandchildren. Gerhard grinned and readily promoted my cause in his unintelligible dialect seeing the humour in every comic situation which involved an opportunity for practical jokes. He then charged the glasses of the musicians and proceeded to astonish us all with his own song.

The evening developed into a concert selection of political, social and humorous 'Schrammler' songs including a comedy classic about learning English. There were plenty of similar examples of professional busking musicians in England including Cockney pianists, street corner fiddle players, and traditional Organ Grinders but this was Austrian and it was ethnically pleasing to the trained ear and my pierced pickled auricles.

"Here is twenty Euros for the first copy of your children's book on Schrammlers."

I slurred a bit but I knew what I meant and it was a huge tip by their standards. The spontaneous reaction was predictable and whilst they continued to sing for their supper my thoughts drifted back to waiting for dinner for two in Luxor with my wife in another old leftover Egyptian hotel from the imperial past. The music was from an old record player with a scratch which jumped just at the point where the duet reached its climax. I had drunk rather too many gin and tonics and started singing on the veranda and then I noticed her smiling behind a pillar at this eccentric Englishman. It was a seduction at first sight on my first night.

****

The next day was not conducive for ski sports as the green lowlands were devoid of snow and the uplands were marred by intermittent freezing rain. We had visited several ski resorts including Warth and Schoppernau which were full of cold wet tourists. After being frozen to the chair lift getting chillblains in an icy alpine wind tunnel and then being soaked to the skin by the driving hailstones interspersed with the wettest of winter rains there was a point where we accepted the old saying; 'When in Rome do as the Romans do.' So we decided to cross the Rhine and invade Liechtenstein renowned for its Royal Princes and infamous tax haven booty for other rich and more famous media personalities.

At first glance at the border most tourists might mistake it for a quaint province of Switzerland but Liechtenstein is actually a sovereign state with some interesting pretensions. According to the abundant literature supplied beforehand there is an approved evolutionary history for one of Europe's smallest but most popular constitutional monarchies. It stems from some shrewd land purchases of Schelenberg (1699) and Vaduz (1712) and subsequent fortunate proclamations from Habsburg Emporer Karl VI (granting the title of Principality in 1719). It survived the hapless alliance with Emporer Napleon's Rhine League in 1806 by quickly joining the German League after his defeat at Waterloo in 1815. Bismarck's Reunification in 1866 united it to Germany, and then more recently it became a financially Federated but Politically Independent State adjoining Switzerland. It was more a case of chance than diplomacy as several of these great European statesmen simply failed to read the small print and when they did find time to look at an alpine chart, it was pointed out to them that the Prince of Liechenstein had not in fact actually acquiesced to them.

I read the impressive Princely genealogy of the Fürst Hans Adam II and his extended royal entourage who all seemed to profess the finer qualities of monarchical traditions supporting the arts, charities and the care of adoring subjects (who had been ruled by an agent who preferred to abide in the civilised neighbouring Austrian town of Feldkirch). I presumed that his grandfather Franz Joseph II must have made another good excuse about Adolf Hitler's Reich Reunification maybe he looked back to what his ancestor, Johann I, might have said to the first dictator, Napoleon as his troops famously reached but were repelled in Feldkirch.

'There's a horseman here from Liechtenstein' reports a French Grenadier.

'Where is Liechtenstein and what does he want ?' replies Napoleon looking puzzled.

'He has a letter saying the Prince of Liechtenstein can't acquiesce his sovereign state to the Rhine League as he has another engagement to appear on a new postage stamp.'

'We'll give him the boot later if we can find him after I've dealt with Wellington.'

The Liechtenstein family photographs retain that country gentry wellington boot look probably because their saviour invented them as it would seem that Napoleon failed to rewrite the small print as he was down trodden and crushed at the battle of Waterloo. It was definitely the defiant diplomatic type of monarchy that I adored. I wanted to see something of the tiny Nation State of around 160 square kilometres with a National Anthem based on the tune of the British National Anthem by H.Carey with corny clerical lyrics from an appropriately named Jacob Jauch pronounced 'Yowch' which about sums up the politically corrected text.

We had visited Vaduz many times before and it is most definitely an excellent but overdeveloped base from which to explore the tiny country. I can recommend the new art gallery with a small but very fine collection of old masters loaned by the Prince. The collection was founded by his Ancestor Karl Eusebius (1661-1684) and his bachelor Great Uncle Franz I saved it from wartime destruction by giving them to his lately departed father for safe keeping in the Castle Vaduz. The Princes only ever really resided in their kingdom in the latter half of the last century but their wonderful residence is still the top drive through tourist attraction of Liechtenstein after the ski museum and of course, the stamp museum.

The exclusive views of the river and snow painted mountains of Switzerland from the privately guarded castle can also be enjoyed at various viewpoints along the steep road above Vaduz. It climbed beyond the palisades and colourful shutters of the Castle along a narrow wooded road and eventually reached our intended destination of Triesenberg. The reason that we had come to this sprawling but pretty town on a plateau high up above the Rhein was not just because of the spectacular sunlit Autumn views. We inspected the church of St.Joseph with its huge wooden cross and strange strutted dome but the real prize was across the square.

The community of Triesenberg is one of the original upland Walser speaking settlements formed in the late 13th Century by immigrants from the then overpopulated Canton of Valais along with much of the Grosses and Kleines Walstertal valleys on the other side of Feldkirch and parts of Northern Italy too. One of the admirable achievements of the Princes of Liechtenstein (and to some extent the Counts of Hohenems before them) was to tolerate and foster this 'free speaking' population which had some quite unique independent customs. The sadly missed Fürst Franz Joseph II was the first Prince to set up residence in the Castle of Vaduz. He was particularly fond of this 'common alpine affinity' and encouraged a biannual reunion of the Walser settlements as a Germanic rather than Romano-Celtic people.

The Walser Museum was founded as a tiny but proud and perpetual reminder of how indigenous populations can tolerate and prosper alongside refugees. There are still many wars being waged today where the prosperity and technological advancement that the refugees bought with them has caused a severe imbalance and then the eventual loss of political and religious forbearance. The Walser people survived on the poorest uplands but their sense of independent pacifist affinity within a wider community still survives throughout the world.

This is only one possibly contested purist perspective. It takes two intolerant sides to start a war and some communities might take fifty years to change a light blub without blowing it up with a suicide electrician or flattening the whole house with a tank. The interesting message of the Walser history was not so much their autonomous agrarian survival due to the natural untamed topographical disconnection from politics (as roads only reached Triesenberg in 1867) but their long resistance against change from a mountain co-operative society to a now sadly overdeveloped commuter community. This evolution was captured in this extraordinary Heimatmuseum not so much by the rather traditional rustic agricultural exhibits (although their simplified interpretation of goat herding and cow bells could be adopted by some of the larger

Appenzellerland museums) but by the slide show in the cellar.

"Daddy, why are we sitting watching a slide show ?" said our bored daughter Emily.

"Because we are witnessing the last rare social pictorial record of the peaceful extinction of native alpine people" I replied enjoying the quite unique tourist presentation.

I studied the smiling faces of the children which already showed distinctive genetic dilution from the original Walser people. Other black and white photographic records of the late nineteenth century showed child characteristics with a smaller skull and skeletal frame usually with prominent ears and front teeth. Fortunately the slides had not been selected by interfering politicians wanting to promote minor racist, sexist or disablity concerns caused by forty years of external immigration. It was the ultimate untainted pictorial chronicle of the last recognisable living Walser 'Heidi' and her classmates. The guilt of the taboo wartime selection and extermination by genetics had long since been washed away in the tide of modernism. The world media was now full of cloned babies and the continuing wars of religious bigotry and political pragmatism. It was clear that none of this turmoil had ever really affected this peaceful remote little commune on this lost plateau at all. The grinning faces of the future would not be able to save their community as that land that time forgot but they might still be able to preserve some record of it in their Walser customs and language.

"That one looks a bit like a dinosaur" said Max, trying to understand.

"The Walsers are the last wandering alpine Aborigines" said my astute wife.

"You could well be right as these dinosaurs accepted natural extinction" I quipped.

My wife had a much more worldly explanation of the Walser upland migrations and there were very few physical artefacts to distinguish them from the Appenzellerland dairy and goat farmers. It was too late and too boring to discuss the mutual social merits and acute political disadvantages of a nation built on vernacular variations, colloquial idioms, and dynamic dialects. Smiling children have a special way of simplifying things that scholars often overlook and the charming lady called Elsie Schadler at the reception presented me with a signed copy of a town book in which she had inscribed in italic Walser Script the following simple words adapted from a phonetic to a European alphabet:

'Fur da Bsuach i unscham Museum viela Dank.'

If you are an expert in social semantics you may wish to correct it but Leopold said it said:

'Dinosaurs can waltz but nobody will dance with them because they x stink.'

****

"Darling, I have a sporting engagement this evening with Georgia," I announced.

"You're flying off to show them your ice skating routine" quipped my spouse.

"Not quite but I am going to the Handball Qualifying Round between Austria and Georgia next to the Ice Halle in Lustenau" I said waving my special sporting invitation.

"I had a very handsome boyfriend who played Handball but watch for fouls."

The idea of a handball hunk with his hands all over my wife instinctively made me self-conscious but a cold beer and a couple of cheers soon snapped me back into the macho grove especially when I saw the row of gorgeous unofficial cheer leaders. News of the diary had spread around the sporting world and I was given a VIP ticket to join the suprisingly sober and subdued press corps in their glass box overlooking the raked back benches of over fifteen hundred spectators with the best view of the new indoor Gymnasium. The smooth talking ex-professional handball player and commentator from ORF called Christoph Waidel patiently pointed out the two teams and the star players as they charged down the wooden gym throwing a miniature football at the two metre high by two and a half metre wide goals in orange painted semi circles at either end.

"The sport has grown tremendously here in Austria in the last four years but the top teams are in Germany, Sweden, Denmark and Spain. This is the first of the pre-qualification rounds and Austria has to beat Turkey, Cyprus and these Georgians" he said informatively.

I kept very quiet as quite honestly this was not a game that received much recognition in England but I adored the drumming fans and the loud 'ooohs' from the spectators as the players made physical contact normally at full stride or in a mid air collision. There seemed to be five players and one goal keeper on each side. A similar number of substitutes sat on the bench not to necessarily replace the injured unprotected players but more to supplant the banned players who regularly got shown yellow cards for fouls by the two referees resulting in two minutes time out or replacement. It was a fast, furious and yet friendly sport where players had to pass the ball after three steps or bounce (or 'catch') it then 'pass' it after three further steps. They were not allowed in the opponents orange semi circle unless they were in mid air throwing a shot at goal. The green shirted but not so 'green' Austrian team did this with a regular lucidity taking advantage of the loose ball and poor passing of the red shirted and red faced Georgians. The resulting massacre was scored at forty to the home team and a hard fought nineteen to the smiling but outclassed foreign victims.

"I'm going to interview the players" I announced trying to sound like a sporting hack.

The second thirty minute half had taken its toll on the players resting on the benches. Whilst the spectators converged on the bar for post match postulations I approached an exhausted Austrian player armed with my press sheet which identified him by his shirt number as Roland Schlinger. I politely requested a couple of minutes of his time which he readily obliged unlike some professional footballers I had met on my travels around England.

"They tell me that a Swedish Handball hero earns 200,000 Euros per year" I began.

"I'm lucky to earn 20,000 and footballers earn more in a week" he laughed.

"I guess I'm not cut out to be a sports journalist. I'm off for a beer" I apologised.

But he was right as I had met a soccer player playing in Austria who had earned several times this figure playing in München. American Basket Ball players earned a further multiple of this figure playing in the leagues let alone for their country of origin. It wasn't the money that motivated him it was national pride which greatly impressed me.

"HANDBALL"

THREE KINGS DAY BIRTHDAY, HAUNTED HOHENEMS AND ANGELICA'S LOST LETTERS

Snowflakes are floating masterpieces of natural water crystallisation according to weather pundits. My children preferred shaking the plastic water filled crystal balls with imitation snowmen in a synthetic snow blizzard. But whether you are a crystal ball gazer or a crystallographer studying the glaciers, the predictions for the future of our current winter snow patterns is pretty bleak in the face of global warming and the statistical probability of no snow below 1000 metres in latter half of this century. I cared more about the melting process than the actual sprinkling of this sweet looking but wet icing sugar. The icy water always managed to trickle into unguarded orifices sending a cold winter shiver down my spine.

"Daddy, I think it always snows in heaven" said my day dreaming son.

Leopold was now securely attached to the T-bar after several failed attempts which had resulted in chaos as several foreign skiers cursed behind him as they had to also prematurely disembark prior to reaching their intended destination.

"If I let go we could fall down to Hell !" he added waving his ski poles.

I didn't need a crystal ball to predict what was about to happen next. The blasphemies and profanities from German tourists trying to enjoy the fresh snow on the Bödele above Dornbirn was pretty near to Hell. Still I supposed in a churlish childish way that it was just another form of torture for this summer bath towel brigade who had already braved a fried fake winter tan on sun beds prior to fighting with the traffic jams to reach the even longer lift queues. Three Kings Day was a public celebration of the arrival of the Three Kings to visit the first true born baby Jesus in Bethlehem. It was also an excuse for these 'flatlanders' to play Kings of the slopes in the Bödele mayhem of the first real snow holiday of the season.

I was trying to maintain my balance keeping the bar around my knees so as not to topple him over whilst gripping him around the waist as we wove from side to side on the bumpy stairway to Heaven. Then the phone rang just as we reached the summit. I let the bar fly into the red sticks known to my children as the final buffers. Being a bit of a fumbling old buffer I forgot about my son as I scrambled to answer the call and luckily the poles did not impale him as he shot sky wards holding on to the recoiling spring bar. It was a close call and consequently the lift stopped dislodging the same pair of German skiers forcing them to make another untimely exit in an ungraceful pile of skis and poles.

"Hello. Can I help you ?" I shouted down the telephone.

The expletives from the tangled pile of tourists drowned out the person on the other end of the telephone. I was impressed with their English even if they had got crossed wires with my phone greeting. The telephone signal was better than their vulgar hand signals too.

"It's Lothar. It's a baby boy called Leon born at twelve o'clock" said the proud new father.

"Well done on Three Kings Day. I'll try again later" I said returning the semaphore of the dislodged "Flatlanders" with distemper.

My terrible German reply was misinterpreted by the now upright and downright furious couple who nearly punched my lights out. I was lucky not to see stars but deep down inside I was so happy for Lothar producing offspring on this day of the greatest biblical star story of all time. I picked up a bedraggled Leopold who was not so happy about the news of a new life owing to the fact that he had just had a near death experience with a large snow pole.

We skied well clear of the 'flatlanders' without any further need for hand signals until tired aching limbs frustrated the children so much as to cause chair lift passengers behind us to hiss at their charming cries of cold and discomfort. A cruel swearing paternal ogre shoved them screaming into the car in front of the same alarmed tourists who complained about child control just as their children threw an ice ball at the window of the car opposite. We did not stay for the crash not wishing to spoil their day. They had already concluded that my children should be house-trained like their yapping dog which promptly bit another passing skier.

Not wishing to spend too long at the Dornbirn Hospital for fear of my children being taken away by Social Services and treated for severe psychological disorder we briefly visited the new born baby who smiled innocently in his crib. When he grew up he too would strain his limbs in the same pointless snow pursuit but his calming complexion like a child in a clinical Christmas crib had the desired affect on my children too. There was nothing better in the world than a new born baby to illustrate the tale of the Three Kings to three tired children.

The feast day of the Epiphany or the 'Drei Königs' known locally as 'Kaspar, Melchior and Balthasar' marks the end of the traditional Christmas holidays. The waning holly and browning pine needles of the 'Adventskranz' with the four burnt out candles of advent is cast out onto the 'Biomüll' compost heap along with the last scraps of the delicious pre-Christmas 'Lebkuchen' and 'Stollen'. Only the 'Tannenbaum' or Christmas Tree waits wilting sadly like a tired party guest to be unceremoniously stripped of chocolates and edible decorations. The streets of every village in Vorarlberg were teaming various groups of grinning children dressed in cloaks and crowns to feign the story of the visiting three kings. Some were led by a fourth 'Sternträger' symbolising the star that led them to Bethlehem.

They spend around three days visiting all the dwellings in Höchst and Gaissau but it is considered essential by the church that they bring a little light into every household. There is a ring at each doorbell and then each king recites or sings a set piece from the story about the gifts they have bought to honour the King of Kings. Then one of them reaches up to the door mantle with a piece of chalk and inscribes a blessing in Austrian script as follows:

$$'C + M + B - 2003'$$

This is little confusing as it could mean the Latin blessing of 'Christo Mansionem Benedictit' or Christ bless this home but it also could mean the Latin names for the three kings: 'Casper, Melchior and Baltasar'. Whatever it meant did not matter to our children who idolised the king with boot polish on his face and the long gowns which were often hemmed in to avoid being dragged along in the wet snow. Thousands of brown muddy and red ruddy faced urchins became migrant nativity play street entertainers receiving polite applause and goodies from every welcoming household. It was all in aid of charity fund raising but it was fun spotting the ninja star-stave carrier coercing sweets from his three accomplices and another team that was throwing snowballs at their accompanying adult. It was an exhausting but entertaining tradition which had been completely forgotten in England.

"There is also a special bread ring known as Drei Königs Brot. Try some."

My wife knew that we would all like the sweet white ring of buns with a brown crust caramelised with a glazed sugar topping. The idea was to break off a bun segment and then tear it apart in search of a coin or trinket as this was the person who got the prize of being crowned the king of the household for that day. The ensuing scramble reminded me of my efforts to entertain a theatre full of thirty bored children with pass the parcel.

I recalled that I had directed a series of touring puppet companies in the theatre in Lincolnshire and it had developed into an exceptional programme of children's puppet parties. After much coaxing of the town based puppet companies who regarded Lincolnshire as a cultural desert we produced some first class shows from the Little Angel Marionette Theatre from Islington in London, the Presto Puppet Company from Buxton in Derbyshire and many other visiting artistes. These shows included a tea party afterwards with assorted similar sticky buns and cakes followed by a visit from Santa with a large corn sack full of goodies. The largest show was for two hundred excited children but it was this small show of thirty children that proved the most challenging as the puppeteer's vehicle broke down in transit. Once again I was left to tread the boards for two hours of impromptu children's party entertainment owing to the fact that most children were abandoned due to my good nature in letting the parent's have some child free time.

The most obvious solution was to take them all around the zoo for a pre-Christmas treat which was quite a successful ploy until it poured with rain and I discovered most of them had no waterproofs. I remembered some of the tricks from the Festival entertainers but I was pretty hopeless at plate spinning, my juggling was a disaster and there was no magic hat. But then I realised that if I couldn't take them to the zoo I could certainly bring them a magic rabbit, a scary spider and even dance with a snake. It was a run away success especially when the rabbit escaped and the snake bit my finger. So it was that these three insignificant pets became kings of the stage along with a huge game of pass the parcel which the children had carefully wrapped whilst I fetched in the pet show.

"You're in that dream world again, Daddy" said Leopold with his cardboard crown.

Leopold's nails dug into my hand reminding me that it was unwise to hold an excited bunny by its ears and much more sensible and sensitive to stroke it into submission.

****

The telephone never stopped ringing as more and more people became embroiled in the Opera, the Chronicles and indeed the farm house reconstruction where the invisible spectre of the plumber had unexpectedly materialised. This latter revelation and his apparition and ascension into the attic was a complete mystery to us but many devout parishioners of Gaissau had warned me of 'morgen syndrom'. This was not a religious experience but a local slang for the incurable affliction attributed to builders which in English circles was normally diagnosed by other speech recognition patterns like the immortal words:

'See you tomorrow maybe all being well or next week at the latest, Luv'.

The concurrence of this completely meaningless statement and associated symptoms like the leaving of a huge mess of pipes and no hot water normally resulted in a fatal outbreak of phantom plumber's disease. The death of the patient unwashed customer could occur without the protagonist even noticing rigor mortis had set in when he returned one month later to request permission to brew a cup of tea. Austrian plumbers might even ask for a beer to help them bend the pipes and occasionally simply retire at midday to prepare for another bender in the bar. I fully expected our rediscovered and recovered water installation expert to have this additional carrying capacity expected of such a liquid profession.

"Whilst the phantom plumber checks your water works, I'm off to Hohenems."

"You make him sound like a ghostly gynaecologist, darling" scoffed my spouse.

I was in fact going to meet a family genealogist whose Palast in Hohenems was reputed to have ghosts and it was probably, like many such historic houses in England, a plumber's nightmare too. I arrived punctually outside the great palace previously the home of the Counts of Hohenems who once ruled a sizeable part of Vorarlberg from the Bodensee to Tyrol. I gazed up from the square courtyard at the remaining Renaissance arches and statutes in the alcoves of this once opulent residence built by Martino Longo in the 1560's for an eccentric and affluent Cure Cardinal and Bishop of Konstanz (and the younger brother of the infamous Carlo Borromeo) who never took up residence. A copy of a painting of the period showed the Palace plans with follies, carefully laid out Renaissance gardens and a small zoo which were partly completed by the Cardinal's nephew, Caspar (possibly named after the most opulent of the Three Kings). Interestingly it was after his death in 1640 that things went rapidly down hill even resulting in the sale of Vaduz and Schellenberg to the Liechtenstein family in 1710. Then the title of Count died out in 1759, the paintings moved off to Bistrau in Bohemia in 1804 and the Palast itself was almost ruined. It was then sold to the Walberg-Zeil family from the impressive Schloss Zeil which can be still seen shinning white in the midday sun on a hill by Leutkirch in Allgäu from the motorway from Bregenz to München.

"It's a long sad genealogical history and I had to buy the ruined Palast back again from my cousin Clementine" said the charming and cheerful Franz-Josef Waldburg-Zeil.

We walked around this clearly much loved family seat now partly converted with an antique shop for his son, a state of the art municipal town gallery in the attics (noted for tapestry exhibitions) and a restaurant (noted for mediaeval banqueting). It was like my home where I had grown up in Lincolnshire. I had lived in that painting with an animal menagerie, a wonderful theatre (also featuring banquets for hungry revellers), and similar pretty gardens whereas the Palast was now surrounded by a modern Hohenems with its back against the cliff. I had seen many such historic houses struggling to keep afloat relying on the impoverished owners goodwill to share their home with often noisy guests and draining the last drops of a landed income into the plumber's sinking fund. Still I yearned for this life knowing too well that the other option of living on the laurels of a prosperous ancestor was a recipe for disaster. My father had avoided this by opening his home to visitors and managing the estate assets rather than manicuring them in the pursuit of trivia. So many such places were squandered through the vanity and the blind belief that such places were playthings of the idle rich.

"I am a second son and I lived in a pretty little castle near Lindau but I fell deeply in love with the 'Palast' which was almost demolished" he said showing me his life's work.

"I know how you feel and you have worked hard on your dream" I acknowledged.

I knew just how hard I had worked with a zoo in the daytime and a theatre at night and his stamina reminded me of my father. He was older but seemed just as committed.

Franz-Josef Waldburg-Zeil had all the paternal aristocratic mannerisms of my father, right down to the tweed jacket with a slightly maladjusted collar. His corduroy trouser and woolly jumper clad son was also an energetic antiques dealer with some pretty examples of the furniture that might once have adorned the palace. My father must have had pretty much the same problems when he first came home to an abandoned historic house after the war. Much of the furniture from my Great Aunt was no longer there either due to wartime occupation as anti-aircraft regional headquarters, and most of the family portraits were installed in other family houses. He had also to condemn another great empty family historic house to be demolished to make way for the urban sprawl of Northampton and only just managed to save a third family house by encouraging its division into multiple dwellings. I could see the problems of this great now stranded and desperate Palast hemmed in on three sides by a rapidly developing modern town with its back against the craggy rock face. It was definitely a labour of love.

"This is the Rittersaal" he said unlocking a large oak door.

The banqueting room was used much as it might have been in the romantic heyday of the Borromeo connection and there was a reproduction of the Cardinal's painting hanging slightly lopsided on the wall. The room had an especially high ceiling for a timber beamed music room with two balconies and it was easy to imagine the banquets that had been witnessed in this remnant of a wonderful Renaissance past. A guide in a North German Palace once told me that the balcony seats were normally occupied by local townsfolk, clergy or honoured gentry who did not participate in the proceedings below but who acted like 'word of mouth' eyewitnesses recounting the great magnificence of the occasions to the generally illiterate population. Other English houses of a slightly earlier period used the gallery as a refuge for the host and one Old Hall in Lincolnshire even had a peep hole from an adjoining bedroom. The musicians only took to the balcony when dancing became more fashionable and it was amusing to note that a modern stage for concerts was now back downstairs in a new age where music was now a foreground rather than a background entertainment.

"We had the Schubertiade here when it first started but one day it just got too big and moved to Feldkirch and then onto the wonderful new Angelica Kauffmann Halle in Schwarzenberg" he said with a note of resigned disappointment. "But now we are alive with new concerts from the Kammerorchester Arpeggione series with new music and exciting talent. It gives a new life to a room built for entertainment."

Having spent eleven long years producing an Award Winning Classics by Candlelight series and sponsoring the Percy Grainger String Orchestra in a similar acoustically challenging but impressive music room I instantly saw the possibilities for the first reading of my opera on Angelica Kauffmann. The grand piano stood abandoned under the magnificent standard wax coated candelabra with the melted remains of a great evening dripped all around its base.

"It's a problem with these candles but they will insist on using them" he complained.

He coughed with embarrassment just like I used to do with prospective wedding clients when the cleaners had inadvertently left the remnants of the reception from night before. He led me into a small banqueting room laid out for a mediaeval banquet not realising that the candle wax was the actual attraction rather than the distraction. Once again I was reliving my past tensely trying to look at the copies of the family paintings but so tempted to jump into my tights ready to introduce the next dance of the seven veils. I smiled as I remembered that I had worked with an extraordinary belly dancer who rippled due to her voluptuous figure and her huge cleavage always mesmerised the audience. Then the sadly departed Baron De Maine (who always wore a full suit of armour and then made assorted costume changes as a saucy sorcerer and a very randy bear) appeared in my daydream like another ghost from my past. I was just worrying about the mono-cycling juggler setting light to the curtains again with his fire clubs when he brought me back down to earth again.

"We could launch your opera here if you think it will suit you ?" he said.

"I would like that very much indeed" I replied with a polite grin.

As I pondered over some of the Bishop's old library books at the end of our tour, I returned to my theatrical past. They were already partying in the Rittersaal and I imagined them sitting with my late father on the balcony above smiling down at me. The Hohenems Palast was probably haunted; at least it had been possessed briefly by the ghosts of my past.

****

My discovery of the past had now become a potential future and work on the travel book administration snowballed and just when the snow was beginning to make travel difficult. My son Max had joined a ski jumping club in Dornbirn and whilst he practised springing for his flying debut in a gymnasium I had more time to visit the town centre. I explored the interior of the famous Rotes Haus whose eaves had sheltered us during the soaking wet Martinimarkt. It was a restaurant of some reputation and the busy waitresses were setting up for the dinner time rush but they kindly showed me around this remarkable mediaeval structure with low wooden beams, curved wooden floors and original sliding windows with bottle-end glazed peep holes. I had eaten here before and judging by the delicious smells wafting from the kitchen it was still an enchanting gastronomes hostelry.

I found a swish designer-look bar in an impressive old building across the square and joined the local after-work drinkers on the bar stools enjoying the local brew. A dark suited slick dresser with rounded spectacles was cordial towards strangers of a foreign tongue and he invited me to the launch of the Dornbirn City Guide the following evening on the grounds that he was responsible for tourism in this cool and vibrant expanding 'City'. Of course no writer could pass up a party especially in the ORF media studios which I had visited for interviews and its strange ship like architecture seemed to lend itself to chic parties.

I was not disappointed as the doorman released the peculiar glass ship's watertight doors and I splashed into a flood of smart young socialites sipping sparkling 'sekt' and flashing fashionable underwater watches. The booze flowed in a bacchanalian celebration of a particularly well written tourist City Guide which pushed the bounds of revealing reportage into the uncharted world of underground culture, aesthetic architecture and techno-tourism. It was a great credit to my host who was enjoying the vast array of live pop and cabaret acts in the television studio. He sipped his soothing drink as it was his big night and I carefully left him to mingle with the new assorted glamorous figureheads of his new 'City' culture.

"Well I'm a psychiatrist" said a tall suited man whose poker faced gaze froze out any further conversation. "I like climbing because I can look down at all the little people."

"Really, that is a relaxing hobby for a shrink" I murmured shying away tactfully towards my couch by the bar before we delved any deeper into my vertigo problem.

"Hey, an Old School Englishman. What are you doing here ?"

The discernibly Irish but definitely American voice came from a radio presenter who had his arm wrapped around a blond high cheek boned fashion model. At last the party had started and before long we were into ghost stories, computerised translations that made James Joyce's poetic visit to Feldkirch sound like a Chinese translation of his 'Finnegans Wake' and other pretty sharp city slicking finger licking repartee. Just as the audience was beginning to swing in with some good new anecdotes a polite pretty middle aged respectably English lady tapped me on the shoulder and spoke to me in a home counties English accent.

"Are you really writing an Opera on Angelica Kauffmann ?" she asked.

"I am working on the libretto which is now translated into German" I replied.

"Well if you are who you say you are, my father-in-law still has some of her letters."

All summer long I had travelled repeatedly from Dornbirn to Schwarzenberg to sit in the village to write the first libretto in Angelica Kauffmann's Heimat in search of the raw material and inspiration for the opera. I had heard the villagers speak of an English Lady and the museum staff in the pretty little Heimat museum (which has some excellent records of Angelica Kauffmann) had spoken of these letters on several occasions. I had in truth pawed over photocopies of the mundane but crucial correspondence. Here was my chance to see the only real living proof of her connection to Schwarzenberg apart from the altar piece gifted to the church and possibly some of her ceiling paintings mostly attributed to her father.

I knew that she had something interesting to offer not least my chance to see the writing of my heroine first hand which unless you write frequently is a difficult thing to explain.

As we chatted I made up my mind to research a second opera on the early life of Angelica in Schwarzenberg which I had avoided due to lack of written evidence. Every tale has an unexpected twist said the great Roald Dahl and my head spun all the way home. Those who still write letters to loved ones or pen friends will probably use the computer but for those who compose putting pen to paper this was a calligraphic call from the past.

A FASCHING CLOWN MEDAL, SCHWARZENBERG SURPRISE AND SKATEBOARDERS

The winter sunset makes the mountains seem like delicious ice cream sundaes with a delightful drizzle of freshly squeezed orange juice and if you prefer to wake at dawn you can sometimes see a red raspberry topping. Personally, I preferred the tangy taste of orange zest possibly with a touch of an associated liquor to be savoured long after the musical moon and the stars of the night have come out to play. On very cold evenings the snow glittered and glistened giving me a glimmer of hope that the party season was not yet over like in dull and depressing old Protestant England where society simply hibernated until the Spring.

There were increasing signs of strange activity in the two villages of Höchst and Gaissau and that did not include the phantom plumber who did his usual vanishing act. The season of 'Fasching' or 'Karnival' would make the next two months like one long party under the guise of throwing out the Winter. This was especially true of all Alleman countries where pagan traditions had not only survived religious Puritanism but they had also become firmly embedded in the conventions and clubs of nearly every community in the now blessed name of Carnival. Some of the greatest parades are in riotous Rio and on the gondolas of Venice but the Bodensee boasts a combination of the best of both of these 'Karnival' shows with the benefit of both masked musical pageants and water-based spectacles.

I was having my hair done at the Unisex Hairdresser next door as most mid forties males tend to do after examining themselves in the mirror after one party too many and a good wifely tongue wagging. The teenage girl with studs in every available orifice at the neighbouring wash basin was having her hair dyed strawberry red and there seemed to be trickles of blood dribbling everywhere like in a very gory horror movie. There were also gentile local ladies being given orange hair tones making them look like old hags and witches. I had to rub my eyes in case I was dreaming again. Even the slim, sleek hairdressers with their skin tight trousers had purple tints and there was an air of unusual frivolity.

"We don't normally open on Saturdays but we will have to cope with Karnival."

My hairdresser was a single mother with very supportive relatives who not only offered child support but who had also helped her to build a new salon in the back garden that would be the envy of even London's finest hair stylists. Her figure, sensitivity and charm left no doubt that she would not be unattached for long unless by personal choice and perhaps preferred experience. She spoke excellent, almost faultless English with a slightly subdued Somerset accent subtly blended between the 'Höchster' slur which made her sound like a nightingale singing after a night out on the cider.

"That explains the hairstyles. Do they have any parties ?" I said sheepishly.

"You must come to the Ball as we are all going to dance for the football boys."

I walked out into the freezing cold after having tactfully purchased two tickets for the Football Ball in the 'Rheinhalle'. There was obviously plenty of fun to be had in 'Fasching' and I was now fired and inspired to further my purely religious education in this respect. A few days later I heard the first distant bass drum pounding in the Church Square outside my window. My heart thumped in beat as I jumped out of my chair to investigate the sounds of the blaring brass instruments that now accompanied the pitter-patter of kettle drums.

When I arrived the square was full of costumed revellers and tightly wrapped spectators gossiping, laughing and making merry after the 'Narrenmesse' church service in the freezing cold. The warm 'Glühwein' helped soothe the cold and the sweet smelling vapours rose with the cigarette smoke and excited sounds of the gathered throng. It was not long before a large group of 'Fluhar Nollatruller' took over a flower bed on the corner of the Church steps and then proceeded to give an impromptu trumpet and cornet concert. Their costumes looked like a French Clown outfit with puffed and fanned silver glittering padded sleeves and flared leggings like a 'Flash Gordon Movie' or an advert for iridescent quilted but very cute and cuddly Elvis Presley dolls. They certainly looked warm and ridiculous which was ideal for 'Karnival' parades on cold winter's evenings in the snow.

"How long does Karnival last ?" I asked a smiling silver version of Gary Glitter.

"In France it can last all year but here it is around two and a half months."

He turned out to be the President of the Insel Show Orchestra Höchst which was hosting the party and which was also one of many spontaneous instrumental clubs formed around similar musical aspirations of making 'Lärm, Krach und Chaos' during 'Karnival'.

The noise, din and chaos then developed further as the 'Schalmeienzug Höchst' decided to mount a musical return barrage on their curious silver plated wind instruments noted for their astonishing sounds and technical origins. The music relied on the wind passing through a multiple of pipes giving the 'Schalmei' a shriller sound more akin to miniature organ pipes. The alto and bass instruments widened the band's musical range but added a sharper intonation. The nearest description to this extraordinary music which was always accompanied by military drumming would be something like a Brass Band from the Coal Pits that had broken a vow of abstinence not to imbibe halogen prior to a performance.

"Daddy, look ! There are some clowns !" said my daughter pulling my arm.

"Well let's go and talk to them then" I said sipping my second 'Glühwein'.

"But your Deutsch is terrible, so I'll translate" Emily said bossily.

We approached the good looking clowns in black jackets with multicoloured flecks and matching trousers. Their red bowler hats had lots of small badges from other Carnival Clown Clubs that they had visited but they were from the

'Narrengilde Unterfeld Lauterach' which was printed on their hat brims. I chatted with the male clown about my experiences with the Hospital Clowns whilst my daughter seemed engrossed in conversation with the other clowns. It was clear that this club was set up around 1982 purely with one objective of making everybody happy during 'Karnival'.

"Do you entertain the children ?" I slurred in a very poor imitation of his native tongue whilst breathing potent alcohol fumes out with my steamy bad breath.

"We entertain everybody; young and old alike" he grimaced.

One of the girls in the group whispered something to her fellow clown and then proceeded to take off a treasured medal from her large chest. Then she grinned and cordially hung it around my neck giving me a little peck on the cheek.

"Your daughter says you are a famous writer from England and so we'd like you to have this to remember us in your book" she said with a wry smile and naughty wink.

It was a great and unexpected honour which I gratefully received in a state of bewildered intoxication and incredulity at my young interpreter's exaggeration on my behalf. I flushed red with embarrassment just as I had done when I was awarded my blue nose by the Cliniclowns in Bludenz. The brass medal had a portrait of a smiling clown with a green hat and a bright red nose. It certainly made me pleased as punch and I didn't need a red nose.

"You awarded it to me because my nose is redder than everybody else" I stammered.

She smiled and gave me a little wave and a wiggle as she tottered towards her taxi.

"Your German is terrible, Daddy" said Emily as we sauntered home.

"You're quite good now. At least I won a medal" I teased.

We arrived back in time for the sweet succulent smell of a simmering supper and sat down to tuck into a hearty meal of an odd looking chicken.

"That was great fun and there's lots more to come in Karinval. Darling, this is delicious chicken but with a very strange rib cage" I said serving it out to the children.

My wife glowered at me as though she had tried me but the court had declared an open verdict. I had not drunk more than a little of the heart warming wine and I rubbed my numb red nose to check that I was in fact as sober as a judge. But I knew when it was wiser not to make an appeal in favour of a latent repeal of my death sentence. The due romantic pleading process when the children were out of hearing in bed might stay my execution.

"There were clowns too, but no magicians" said Emily as she went to bed.

"Plenty of fun but nobody to pull a rabbit out of their hat" I smirked obtusely.

We lounged lethargically on the sofa half watching the first of the politically satirical comedy television shows that were encouraged during the 'Karnival' season.

"I could have shot you when you almost upset Leopold" she frowned.

"But you're a medal winning magician too pulling that *"rabbit"* out of the cooking pot."

I was granted a pardon and the rest of the evening was spent clowning about.

****

The second opera libretto was now being researched in earnest in Italy and I struggled to keep the composers moving on with the chorus and duets from the London Opera. There was also a new English course for businessmen in Lindau and a diary full of appointments as gossip spread about the Chronicles to the far reaches of the Bregenzerwald. This latter invitation was to prove the most rewarding distraction. A white carpet of snow rolled out in front of me as I struggled with the tired gearbox of the biscuit tin climbing over the winding road from Dornbirn over the Bödele. If there is one place in Vorarlberg that could be described as a winter Heaven on Earth then I would always choose Schwarzenberg.

The sprawling village of traditional wooden farmhouses was well distributed in a mountain pasture idyll and it had been carefully conserved from the onslaught of modern concrete architecture much to my hidden pleasure (but often to the open displeasure of those often non-resident entrepreneurs wishing to profit from tourism). I had listened to many diatribes about the isolationist ignorant rustics of this part of the Bregenzerwald. Even local inhabitants were ashamed about their appearance to the modernist world of the Rhine Delta over the Lank. But my summation of the situation was simply to ignore those simpletons of the suburban myth for if there is an alpine paradise on this Planet, it would look like Schwarzenberg. An unspoilt, unique, and as yet unconquerable harmony of nature in a vast world of human excrescence. There was not one pimple in this perfect snowy panorama.

"Excuse me, I have come to see someone up the road, but he doesn't seem to be at home ?" I said to a gathering of pleasant 'peasant' pensioners playing jassen in the Gaststube zur Buche. "Maybe he has forgotten my meeting with him ?"

"Did you hear his dog ?" said the voluptuous landlady who was supporting a full tracht. "If the dog is there he is not far away."

After struggling with the door bell of the roadside farmhouse in between dodging the spray from passing cars I gave up and put it down to 'morgen syndrome' which was quite a common Vorarlberg disease. It was a sort of aboriginal alpine amnesia where the natives were often apt to forget their appointments and go off on a 'walkabout' so I adjourned to reminisce.

Having spent nearly a year in Australia working in remote Queensland sheep shearing sheds and cattle stations I was prepared for this long before visiting the Bregenzerwald. I had travelled hundreds of miles around the 'bush' on assorted aged scramble bikes, and an ancient Holden utility wagon as well as sailing backwards into the trade winds on a 'jerry-built' catamaran down the Great Barrier Reef from Thursday Island to Cooktown. I once spent eight days driving a combine harvester across New South Wales as a wager which won me considerable notoriety with the radio stations and 'road train' truck drivers who had nicknamed me on their CB radios as 'the mad Pom with the header'. Every truck stop along my route used to cheer me in the bar and offer me drinks as they could not believe that I was going to drive such a slow agricultural machine over five hundred miles. I had just read a very funny book about a comedian who travelled around Ireland with a Fridge. I wondered what he would have made of my experience especially when I called the breakdown service to jump start the temperamental beast only to finish up push starting the tow wagon.

This was one of my fondest memories of my many months of travelling as well as winning a rodeo bet by default with an extremely drunk indigenous aboriginal 'Ringer' or in Queen's English: a sozzled native cattle hand from the outback. I was awarded a whole tray of 'stubbies' (beers) by the barman at the rodeo for being foolhardy enough to turn up to take on my illusive big mouthed challenger. Then I was shown the fierce snorting bullocks in the pen which I had chosen as my choice of weapons in this macho duel. I was brave and stupid in those youthful days but the tale ended when my challenger resurfaced to help me to consume the beers. The barman laughed, not because I had won by default but because my opponent was in fact a famous rodeo star from the Northern Territory.

I wandered around the village on my own 'walkabout' knowing better that there was plenty of time to wait for him to reappear. I visited my favourite opera researcher and the Bürgermeister's very capable and pretty tourism assistant. Then I realised that my diary had referred to Schwarzenberg many times as my place of business and second summer home from home but that I had never really described it from the viewpoint of a foreign visitor. It too was famous for cattle walking rather than riding and for a phenomenal woman.

A most remarkable church forms the central pivot of the three way village of Schwarzenberg. This once lost rural idyllic civilisation was connected in one direction to Dornbirn by the first passable carriage track in the 1800's and later by two high bridges firstly in the direction of Egg and latterly in the direction of Bezau. There are no street names as everything is still identified by a landmark, family dwelling or building which a traveller might use for guidance. This is a street system peculiar to Schwarzenberg where there is invariably always somebody on hand to give you detailed directions if you can follow the local dialect.

The village is also famous for the Angelica Kauffmann Saal which hosts the Schubertiade concerts (and hopefully one day my opera) and a tiny but pretty converted farmhouse museum featuring local history and copies of some of Angelica's work and letters.

I had just left the bank after chatting with a local footballer about the next Fasching frivolities when a large black shaggy Newfoundland hound started sniffing my leg.

"Ah, the Englishman with the Opera, I'm sorry but I was taking my grandchildren to the dentist and I forgot" said an extremely apologetic elderly man at the end of the overtly friendly dog's leash. "Don't mind my dog, he is as soft as butter."

"Hop in." I gestured to my biscuit tin and we headed off with the panting dog back to the Gaststube to enjoy a traditionally warm beer together.

We talked about his work with the Heimat Museum and my opera project as he was a well known and respected source of information for writers like myself. I should say that it was rather more me doing the talking as he was infamous for his few well chosen words and long thoughtful pauses. I assumed this was out of modesty or due to his infinite wisdom but I was later told that it was because he had worked in Bregenz Museum noted for its silent strutting curators and seated sleeping ushers. Once I had tried to wake one of them to ask about the Angelica Kauffmann paintings to receive no recognisable response, apart from a finger being raised to his lips as though I was in a reading room or a gentleman's club. The museum in Bregenz had reopened the Schwarzenberg Museum in 1985 after nearly fifteen years of closure and the curator had sent him to manage it. This was possibly on account of his local interest being a native by marriage but perhaps also due to his endearing style of conversation as his modesty and tongue were only eased by the end of his beer.

"Can I see Angelica's letters as it would be nice to see the originals after spending so long writing the Opera ?" I said after a tiring, lengthy but hopefully interesting monologue.

"It would be my pleasure" he said with a smile and we walked to his house.

There are many ancient houses in Schwarzenberg and indeed some excellent hotels where you can experience farmhouse hospitality and associated countryside culinary delights. However, this two hundred year old house was quite the most remarkable example in the village. I was shown into the cold panelled guest 'stube' which was obviously not used in winter in favour of a more modern snug 'stube'. The enormous green and cream white tiled 'Kachelofen' in the inside corner of the room was typical of this region but its shiny brass oven doors along with the now unpolished brass door handle showed that this family had once been quite prosperous farmers. I sat in the opposite corner in the 'Herrgott's Winckel' admiring the carved crucifix and two engraved glass cases that hung on either side of it. One of them contained a nativity scene with beads and golden thread stitch work whilst the other celebrated a local saint, both probably souvenirs from a monastery or a pilgrimage.

"Here you are" he said carefully removing three letters wrapped in an old envelope in a plastic carrier bag. "I hope you can read them, but I also have the typed version."

"It is the original that can tell us so much more about Angelica. Looking at the dates you can see that she signed them with her surname with only one 'n' and later adjoining her husband's name of Zucchi" I said enjoying the real feeling of being in touch with the past and with my operatic heroine.

Her italic ivory pen or perhaps even a quill had inscribed these letters to Joseph Metzler without a single mistake in neatly formed lines. She could have been a chronicler like me as well as a renowned painter and an accomplished singer. However the real surprise then hit me like a thunder bolt as he withdrew a dust cover from a painting in the corner.

"Of course this is one of her paintings that normally hangs over my bed."

As I left we admired a beautifully painted cupboard 'Hochzeitsschrank' from the man with whom Angelica had corresponded and I recalled how they used to carry them over the mountain passes to the bride's new home. He had some good examples of the work of a local unknown painter born in the same year as Angelica called Gabriel Ignaz Thum, but it was plain to see why my heroine was a child prodigy. Then a little girl crept up behind us with black curly hair. She had a beaming white mischievous grin and I regained my composure asking her if she spoke English. She shyly clung to a wooden pillar and proceeded to giggle.

"Hello, Goodbye, Yes and thank you" she repeated like a nursery rhyme.

I crunched back through the snow with her haunting image and that of the exquisite masterpiece painted by her famous ancestor in my mind. I was reminded of the fact that 'My Little Mountain Angel' was the title of my opera and perhaps a little ghost of the past had peeked out at me to guide me on my long journey to its fruition.

****

The biscuit tin coughed and spluttered in the freezing evening air and then it growled and moaned as I ground my way back over the mountain pass to Dornbirn. This momentous day in the life of a middle aged libretto writer and corny chronicler was not over and the sun had not set on me just yet but it dawned upon me that I was heading for a total contrast from the naïve and surreal Elysium of the tranquil Bregenzerwald into a teenage hell.

"Welcome to Halle 8a, my name is Cle" repeated a young slim student so that his voice could be heard above the deafening sound of punk rock and the roaring wheels of several spotty teenage skateboarders. "Make yourself at home."

I ventured further into a small but impressive hangar-like sports hall which was a part of the Messe complex in Dornbirn which included conference halls, an ice hockey rink, an indoor tennis hall and several other sports facilities.

This 'Halle' had several quarter pipes, ramps, fun boxes and flat rails upon which a multitude of teenage boys were riding their skate boards to the limits of their well advanced sporting skills. There were a few spotty spectators lounging on old sofas with woolly hats, revolutionary red sixties streetwise t-shirts of 'Che' and unwashed jeans that appeared to sag significantly around their butt cheeks.

"So, who is the cool skateboard king of this den of iniquity?" I joked.

"I'm not quite sure what iniquity means, but that kid 'Chris' is the best as his deck is sponsored by Yama and his trainers are sponsored by Vans. He's cool" replied Cle.

I wondered if his shoes and skateboard were so important to youth commercial exploitation why the rest of his scant cheap market stall clothing looked like it hadn't been near a washing machine. Cle waved him off the ramps. It was quite clear by his stylish 'ollies', an absolutely awesome 'slide' on a descending rail, a really astonishing 'One-eighty', and an ice cool 'wheelie' in our direction that he was a 'cool' king of the 'Halle'.

"I was in Africa so I speak English. So what do you want to know ?" he said politely.

We chatted about his World Cup in Prague and Eurocup adventures in Basel and then we amused ourselves learning the skateboard language which had grown this street based hobby into an international sport but still with an associated club music culture.

"Well my grip tape is wrecked and my board is kicked, means that you need a new surface on your deck, but probably a new deck too" he started with a patient smile.

I scribbled in my yellow book pretending that I understood exactly what he was talking about although it was like technical teenage trite to my untrained ears.

"We tend to hang out here in Winter on Wednesdays and Fridays and when the weather is cool then we go snowboarding on Sundays" he said cooly after explaining his craft.

I thought of all the bored spotted teenagers in England that professed to worship this skateboard culture including my very capable son, Max. It was clear that the Vorarlberg kids had so much more fun as they had snow to slide on as well as wood and concrete. He flicked the wheels on his 'trucks' as he talked and then flipped the board with his right foot before he headed back to his royal perch on the top corner of a large wooden quarter pipe.

"You are coming to our contest in February as we have the best of the best."

"You can bet on it!" I replied to an over-enthusiastic Cle. "I'll bring my son, Max."

ANDELSBUCH CHEESE, A PHANTOM ROLLS ROYCE AND A BLUE POLICE LIGHT

The various subsidiary provincial tourism offices eventually began to learn of my harmless menopausal madness and prominent politicians and other departments from the local government 'Landesregierung' for Vorarlberg were becoming interested in the chronicles.

It was becoming quite amusing to read the incoming Emails as it was clear that grammar was not always taught correctly in such prominent governing circles. The use of computerised translations were becoming more unintelligible and I simply chose the invitations that made me laugh the most. My favourite garbled message was supposed to read: *'We will organise your trip to the cheese road in Andelsbuch'* The lovely lady must have got frustrated in translation and it 'came' out as : *'We will orgasm your tip to the KäseStrasse in Andelsbuch.'*

This most definitely attracted my attention and went to the tip of my list although I was concerned about such a cheesy experience in street in such snowy conditions and whether I should read Andel's book beforehand. Quietly giggling about the unfortunate but hilarious Email message I set forth into the Bregenzerwald to visit a new 'Käsehaus' with an ecstatic feeling of wild anticipation. At last I had found somebody who really understood my sensitive if not perhaps sensuous midlife predicament. I had heard that many males suffering from my debilitating midlife disease had found comfort eating a successful cure. Cheese was probably not the food at the top of my list but her idea might be the cure that I needed.

"Welcome to our cheese show and I hope you are comfortable. Please let me know if I can help you in any way" said a young girl hostess in a very short skirt.

The young naive waitress was blissfully unaware of my unusual invitation to her establishment and she poured out a welcoming glass of local Schnaps which I rapidly consumed. The show was fascinating and Hubert with his dazzling white wry smile and peaked hygiene cap that was slightly off skew explained the cheese process. He stood in front of a huge heated cauldron called a 'Kupferkessel' full of eighteen litres of milk which he stirred with his exceedingly long 'wobel'. I was becoming a bit squeamish about his other tools especially the 'käseharfe' which was used to cut the thickened pudding. So I stayed back from the action nibbling the local dairy delicacies notably a strange beige caramelised 'molke' and butter mixture which was called 'sig' but appropriately enunciated like 'sick'.

"Hey you are from England" said a large booted young farmer with an earring.

The 'cheese' show was full of an extrovert crowd of agricultural students from Schluechhof but I took it in my stride having spent three years at the Royal Agricultural College in Cirencester. This notorious English establishment for young aspiring landed gentlemen was a little different from his Swiss pastoral retreat for loudmouthed peasants. It was wise to humour him as it was clear that the chance of meeting the person who had offered to organise my trip was now quite remote. I had an empathy with their good-natured banter as I too had learnt precious little about agriculture during my wild misspent days of study.

"Do you know Prince Charles ?" interrupted another unshaven student whilst pointing a large television camera in my direction. "He likes cheese too."

I could only speculate on the royal pleasures of cheese but I did recall being once apprehended for raiding a girls school in the vicinity of his country seat during those untamed college days along with several now titled students of the realm. The Principal was well used to finding motor cars in his study and loose cheese producing cows, not to mention looser young ladies wandering naked around his educational establishment. He reprimanded us for our exuberant indiscretion and accepted our dubious excuse that we were trying to air some leather trousers on the school flagpole. We were young full blooded bloody hooligans but in a College that was then single sex he could see the funny side of our endeavours and probably then changed the new intake to a mixed sex establishment for fear of further incidents.

"No comment but they nickname me 'the Silver Spoon Schuhplattler'. I can show you an old English custom" I said picking up a spoon as the camera focused on my plate.

I began to spread a thick layer of 'sig' with the reverse side of the utensil. This exhibition of traditional English manners was an amusing distraction from their education.

"You spread it with a spoon. We use our fingers" said one of them sarcastically.

"Maybe you should ask them what they do with it in Andelsbuch" I retorted.

****

This first glimpse of Swiss humour was a light relief on a very busy day and the shop prospectus had a photo of the head of a cow with the caption; 'Frieda-Employee of the Month'. I laughed and jumped back into my biscuit tin to grind up out of this attractive village set in a valley basin and back up through the snow towards Dornbirn. I was heading to the only museum in Vorarlberg that could be regarded as of international standing and quite outstanding. It was hidden along a long ravine on the way to Ebnit. I had visited it on many other occasions as it housed a veritable collection of English National treasures and was in fact the largest single accumulation of Rolls Royce Phantoms in the world.

A strikingly handsome and eligible young gentleman escorted me up to the museum restaurant which would have put to shame many English Country House dining rooms. We sat at one of several mahogany tables with matching chairs.

This was the home from home for an extraordinary Austrian eclectic collector and an exclusively eccentric accumulator of everything that made you proud to be British. The attention to detail included fresh washed hand towels in the Gents, a Play Area akin to a Victorian Nursery with assorted dolls prams, wooden horses, a cute camel and a computer game about racing an old timer like a Bugatti or a Napier Railton around the old Donnington Parkland circuit, and a charming grey china cat lying asleep under our table with three furry blind mice.

"I'm Franz-Ferdinand. Please make yourself comfortable as my father will join us shortly. I help him restoring the Phantoms" he said politely offering me coffee.

It was such a marked contrast from the previous alpine farming jibes, but he was quick to show that there was humour in the world of Rolls Royce restoration. His fashionably grey haired father, also called Franz or 'Frank' Vonier with a neck length wild indian hair style and a white knotted cowboy cravat eventually made his entrance as I was studying the story of the Hon. Charles Stewart Rolls and Sir Frederick Henry Royce. He helped me to copy down a wonderful understatement from an ironical advertisement which read:

'From Silver Ghost to Silver Shadow, the Rolls Royce has remained supreme for more than six decades as the universal symbol of timeless excellence and man's ceaseless striving for perfection.'

He enthusiastically shook my hand like a champion receiving his laurels on the podium after one of those nineteen twenties races in Monza or Tripoli and judging by his attire it was clear that he spent more time under the car than driving it. We strolled around his phenomenal Phantom Hall of Fame which he jokingly referred to as his residential home for old Phantoms of the past. We looked at his workshop where he explained why the Phantom One would still outlast the modern equivalents because of its innovative engineering with effortless steering, electrical sophistication that permitted it to run on the battery without an engine, an early servo-clutch with IBS and a gearbox which never wore out.

"A vintage Phantom is the only Oldtimer that has proved its power, reliability and most important its usability" he said as we toured these last rolling voices of the past.

He smiled as he stood on an old chassis showing me the technical advantages of his beloved classic car. We looked at another Phantom under restoration from the Lawrence of Arabia movie and admired the painstaking shaping of the wheel arches which were beaten by hand on a carpenter's wooden 'model'. He lovingly patted another battered hulk that had seen better days as a chicken coup in a farmer's barn.

"I drove that one from the North of England and the Belgian Police stopped me but they couldn't find anything wrong except for the wooden coach work" he grinned.

We strolled around the other displays including the complete workshop of Stewart Rolls shipped over from Manchester complete with a generator and pulley powered drills and lathes. He powered them up and we talked about the development of car tools. It was later as we stood admiring his first wedding car that he told me the story that should inspire all young Vorarlberg entrepreneurs to follow their instincts. It certainly left me with a much better understanding of his passion and seemed so fitting after my cheese tasting episode.

"I was a naughty farmer's child in the Montafon Valley. I used to pour water on the road so that the cars would skid and I could then go and help them. One day I was asked to look after a Rolls Royce and I fell in love with its strange radiator. The very next day I told my father that I was going to buy one when I grew up. He said it was better to buy a cow."

****

The next day my special permission to ride in a local police patrol car arrived and I strolled past the church to the Police Station or 'Gendarmerie'. It had taken a lot of research and courtesy calls to even get permission to look at the most notorious Vorarlberg chronicle in the 'Gendarmerieposten' in Höchst. This was partly to do with the nervousness of the police after an unfortunate but legendary incident in the old police station in 1979 when a prisoner in the nearby but not adjoining cells had been forgotten for a staggering eighteen days. There was also the hugely bureaucratic paperwork process that ran through every government department in Vorarlberg. I had only encountered a worse system before in India where it took sixteen rubber stamps just to authorise a traveller's cheque refund.

"Welcome to our station. Here is the legendary Chronik" he said shaking my hand.

Bezirksinspektor Bernd or 'Bernie' Rhomberg was also interested in the history of this rural outpost that had served Fussach, Höchst and Gaissau since around 1880, not very long after the Tirol and Vorarlberg Gedarmerieregiment was founded in 1850. The records were quite remarkable and unique and later entries even included photographs of crashed cars and biplanes. We studied the entry of an old murder story of a crime of passion in a Stickerei in 1910 and talked about what the now thirteen strong twenty-four hour post did in this last landlocked part of Austria. Then we toured the station taking great care to visit the new metal barred cell which reminded me of a cowboy jail. I was more fascinated by the children's paintings dotted around the station and impressed by the completely open reception counter which was almost unheard of in England where you were lucky to hear the muffled voice of a British Bobby behind toughened finger smudged bullet proof glass.

"Shall we take a ride in a patrol car?" he grinned as he opened the garage.

"It's the moment I've been waiting for all my life" I said with a smile.

I had ridden in several police patrol cars in the past in many parts of the world but normally in the back seat as a passenger awaiting charge. The funniest episode was in America where I had driven through a toll booth in New York State without paying because my motorcycle was running out of petrol. I pulled up at what turned out to be an abandoned Gas Station and saw a patrol car screeching by with its siren on so I instinctively waved to it for assistance. The patrol car did a spectacular about turn and before I could greet him the cop was standing behind his car door pointing a pistol at me. After the usual 'freeze' and 'spread them' routine it turned out that he was in hot pursuit of a toll jumper in a yellow sailing coat and a helmet with GB on it which suitably fitted my description. As I took a ride in his 'cage' back to pay my four dollar toll and to fetch some petrol we became firm acquaintances. He asked me if he should give his visiting English cousin tea and cucumber sandwiches to which I retorted with the immortal adapted lines; *'When in New York do as the Yankies do'*.

"Well, I thought we might start by going to the border" said Bernie starting the car.

We drove to the border in Gaissau and stopped by the footbridge that had nearly caused my unwitting arrest by the border guards on my first evening walk in the village. He explained about the problems of illegal immigration and asylum seekers which was made worse at night time and considerably increased in times of war. The 'Schleppers' who ran the people smuggling were normally in the country of origin notably Afganistan, Russia and its many Republics, and Iraq at this time. They made life difficult by pointlessly stealing the identity passes of the 'illegals' which only made matters more tedious for the 'Dolmetscher' interpreters and they were nearly always returned to their country of origin anyway.

Then we drove through the pretty snow covered nature reserve around the edge of the Bodensee where the police had to control cars to keep the lanes free for hundreds of walkers and cyclists. We eventually stopped at a wooden hut in Fussach marked simply as 'FKK' where he said he was occasionally called out for people who had lost their car keys or purses.

"You mean: to catch pick pockets" I said naively.

"I don't think they would find many pockets in this nudist colony" he laughed.

This was typical of his charm and wit which reminded me of a rural policeman in England who always used to have a joke after we had thrown out drunken stragglers from my mediaeval banquets. Once we had a difficult situation where two women had fought over what turned out to be a misunderstanding over the identity and seduction of one of the protagonist's husband and he asked the other party to replay the foreplay from the beginning.

"Every village has it's little kings and we try to keep them happy" he smirked. He was referring to several self made popular industrious entrepreneurs who had brought recent wealth to an area that had once survived on agriculture, textiles and smuggling. Along with the increasing overpopulation and industrialisation of the Rhine delta there were now other crimes to contend with in a spreading concrete jungle which he predicted would soon be a suburb of a large sprawling city. He was thankful that these popular uncrowned figureheads wanted to protect nature but I wondered once again whether we would see much more than a small coastal nature reserve on his 'beat' in twenty years time.

"Anyway," I joked, "there may be little kings in these three villages, but you are the only one with a title, Herr Inspector."

We then drove on to see the Harbour Police or 'See Gendarmerie' in a relatively new building (from 1995) in Hard. The twenty metre long Police launch called 'V20' was moored up for winter next to a pretty old paddle steamer called 'Hohentwiel'. The patrol boat served the twenty-six kilometre long coast of Vorarlberg mainly as a lifeboat and to check up on seaworthy certificates of registration for all the boats. This was something unheard of in an English seafaring nation where we had separate lifeguards and anybody including the Owl and the Pussy Cat could to go to see in a pea green bathtub.

Two experienced water policemen who looked suitably nautical entertained us with a tour of the tiny station. Then we left to see where the old 'Puff House' or brothel was in the 'Old Park Café' which had an interesting illegal history dating back to the nineteen seventies until it was finally destroyed by fire in 1995. The road to Bregenz had been famous for street prostitution since the swinging sixties, although now it had mostly disappeared underground after a political campaign citing 'Our Clean Land'. He recalled many fights between 'Zuhälter' or 'Pimps' and that 'Buckel' watchmen used to stand in the street to watch for police cars with walkie-talkies. There was even a 'Puffhändlersprache' which was like the smuggler's 'Pumpeulusisch' and similar to the pimps talk in New York. The pimps often drove over from Switzerland in huge American cars and were always seriously overdressed.

The radio crackled just as we were on the main road. Before I knew what was happening, the blue light was flashing and we sped off to the scene of a nasty looking accident. A motorcycle was lying in a side road with its front forks under the wheel of a bus just over the bridge in Fussach. The ambulance was loading on the unfortunate injured motorcyclist and I carefully avoided staring at the pool of blood near his shattered dream. There were several policemen already at the scene taking statements and measuring the accident site marking the vehicle positions with spray paint on the road. The patrol car was well equipped with flashing beacons, signs, and a dated accident camera. It also had bullet proof vests and a speed camera which we did not require.

There was a press photographer taking photographs with his digital camera for the local Vorarlberger Nachrichten and also interestingly taking mobile telephone pictures for their internet newspaper. The Police relationship with the press was genial and we chatted whilst the Policemen took photos for their accident report. Interestingly the press often helped on these occasions and there was a lot of smiling when they took a picture of me shaking hands with my very prompt and capable driver and his blue flashing lights. A proud moment for me but sadly a daily occurrence on this busy road with additional dangerous (and I certainly felt unnecessary) heavy traffic travelling between Switzerland and Germany.

The reason why they had not built a motorway connection between the Austrian motorway and the Swiss motorway was a mystery. But it was clear that the longer it was delayed would result in so many unnecessary injuries and loss of life. I had had an accident on this dangerous single track road and the pollution must be doing untold damage to the local residents, but then passing trade was important to shop keepers even if the prostitutes no longer benefited from it. I was not going to solve an age old political problem but somehow that catch phrase 'unser subers ländle' rang hollow as I saw the blood on the street.

"Well I hope you enjoyed our patrol as it was nice to have company" he said.

"Thank you for taking so much trouble over an eccentric English chronicler."

"I like your idea of a travel satire" he joked putting his peaked white cap on to formerly shake my hand. He reminded me of a laughing Lilliputian with his ermine crown.

"THE PURSUIT"

LANDESBIBLIOTHEK, SKI JUMPING AND LONGING TO BELONG TO AN ALPINE LILLIPUT

For those who might not have been lucky enough to enjoy the wild childhood fantasy adventures to be discovered in a musty leather bound tome in one of the most beautiful historic house libraries in Lincolnshire, I can recommend the next best thing in the stunning beautiful baroque Landesbibliothek in Bregenz. It is a unique library in a converted and extended redundant church and monastery formerly known as the 'Stiftskirche' designed by a sympathetic architect and built by my cousin, Gerhard and his building firm. It is a credit to his accomplished skills and the Vorarlberg vision of the future of this Alpine Lilliput.

There are many forgotten travel tomes hidden in the shelves of this exquisite library but amongst the rows of fantasy fairy tales is a literary bible for all children like me who struggled with dyslexia but desperately wanted to delve deeper into another day dream. I remember my first ever experience of being finally able to cope with not only seeing every word as a mirror image but also being at last allowed to escape into that looking glass. Most English children read The Lord of the Rings, the Tales of Narnia or perhaps Alice in Wonderland all of which I would commend to my children but my favourite book was hidden on the top shelf of my father's library only accessible by wooden library steps.

I would hide under a mahogany table so as not to be discovered by my three wild brothers and jump through the magnifying glass into the fairy tale world of Lilliput and Gulliver's Travels by Jonathan Swift imagining what it would be like living in the tiny world of the little people. I grew up to become taller than the average school child which meant that the bullies gave me a wide berth at my prep school but unfortunately I could never hide in the crowd when it came to selecting cannon fodder for loathsome rugby practice. I hated my prep school in a draughty old castle in Yorkshire and tried hard to escape but was always recaptured by the masterful monks who melted down my resistance and moulded me into a young gentleman.

The mythical world of imagination played a huge part in my new opera as I had always learnt that the best libretto and indeed the greatest plays and ballets allowed the audience to effortlessly slip into a world of fantasy. Yet somehow I was also writing and composing in another forgotten world where I seemed to grow taller in my self esteem and at the same time the bounds of this charming Alpine Lilliput could not tie me down. My originally private daydream biosphere was blowing up like a balloon within the very real world of Vorarlberg and I blew as hard as I could to keep afloat amongst the menacing mountain peaks of my new writing career as I sailed on an updraft of artistic ego.

There were many meetings with infamous local representatives but I now increasingly reverted to my childhood reverie of a giant in Lilliput. I half expected these officials to stab me with a pin to force me to submit once again to triviality of real life. I received a letter from the 'Landesbibliothek' inviting me to a 'Termin fur eine erste Zusammenkunft' with a flamboyant scholar know as Dr. Wilhelm Meusburger. He had studied the Bregenzerwald dialect but he also confusingly possessed the same surname as my incredibly patient bank manager. By chance of my wife's efficiency I managed to accept his invitation without the embarrassment of sending him the wrong letter apologising about my withering bank balance but the mystery remained whether he would look like his kinsfolk.

I entered the Landesbibliothek having paused momentarily to take in the view from the extraordinary car park which overlooked the now barely recognisable historic town of Bregenz. The builder's cranes hung over this modern cement, asphalt and concrete nightmare which was once a beautiful mediaeval town like Lindau which I could see over the shimmering Bodensee. The modern world of commerce had optimised the limited space below building ever higher to catch this glimpse of the lake but I could still just make out the last few bell and watch towers that signified the remains of a once famous architectural town. Then I turned my back on the wretched overwhelming towering glass bunkers to seek solace in a last lost celestial heaven of books and to seek out my destiny.

"Well hello Englishman. I will be with you in a moment" said the flying 'doctor'.

I shrieked with shock as I immediately recognised that my future lay in the hands not of a suited bank manager that I had imagined but with no less than the wild Chocolate Mountain Santa that I had met at the 'Kulturtreff' in the Thurn and Taxis Palace in Bregenz.

He was obviously used to this type of greeting as he wore another flagrantly outrageous attire complimenting his swirling moustache and a full face beard with a wild curled coiffure. A huge Santa smile shone out of his friendly facial façade and I half expected him to give me a Christmas chortle. He glided past obviously in a hurry to catch his reindeer but not without reminding me to sit down before I fainted with amazement. I was finally going back into my childhood fantasy forever as my daydream was now undeniably actuality but then who better than this strange suited Santa to make my mental illusions come true.

"Well I think that we can make your wishes come true" he chortled whilst juggling with a cigarette in one hand and answering a complicated telephone call.

He was not really the image of Christmas that most children would recognise but then the red and white Santa that they knew was attributed to an early twentieth century Coke advertisement and this was the twenty-first century. He still supported a strange silk scarf and a dark fluffy tie that looked like it had been through a tumble drier. It was perfectly feasible that had the originators of the famous advertisement been on coke at the time we might well have finished up with something akin to his irrepressibly incandescent sense of fashion. I was sitting in his tiny lifeless white monastic cell pouring out my wish list like a bewildered schoolboy in a department store grotto and he was actually listening to my requests.

"I think it is an excellent project when can we do the first reading ?" he said.

My mind was agog with wild aspirations of being finally accepted into my Alpine Lilliput instead of being singled out as a strange eccentric Englishman. Then the door suddenly shot open and another bearded bespectacled professor from the 'Landesmuseum' in Bregenz called Helmut Swozilek waltzed in to join our discussion on the first opera about Angelica Kauffmann. Here was yet another legendary academic authority on her life listening to my mythical mysteries of writing a popular libretto which wound itself between the reasonably accurate accounts of her romance with a marriage swindler and the world of Greek Gods and the unrestrained emotion of blind passion.

"I like your ideas as there is a thread of truth and you need artistic licence" he said.

He was a man of a much more conservative appearance with an overcoat that gave him the semblance of a serene serious man of study about to embark upon the discovery of another lost world. If Jules Verne had modelled his professor on an Austrian rather than German professor, then this was the man to lead the journey to the centre of the earth. I was reminded of the lecturers that used to try to prefer their infinite knowledge upon me as an ignorant tearaway student and he had that charming mannerism of lowering his glasses to write some reference material in my yellow book.

I thought back to all those years of struggling with dyslexia to *'dissect the humbug of high jumping hieroglyphics from the hindrance of highflying hippogriffs'*, which had made any attempt at scholarly research like an exploration of an Egyptian fairytale punctuated by sphinxes. The palpitating pages of imperative but indecipherable pamphlets had dogged my dreams of becoming a University Don allowed to walk upon the hallowed turf of the great colleges of England. The disability returned to haunt me yet again as he wrote out his recommended reading material. He had translated many texts into the language of this Alpine Lilliput but he would never be able to read the jumbled jumping letters of my mind. I was a tall dark giant shadow upon which he had cast a dazzling light and it was pleasing for once to jump out of the horrors of the endless crosswords of my criss-crossed mind.

"Thank you for your help and my wife is an Egyptologist better suited to helping me with this original source material" I replied with my fingers crossed behind my back.

"I think you definitely have the right idea and it will be a great book" he grinned.

"Well I promise you a very special place in it" I said with a satirical smile.

The balloon had so nearly burst as I knew that there was no chance of my ever being able to read this biographical reference material in another language, probably hand written like Angelica's letters and undoubtedly ready to jump out at me at every turn of a page. The coffee machine, computer and the dictionary had been my comfort items. Then I remembered once being asked by a naïve radio reporter on a live literary transmission which three items I would like to conserve inside a time capsule for a future generation to enjoy.

'A Harley Davidson, a pair of muffs and naked model' I had unhesitatingly replied.

****

The wild man was back on track with his equally wild son (now nicknamed 'Magic Max the Merlin') heading this time to the daunting beginner's ski jumps on the Bödele and it certainly looked impressive as we looked over the sharply descending piste which formed the earthly landing strip for these flying eagles. My son knew nothing of my hero 'Eddie the Eagle' who was really a flying plasterer when he was not trying to plaster himself all over these daunting landing strips and the newspapers. I think it was actually the high diving board that had attracted Max to the idea that he could fly like a bird of prey some of which were known to reach extraordinary velocities whilst plunging out of the sky to scoop up fishes from the sea. He was much more akin to an Osprey but with his red locks he might have been confused with a Merlin which I had once had the pleasure of flying at my late father's wonderful zoo.

"Daddy when do I get to jump ?" said Max shivering with excitement.

"The commentator said you can be a 'Vorspringer' before the other jumpers."

I looked out over the very picturesque panorama as there was an excellent view of the Bodensee from the commentator's cabin. Then I looked down at the tiny matchstick men that were the Red Cross crew on hand for accidents and crossed my fingers hoping that I would not be spending the next few weeks by his bedside in the casualty department.

"Don't look so worried Daddy I won't wipe out on normal skis" he grinned.

"You've got your helmet. I'll take you up to the start" I said with my fingers crossed.

We trudged up the deep snow that ran along side the two 'spuren' or grooves along which the skis ran on a tramline to heaven. The other 'Schispringer' were sitting on a long log awaiting the judges and marshals to prepare the landing strip by walking up and down it with their skis. Max was only on the first shorter jump along with several local children fitted out with numbered foam suits, crash helmets and jumping skis which dwarfed their tiny bodies. They looked at him strangely as he put on his oversized helmet and snapped his ski boots onto his piste skis still trying to look every bit like it was perfectly normal practice to jump off a two metre jump with a descent trajectory of a falling circus trapeze artist without any safety net at the bottom. This was one small jump but one huge slide for Max and mankind.

The commentator's microphone echoed out over the sheer mountain side and the judges took their places along the line of descent to mark off the landing length. I looked down the two tramlines which descended steeply downwards towards some conifer twigs which marked the point where the jumper leapt into the air and then straightened his body as the skis formed 'v' shape wings to fly through the sky landing somewhere out of sight from my vantage point. Then the marshal's radio crackled and Max lined himself up on the tramlines and crouched down on his skis.

The blue flag of the marshal at the side of the jump dropped and the smooth toned commentator sounded the formal alert that there was a 'Springer' now launching himself towards an unknown future. Max set off down towards the green twigs and then he did his best to jump up to his full height for a split second of flight before landing with a loud thwack and then hurtling downhill as fast as his brave little skis could carry him. Then the judges radio crackled out and the Commentator said;

"Max aus England ... Elfmeter." Not bad for his first jump.

It was a proud paternal moment like the first time I had seen him jump from an eight metre diving board. Then he had resurfaced and paddled to the side of the pool complaining that he had hurt his hand whereupon I had suggested that he tried it again which he dutifully did to my complete surprise. There are stars and heroes that everybody knows but I was privileged to have a brave and foolhardy son who took a delight in dangerous pastimes including skateboarding, diving and now ski jumping.

'Magic Max the Merlin' returned to the commentary box with a huge grin as wide as the strap around his helmet and we all congratulated him on his first jump.

"But Daddy they get three jumps so can I go again ?" he said so enthusiastically.

"If you want to.." I said hesitantly and the commentator nodded. He was hooked.

We drove home with Max the Merlin's trophy headband presented for sheer gall and courage by a smiling commentator. He wore it until it wore out like a British Victoria Cross and I was thankful that it was not that medal which was mostly awarded posthumously.

****

Whilst I was flying to the moon in my daydreams in search of another fantasy diarist for inspiration or escaping in a balloon constructed of ladies underwear like Baron von Münchhausen, my wife was struggling with the very real world of builders and child welfare. The footprints in the snow from those first steps of the phantom plumber had now disappeared as more contractors appeared in a frenzy of activity. Worse still, the children were starting to experience difficulties associated not only with the different languages, pubescence and dyslexia but also with xenophobia and jealousy. This filled every available hour of the day for my distraught wife and her reluctant but enchanted husband visiting educational psychologists, child psychiatrists, and even herbal physicians.

"Darling diarist, you need to help me or I will freak out too" she screamed.

"Just send me on a mission to fight the Sultan's army as they don't call me the bravest and most courageous Baron in the universe for nothing" I recanted from the depths of another wonderful fantasy fairytale diary which had crept onto my desk from the library shelf.

"You can help your daughter who is feeling lonely in her new school" she ordered.

Diffidently I set off to the school in Lustenau to attend another meeting with my daughter's teacher to explain the tears that had trickled down her cheeks the night before in her mixed up and hormonally challenged mind. She was growing up quickly as a born survivor in an extremely demanding academic class with increasingly higher grades and I was a pretty ineffectual, redundant but caring father who had no idea what it was like to become a woman. I couldn't contribute much, although I had cross-dressed as a Jester in my theatre days and my green taut tights gave the ladies an unexplained lust for my otherwise hairy legs. Such flattery however was often accompanied by fonder fondling that could compromise my marital status so I wore a cod piece which was an old cricket box for additional protection.

I strutted out of the cordial meeting where my distracted thoughts were reminiscent of the age old midlife desire to change sexes with my heroines so that I might just once actually understand my daughter and myself. But there in the polished stone temple of the central hall was something I never expected to encounter in an Austrian school. A manifestation of a diarist that was so infamous yet so horrifying that my eyes filled with emotion as I confronted her life story on the magnificent display boards.

'We were the hunted animals of the night' I discerned on one of the boards.

'I was proud of my nationalism but now I am ashamed.'

It read above a sepia tone picture of a family on the beach with a Swastika flag in their sand castle.

The sands of time had not buried the Holocaust and the dairies of a little girl had helped to keep the candle of enlightenment burning brightly in an increasingly xenophobic and racist new world. Tears swelled in my eyes as I followed her sad story from another time and now another century but still able to send a chill down my spine.

The depressing reality was that many of the photographs of the bone structured shadows in the extermination camps were more emotionally charged than almost any picture in words that I could ever create. There were six million murdered fellow human beings crying out for forgiveness for a genetic crime that they did not commit through the symbolic chronicle of an innocent child who chose to preach about reconciliation and remembrance.

Learning about the Austrian past was a traumatic, terrifying, and tumultuous time for most children of the chocolate mountains but I found this obvious open expression of emotions entirely invigorating. The invisible was now transparently indivisible from the highly visible with a vision of the future derived from a diary of a discomforting history of anti-Semitic hysteria. It would endlessly enlighten and emancipate the green Elysian fields of this alpine heaven by telling the tale of the austere killing fields of Auschwitz. My poor puny, pusillanimous and purblind pen could never hope to conquer this peak of pure perfection.

"Are you alright or do you need a psychiatrist too?" my wife said sarcastically.

"You might say that I have just seen six million lost souls of the past."

She knew that reference which was imprinted on the 'soul' of her feet. She too had learnt of the shame for this bygone but not forgotten genocide at school. It overshadowed every succeeding generation who were also as innocent of this past as the six million souls whom they now commemorated. Later I wept salty sad tears like my daughter, but not for her but for another little girl who had saved six million souls at the stroke of a pen.

"ANNE FRANK DIARY"

FELDER THE FREE WRITER AND FELDER THE STOOL MAKER'S BREGENZERWALD BEAUTY

The soft white untainted snowflakes drifted across the road covering up my alpine paradise and shrouding darker secrets of the terrible times of the Diary of Anne Frank. There was no country that did not have its faults, including the little Lilliput in my daydream world but despite the past, I felt the new freedom of a bright new future. I looked out of the steamed up windows at the last of the sun glinting through the glistening branches of white robed trees. The snow drifts looked like fresh sweet smelling sheets laid upon the bed of a restless giant. I peered through the icy windscreen, half expecting this roaming leviathan to leave a trail of massive footprints in the drifting snow in front of me as I fought to control the whining beast on another expedition into the remote regions of the Bregenzerwald.

My two sleeping tigers were snuggled in the back, doubtless dreaming of a fresh fantasy; such was the innocence of childhood whilst the blizzard blew fiercely fanned by that colossus that haunted my consciousness. I felt like a classical Greek text book hero setting forth on another epic adventure and this time I knew that I was going to find the face that had infatuated the greatest of the Greeks and Trojans and that had sailed one thousand ships over two millennia ago before Christ. The beautiful legend I was seeking was scarcely one decade old and a creation of my midlife dreams rather than a record of an ancient civilisation, although the genetic history of such genial beauty was a subject of scientific significance.

"Daddy, it looks bad out there. Where are we going to ?" said Max anxiously.

"We are going to find the Beauty of the Bregenzerwald and to see a man about a book" I replied, struggling to control the slipping beast on the winding pass over the Bödele.

"Not another boring meeting. Why can't we go ski jumping again ?" he said sleepily.

The multitude of specialists that my wife had employed to seek out the reasons behind my son's sketches of helicopters bombing churches that had so disturbed the priest and the pedagogic professionals in his school had finally reached a conclusion. It was a great relief to find at last someone who understood that Max was not a manic monster. The report concluded that he was a hyperactive, extremely alert, pubescent, and manipulative child like his rebel father who just needed stability, confidence and a better paternal role model. Being a natural fall guy for all the family trials and tribulations I was dispatched to perform such feats as following him over the ski jumps becoming a rolling model of fatherhood and facing some near death experiences that I did not wish to repeat.

My wife had cornered me on this topic at the first Faschingsball of the Karnival season in aid of the Höchst Football Club locally known as 'FC Blum' after someone had mistaken me for the ultimate English secret agent in my penguin suit and bow tie. The fact that the quite excellent staged satirical comedy entertainment, which so successfully sent ripples of uncontrollable laughter through the four hundred strong audience, was centred upon the theme of James Bond merely highlighted my predicament as the only Englishman present. I still craved for my stage career and my wife knew that this was a weak moment to spring the issue of paternal idolatry and extract rash promises as we strolled home for an early night to relive those film screen moments of passion.

"You can make a snowman whilst I am with my expert guide called Armin Willi." I said trying to avoid a snow plough.

There was a lot of giggling in the back as children have a unique way of seeing beyond the world of titles and academic credits into the funny side of name significance. A new nickname of 'Poor Old Willy' was then derived from the naïve childhood English reference to an anatomical part of their growing boyish genitalia and the more appropriate German word 'Arm' meaning 'poor' suffixed with a natural childhood assumption that all experts must be 'old'. Actually there is something to be said for adolescent intuition even if such an outrageous nickname deserved a firm adult reproach.

My gentle guide could be better described as a genial genius who was also a grandfather well used to my mischievous imps and doubtless his angelic grandchildren. I quickly dispatched them to enjoy the now exceedingly damp snow so that we could get some intellectual solitude in my search for the infamous literary giant of the Bregenzerwald also renowned for his rude efficacy of authority and revolutionary revelations. We retired to the cosy contemporary shrine of a rebel social democrat writer called Franz Michael Felder.

The chronicles which I had so lovingly complied had come close to discovering diarists with more than just a desire to change the minds of mankind, but none of them could be considered as indigenous or indeed revolutionary beyond their time. I was a wild rebellious midlife man and in my small insignificant way I was also an agrarian, well versed, radical 'anti-disestablishmentarian'. At least ever since I had learnt that this was in fact the longest word in the great English game of 'Scrabble' from a wise monk whose grin was greater than his vocabulary. For the great propensity of popular political writers it is not necessarily the texts but the thoughts that they inspire long after their often untimely demise.

This could be said of the short thirty year lifespan of Franz Michael Felder, whose diaries and literary tomes were as influential and provocative but less thought corrupting of the media manipulated masses as say the banned 'Mein Kampf' diaries of Adolf Hitler. For Felder was a man who changed the thoughts of an isolated mountainous region and whose contact with the outside world consisted of little more than the odd trip to Lindau and Leipzig before his tragic early death at only thirty years of age. If he had lived longer, he might well have risen rapidly from humble origins to become world famous but not as a fascist dictator or as a revolutionary despot but as the true free thinking radical of the Bregenzerwald.

"Actually the alcoholic doctor operated on the wrong eye making him blind in his previously good eye and leaving him with one short sighted eye" said my beguiling guide.

But time and again I had seen disabled composers like the deaf Beethoven or even the wooden handed artist Rembrandt struggling with a disability which gave them a discipline to achieve great aspirations which another able genius could not hope to accomplish. My guide took me through the life of this glasseyed rebel in a difficult and complicated conversation which was punctuated by pauses for me to scrawl diligent but deliberately demented and dissipated diagrams in my diary as I really dreamt of being this revolutionary farmer.

The first secret of this writer's success was his private library of over six hundred books which he then created into one of the first open 'Handwerker Leihbibliothek' in this forgotten valley where reading was yet to enlighten the poor farming population. He questioned everything, encouraging unheard of women's rights and Social Democracy with his brother-in-law Kaspar Moosbrugger. He fought the local Cheese Baron (also called Moosbrugger) encouraging local farming co-operative 'sennerei' to break his monopoly with a self marketing ideology. He even criticised the church and a doctrinal and authoritarian priest (surprisingly not called 'Moosbrugger' but called 'Ruscher') such was his belief in questioning the infallibility of traditionalism. This well read nineteenth century novelist who lived in a lost valley of families with the same surnames had changed this poor unenlightened exploited forgotten world forever with books like 'Reich und Arm' and 'Sonderlinge'.

We then set off in search of his memorial in the magnificent setting of the churchyard which was located on a hillock above Schoppernau. It overlooked a splendid Dickensian view of a beautifully preserved but considerably extended wooden alpine village panorama with a backdrop of sheer, steep and miserable misty mountains. The romance of melancholic despair cried out like the echoes of this great man's words as I read his simple epitaph on a large cross with an engraved portrait profile. His face ironically faced out with his good but short sighted eye over his cherished homeland. There written in gold lettering on a stone cross by the wall of the church he had so chastised were no words of remorse, just his name and the dates 1839-1869. I closed one eye and squinted in the rain but I could not see why he had not seen this heaven as heaven but he must have passed on so poetically into his paradise.

It was a wet but humbling experience to feel the presence of a tragic novelist and indefatigable diarist who was encouraged like me out of dejection and despondency in his disability by his pretty and learned wife, Anna (whose maiden name incidentally was Moosbrugger). I thought that there was some hope for me as I struggled to come to terms with disenchanting dyslexia, dismal despair and this disingenuous drivel that had somehow crept up on me again during my opera writing daydreams. The parapet wall looked tempting as I could easily fling myself off in an impassioned statement of sincerity but as usual it was a simple child's view that brought me back from the brink of a desperately depressing diatribe.

"Hey, you said we were going to meet the most beautiful girl in the Bregenzerwald."

"Quite right Max, it is time to see the face that sailed a thousand cheese gondels."

"Sometimes I wonder what you are talking about Daddy" said a perplexed Max.

"Elementary, my dear Max, maybe you will grow up to be a detective too."

There was a great unsolved mystery which required a midlife detective to use all his powers of persuasion to uncover the truth behind a timeless beautiful face that had haunted his dreams whilst scribbling the love songs for an opera by a Bodensee swimming pool. The legend of the Stool maker's daughter was not, it would seem, a story shared amongst the local village mainly because it had been more a figment of my imagination than folklore. The fabled face had formed in my fantasy some twelve years earlier on my first of several visits to Schoppernau to purchase one of its most famous products. I had set out with my new wife in search of Bregenzerwald stools and other hand carved items which were to adorn our new nest in Lincolnshire. It was my wife who had formed the fantasy fable into a living legend by mentioning that the stool maker's daughter was known as the Helena of the Bregenzerwald.

This reference bore no relation to the fabulous beauty of Troy nor to the actual name of the individual known as the Stool maker's daughter. It did not even identify which of the two great, great granddaughters of the famous author, Franz Michael Felder, should carry this honour into literature. The moral of the tale was not one of immortality or indeed immorality. It was just an aside about the genetics of this lost valley where darker hair and moonstone eyes had predominated over the infamous flaxen hair and ocean blue eyes associated with other neighbouring tribes. There is doubtless an explanation associated with sunshine and migrations but I remained transfixed by the tale as the living reincarnation of my opera heroine, Angelica, during the long hot summer afternoons in the swimming pool café.

An opera cannot come alive without focusing on something that lives and breathes in the same space as the writer and my heroine was long dead. It was not possible to choose my wife as the verses would become *'vitiated by the vivification of another personality'* or to put it in layman's words, the real life words spoken might negate the lyrics.

It was therefore important to hold this figure of myth that I had briefly seen to create a living vision without a voice and I could then create the libretto from her lips. I could have chosen past conquests but this was perilous ground for a married man and I could not use television or film stars as they were tainted by past scripting. So the choice of this image of a Bregenzerwald beauty which I had seen, but never spoken to was a sensible and sensitive, not a sensuous fixation upon which I could base my opera heroine. It was akin the fresh but unfeeling flesh in one of Angelica's paintings which I could reanimate and give an additional gift of vocal pleasure.

The Stool maker's daughter, Isabella, was now married to a stunningly handsome smiling chef called Erwin. The Stool maker had furnished their new 'Wirtshaus zum Gemsle' with some classic examples of his fine craftsmanship. All of the stools seemed to bear the hand carved stool backs that had made his workshop so famous throughout the world and the easily recognisable restaurant motive of the head of a mountain goat. They sat together like newlyweds as their son ran riot with my two terrible tigers amongst the wooden tables of this delightfully new yet inspiringly old fashioned panelled guest house.

"Here is a stool that has a carving of Franz Michael Felder" said the shy chef.

I noticed that the author's name and dates were carved on the seat which seemed more appropriate to a man who spent much of his life like me seated at his 'Schoppernau Stammtisch'. I had chosen to write in an architects office in Höchst, surrounded by bottles of wine and building plans whilst he had written his great manuscripts in his library reputed to have a wonderful collection of masterworks. Such was the upheavals of the nineteenth century that he had inspired that I could now sit on him where others for his era whom he had criticised could not. But with his glass eyed portrait behind my back I wondered if I would be the next in line for his wrath for my satirical portrayal of his impassioned and tormented life.

"So how do you feel about being another Helen of Troy? The legend of the most beautiful girl in the Bregenzerwald? The face that sailed one thousand cheese gondels ?" I said trying not to stare at her craven but quite unexpectedly unchanged image.

"Who was Helen of Troy ?" She enquired innocently and studying me inquisitively, flattered but unshaken by this strange revelation from a complete stranger.

"You are not as well read as your ancestor but promise me to read the legend of Helen of Troy" I said laughing.

She was my ship's lucky wooden figurehead in my long epic-voyage.

GHOST TRAIN SPOTTING IN FAIRYTALE FELDKIRCH AND A RANKWEIL REVELATION

A fresh soft and silent snowflurry fluttered past my flustered sanguine face as I stamped my feet in the fairytale Schattenberg Schloss. I was far above the snow covered picture postcard friendly town of Feldkirch in the eight hundred year old fortress courtyard, sheltered by the oak walkway watching the snow fall as though I was entering another flight of fancy in my now fragile and often fickle daydreams.

It had been a hard drive in thick snow to reach this most beautiful city which held so many fond summer memories but somehow it now seemed like I was a bloated bubble inside a picturesque but well shaken snow globe. The dreadful internet English editorial translation which had caused much hilarity in my office had offered an excellent opportunity to follow in the now deep snowy footsteps of the Irish Radical and writer of 'Ulysses' and 'Finnegans Wake', James Joyce, and his 'fellow Irish poet', Sir Arthur Conan Doyle. This was a revelation to my literary repertoire as I always thought of the creator of Sherlock Holmes as a Scottish Unionist and primarily a fiction writer. However, I was well prepared to seek the solution to this riddle and to follow in both their now phantom past footprints in the swelling snow storm especially as the website offered not only this new insight, but also a record breaking twenty five grammatical and spelling mistakes in only two paragraphs.

My favourite fantasy castle stood in an imposing position on a rocky outcrop still guarding the passes to the South and East of Feldkirch and a newer road and old rail tunnel that passed directly underneath it. It was built in the thirteenth century in an era of knights, dragons and aggrieved but attractive maidens by Hugo von Montfort (who apparently bore no relation to the famous founder of the British Parliament). The castle fortress now had a wonderfully eclectic museum that basked in the glory of gothic art and possessed a wonderful statuette of St. George slaying the dragon. Contrary to martyrdom myth of the great heroic English Patron who slew a dragon, the real Saint George was a Roman soldier slaughtered in a Diocletian purge of early Christians in 303 AD. But that did not bother me as a dark daydream believer. He was my heroic role model as the valiant white knight of my enigmatic nightmares riding his dashing steed to rescue my dream damsel in distress and this great fairytale stone castle would always be the fortification of my fantasy.

Inside the Restaurant the solid oak window benches had stark but inviting tables looking out of the glazed gun portals at the stiffening snowstorm. The coffee and chocolate 'kuchen' cheered me up as I waited for my guide provided by the tourist information office. I would highly commend to future visitors to Vorarlberg that this service is so much better than in many other European countries and a bit better organised than the excellent but often inefficient Blue Badge Service in England. The huge beams that spanned the refectory styled restaurant and the wonderful sturdy wooden arched doors gave me a new sensation of security. This was the fortress that had held back Napoleon's advance until the rest of the Austro-Hungarian Empire was crushingly defeated and it was ordered to honorably surrender. It was nearly destroyed by the neglect of its Habsburg owners in the nineteenth century and saved from being sold as a quarry by the citizens of Feldkirch who turned it into a poorhouse.

Latterly a loving resourceful 'Zimba-pfarrer' so nicknamed 'Mountain Father' Gebhard Gunz founded a weird and wonderful fantasy museum mixing strange wall fresco's of heroines with fine original oak floored rooms displaying assorted furniture and painted cupboards, selected musical instruments, the strangest wrought iron locks and handles and a huge armoury better described as 'an eccentric priest's private army arsenal'. It contained a significant church painting of Johannes Kauffmann in the chapel which was painted around the time of my opera setting before he left to join his daughter, Angelica, in England.

"So are there any ghosts here ?" I casually asked my extremely learned guide after settling him down with a fresh cup of warm coffee after he had walked up to the castle through the blizzard.

"Funnily enough there are several in Feldkirch, but actually I was wondering about the lady's footprints that I followed here in the snow" he said reminding me of Dr. Watson, the infamous sidekick to Sir Arthur Conan Doyle's Sherlock Holmes.

I carefully resisted the elementary response preferring to hear his howling ghost tale of the Reichenfeld upon which the infamous but now defunct Jesuit public school of Stella Matutina had been built. We looked out through the snow flurry which seemed to be subsiding, across the strangely named river 'ill' towards a large yellow and white plastered nineteenth century building just visible below the wooded cliffs that surrounded Feldkirch.

"That's the famous school where Conan Doyle studied and might have written some poetry. Above it is the haunted woods where a greedy step father is said to roam in torment having swindled his adopted sons out of their inheritance of the Reichenfeld," he said gleefully.

I could see that it was going to be a Tall Story Day, although he had definitely done some considerable research on James Joyce and Conan Doyle. He was my first English speaking guide with impeccable grammar and such a wide vocabulary and a slight home county haughtiness that made me giggle into my coffee.

"Where did you get that accent as it is 'frightfully' good" I said after a long and fruitful discussion on such a wide range of topics that he was most definitely the right man to ask to dinner to keep Dr. Watson company or to baffle P. G. Woodhouse buffoons with his bantering but dashed interesting conversation.

"Well you could say that I learnt it from a charming ninety year old English girlfriend on my English exploits, but I also taught English here for many years too."

He replied with that look of a schoolmaster, uncertain where the divergent and irrelevant conversation might lead but defiantly ready to make a jolly jingoistic but disturbingly distracted pupil put pen to paper. But I was already back at my daydream desk dribbling chromatographic black ink cartoon silhouette pastiches of him on my invisible thick pink blotting paper. We chatted on about his quite beautiful city but as the coffee wore out I was champing at the bit to get out to explore the fresh snow which I could see out of the corner of my eye through the castle classroom gun port. Eventually I was completely briefed and I was even ready to write out 'I must not rejoice about James Joyce' one hundred times just for one step in that virgin snow that now lay silent and serene on the city roofs and streets far, far below my scholarly study in the sky.

"I'll take you to see the school, but as for James Joyce, there isn't much to see really as the hotel down there has burnt down" he said pointing out of a wrought iron grill that was once a small gate which led down to the stables. "But he was a train enthusiast and trains used to pass right underneath the castle before the tunnel was boarded up and diverted because of the sharp bend."

As we walked down the steep snow covered steps I realised that searching for clues on the great Sherlock Holmes and indeed the great Irish rebel writer was not going to be just an elementary task as the evidence seemed to have evaporated into folk legend. Fortunately I was endowed with an inspired imagination which had not served me well in the classroom, but now was allowed the freedom of the city as we explored the old haunts of these great early twentieth century authors. My wildly enthusiastic guide strode on through the slushy streets exploring the famous mediaeval covered walkways which I remembered thronging with clowns and street entertainers at the famous summer 'Gauklerfestival'. We stopped to admire the interior of the Rathaus where Vorarlberg was formed in 1620 under the lavishly carved wooden ceilings of the Ratssaal and even more embellished angelic ceiling of the Bürgermeister's Ratsstube. Finally we explored the interior of the old Jesuit school which was now a wonderful 'Konservatorium' for young aspiring and inspiring musicians with a marvellous theatre, library and chapel all built incredibly on top of each other.

We stood listening to a young musician playing her abstract homework composition to her tutor on the recently installed organ built in Feldkirch. The pipes gave a shrill haunting echo in the pretty but deserted chapel reminding me of the melody in the Phantom of the Opera but with a touch of the Rocky Horror Show rock classic humour. It was now apparent that there was nothing much in the way of elementary evidence left to associate it with the regimented and austere public school that had formed the childhood opinions of Arthur Conan Doyle. The tourist guide was charming with recollections of the French occupation and disintegration of the great Jesuit school that had brought ice hockey and ski jumping to Austria at the turn of the century. However, by a process of deduction between the by-lines it was clear that there was no material evidence but perhaps a faint echo of an early Holmes.

As I left this beautiful wondrous fairytale city I laughed to myself as it was clear that the sparse evidence was not enough to win my conviction to the story line about the great Sherlock Holmes, although I felt a strange shiver when I thought of James Joyce. As I passed the snowbound railway station I thought that I caught a fleeting glimpse of the great Orient Express but this train no longer passed through Feldkirch. The railway station was mentioned by the great historian Stefan Zweig who wrote about the passing of the Imperial Train carrying the last Habsburg Kaiser Karl I as he was expelled from Austria, but that was on 11th November 1918. Maybe it wasn't the Imperial Insignia that I had seen and possibly it was the Third Reich Swastika and the train was being searched whilst the great playwright, Carl Zuckmayer, was fleeing to Switzerland but that was on 14th March 1938.

The snow was falling again and the squeaking of the frozen rubber window wipers on the icy windscreen woke me up in time to avoid an oncoming snow plough. I pulled over by the side of the railway track, but the train had vanished from view. I rubbed my tired eyes and I squinted through the side window but the station platform was devoid of both people and trains. The station clock was still moving and I checked my mobile telephone against the time and the date. It was definitely Thursday 30th January 2003 so what was it that I had seen arriving at the deserted platform ?

Then I thought that I saw a elderly man sitting on a bench in a dark overcoat wrapped up in a woollen scarf with his felt hat dusted with a sprinkling of soft fresh snow. He pushed up the brim with his index finger to reveal his face and he starred at me through his round spectacles. A sneering smile appeared from under his short nasal moustache and I shivered as it was as though he was looking right through me. Then as though by some extraordinary feat of magic he simply disappeared just as he had appeared into the setting sun.

I set off again to visit the great 'Basilika' of Rankweil, thinking that my imagination had probably got the better of me. I sipped superstitiously from a plastic bottle of cold but refreshing sparkling fruit juice which I noticed was also made in Rankweil. The great pilgrimage church dedicated to 'Maria Heimsuchung' was also set on a rocky promontory with a spectacular panoramic view and I parked in a snow drift at the top of this holy pinnacle of the Catholic faith. My confounded mind was searching for scientific proof of my apparition as I struggled through the knee deep snow to the steps that entered the fortified inner sanctum of this holy place dedicated to another of the great biblical mysteries of Our Lady.

The snow had settled on the scrolled wrought iron crosses and the sun cast strange curled shadows in the snow as I walked up the cemetery steps under the wooden walkway that surrounded this hallowed sanctuary of peace and silent tranquillity. I lit a candle of hope at a crib ironically depicting Christ being betrayed by Judas and I began to repent of my scepticism of my detective investigations in Feldkirch. Then I climbed up the stone steps past the portraits of the past guardian priests of this place of pilgrim devotion and entered the great 'Wallfahrtskirche' with its glorious golden chapel depicting the Madonna surrounded by mellifluous angels and charming cherubs.

I brushed the snow off my shoes and placed my sodden hat on a pew and sat tacitly down to take in this great historical clerical centrepiece of Vorarlberg. The church was not only spectacular because of the extensive views from its famous covered walkways but it also housed several exceptional exhibits including a eerie saint's skeleton and two shining golden relief depictions of gospel miracles. As I stared back over my shoulder at the magnificent Barock organ pipes decorated with gilded carved wooden scrolls, I realised that I was alone in this great white shrine in the great white emptiness of a snow congested countryside.

The nature of my revelation became apparent to me not as a spiritual discovery of my soul but more as an apparition of a free spirit of the past. I had set out in search of a short story that might inspire me to seek solace in the stroke of a pen. In this new era of internet computer scribblers, somebody had called me back to the era of the true fictional freedom writer not sitting sucking a pen at a monastery school desk but seeing through a moving steam spectre of history. My charming guide and mentor had tried so hard to help me to find inspiration in the imagination of the now non existent past. He had in fact revealed much more than a tourist trail in the phantom footprints of two early twentieth century authors.

I had also been ghost train spotting guided by the ghost of the great James Joyce.

"ORIENT EXPRESS"

LANDESHAUPTMANN, SKATEBOARD KINGS, SNOW ZEBRAS AND KETCHUP BORDERS

The snow adorned the giant concrete and glass christening cake like an edging of sugar icing. The Vorarlberg government administration building rose up in front of me in several tiers like a birthday celebration of functional city architecture. I wondered if the architect might have been inspired by Victorian bee hives or perhaps nuclear bunkers as it was buzzing with activity but had all the barren but secure sterility of the Pentagon. Looking upwards in the great pyramidal atrium made me feel like a birthday surprise stripper except this time I was the midget belly dancer from Lilliput inside the Landeshauptmann's gigantic concrete birthday cake. I was in the secret inner sanctum of all that bureaucratic paperwork that drove the rest of the region insane and I wondered if perhaps the architect had used the overflowing drawers of his filing cabinet to arrange the disconcerting asymmetrical floor levels.

As the silent lift ascended to the sixth floor Presidential Penthouse I tried to think of my opening lines for my interview with the Landeshauptmann, Dr. Herbert Sausgruber, who was in fact from Höchst. The top floor lit up on the lift display just as my mind had changed from an opening belly ripple to a more formal Star Trek greeting as it now felt like I was about to emerge on to the bridge of the Starship Enterprise. As I looked over the balcony I practised my inverted vulcan 'V' sign as a science fiction greeting. I quickly decided that this special Höchster might misinterpret this potentially sexual hand signal especially after the lady coming out of the lift after me gave me a very strange glower.

"Good morning Englishman. You are early because of the snowstorm but the Landeshauptmann will see you shortly" said the smiling secretary. She reminded me of one of those extraneous but exotic starship extras in mini skirts that always seemed to greet science fiction heroes before being exterminated by an extraterrestrial.

I settled down for a very long wait in a distinctly uncomfortable corridor where busy bees purposefully buzzed past me offering greetings that made me feel less alien to this deserted science fiction environment of government enterprise. There was little to amuse me in this uninspiring windowless waiting place, except some whiskered portraits of previous Landeshauptmann. The appointed time ran over, due to his busy schedule saving the universe, so I amused myself sketching the facial hairs on the portraits which included a long sweeping top lip moustache and some assorted short fluffy lapdogs tucked under their nostrils.

"You can come in now. I am sorry for the long wait" said his starship secretary.

She showed me through to a unexpectedly frugal office which was quite disappointing considering the remarkable oak carved Bürgermeister's Ratsstube in Feldkirch where 'Voralberg' had been first conceived. However, there were some more comfortable soft chairs reminiscent of a seventies television talk show and the Landeshauptmann was an astute, politically proficient, engaging and enchanting host with a good ear for my opera and even better eye for an amusing interview. I felt relaxed as he seemed like a fellow wild mountain man and certainly as friendly as the Vorarlbergers I had met on my diary star quest.

"I always wanted to drive a locomotive like Jim Knopf" he said with an impish grin.

This reference to a famous children's fairytale book about a train that goes on great global adventures was a sign of something more significant below the surface, so I dug a little deeper to see if I could find the sweeter chocolate mountain secrets of Vorarlberg.

"I am an eccentric wild man in search of something special here in your chocolate mountains. What was your wild childhood like in Höchst ?" I asked with a satirical hint.

"I must confess to being a rebellious child too as I hated school and the shock of loosing my freedom, and all that sitting still" he said with surprising sympathy. "In fact we used to put beetles down the shirt collars of the children in front of us in the church."

As we chatted about his enterprising stamp collecting stories, my mind strayed back, off into a strange science fiction world of a star crazed satirist. He was like Captain Kirk and I was going where no man had ever gone before. When he sat back I started to scan the arm of his easy chair for the control buttons, wondering which one would switch on the transporter beam and whether he would autograph or phase out my inter galactic Vorarlberg travel log.

"I am really at home in Höchst and so are you" he said after our brief chat.

****

The snow was getting heavier as I emerged from the bowels of the Landesregierung birthday cake car park and I still had another appointment in Bildstein which was quite high up above the Rhine valley. The four wheel drive was an essential tool in my writer's armoury as I did not have a special space transporter which could be operated at the flick of my communicator but my mobile phone was full of messages wondering where I had vanished to in the snowstorm. It was a tempting excuse to say that I had been exploring another galaxy with a fellow wild man, but my wife was weary of my daydream excuses and she wouldn't forgive me leaving my daughter outside her school in the freezing snow.

The slushy winding road to Bildstein was marked by stations of the cross and I prayed not to come off the narrow street as I sped up to this remote little snowy heaven. I passed several shadowy snow covered orchards which looked out through the clearing clouds to the now built up dormitory town of Wolfurt.

The invitation had come from another tourism officer who had billed Bildstein as his personal little starry heaven and since I had been aboard a starship it seemed appropriate to pay my respects to his celestial paradise.

As I parked outside the church I noticed a peculiar wooden house with several garden gnomes in the window boxes which was a omen of stranger things to come in this remote settlement not noted for its hospitality. If there were gnomes, then perhaps it was a clue about the nature of this Disneyland Christmas card village. It wasn't long before I had spotted 'Sneezy' on the snowplough blowing into his handkerchief, and then 'Droopy' walking up with his snow shovel. I half expected them to start singing 'off to work we go' as they dug with such inherent and inbred efficiency clearing away the fresh deluge of snow.

The pretty twin towered church was also dedicated to Maria Heimsuchung like the Basilika in Rankweil, but I wondered if I would experience another spiritual revelation or surreal supernatural subconscious attack of some satirical insignificance. The wooden panelled ceiling was inset with paintings and the choir balcony had paintings of mostly standard masculine saints, although a token standing female saint struck a chord with my caustic consciousness. I was now no longer going where no man had ever gone before as I had regressed back to a fairytale world beyond Lilliput into the famous pages of the brothers Grimm since decimated by childhood cartoon characters. The miniature stations of the cross set in the walls outside and inside the church only served to feed this dwarfish fantasy.

I trudged through the deep snow drifts to the front of the church trying not to whistle in case a line of jingling, green felt capped, bearded midgets fell into line behind me. The church still had its crib and Christmas tree so the thought had crossed my mind that if time stood still here I could get stuck with those warbling nauseating marching melodies in torturous perpetuity. Behind the church was an open snow covered parade square with a snow covered soldier solemnly leaning on his rifle which was another worrying portent, so I sought refuge in the solitary shingled house that was sign-posted as the 'Gemeindeamt'.

"Excuse me but I am English and I wondered if you have any information for me." I said looking at a tourist brochure with some small men in felt hats.

The lady behind the counter reminded me of 'Sleepy' but she turned out to be more like 'Grumpy' when I said that I needed some information to write about Bildstein. Eventually she started to transform into 'Happy' but not before a brief display of 'Angry' at my snowy boots. I tried to be the smiling seventh dwarf as we discussed the total lack of literature and access to the local internet site but I was not very convincing. As I left I caught a glimpse of some laughing children looking out of the window so I obligingly whistled and marched of towards my car in the hope of encountering a Snow White to save the day.

The village was deserted so I drove down disappointed but admiring the now splendid view of the snowy plains below and listening to the radio which was playing a popular Swedish military whistling tune called 'Fernando' sung by Abba. The Scandinavians liked little people as well as trolls and little plump pop stars too. I was just whistling along with the merry tune when I spotted something in the corner of my eye flashing past me behind a high fenced field at the bottom of the hill. I stopped suddenly sliding on the snowy slush and opened my steamy side window to check if I was really seeing things again. But sure enough, beside a huge factory called 'Doppelmayr' there was a series of strange animal enclosures full of exotic animals and birds collected by an eccentric local industrialist who made ski lifts.

There in black and white before my eyes were stripy zebras strolling in the snow.

****

The following Saturday was a long awaited day for my son Max as I had made a promise to visit the Skateboard stars with him in the 'cool' Mecca of youthful adoration at Halle 8a in Dornbirn. This loud smoky den of daring was as ever alive with deafening music, indifferent teenagers and the grinding and whirring of dozens of skate boards. There was a small disco this time which belied the sound it blared out and a panel of punk haired judges watching skate board competitors soaring over various ramps and other obstacles.

Max pulled down his woolly hat and his little brother Leopold pulled up the hood on his sweat shirt and they both sat on their skateboard overawed at the awesome display of young flesh flipping, flying and falling off their 'decks'. I sat them next to curly haired 'Chris', the undisputed King of the Coolest Skateboarders, and his shy girlfriend with bright red tinted hair. The atmosphere was full of earsplitting stereo static electricity and the whoops of ecstatic fans as each competitor rolled down the ramps, ground along the rails and tried to get some air above the smog of dense cigarette smoke. I was impressed as the commentator read out the names of sponsored professionals like 'Take It Truppe' and 'Daring Dave' and amateur riders like 'Ja Fur Yannick' and 'The Flying Rucksack'. The tricks were often over-ambitious, resulting in bruised egoes as the competitors hit the hard concrete and their 'decks' sped on pilotless to smack against the wall like those car dummy impact advertisements.

"It can be a quite dangerous sport," said my host, Cle, who sat on the judges panel with a cockerel shaped hairstyle. "But that is part of the culture."

"Yea," nodded the Disc Jockey called 'Truffl' with a snotty punk sniff. "The music is mainly hardcore and punk or triple 'x' straight edge hardcore."

"What's the triple 'x' stand for ?" I said almost screaming over the Sex Pistols.

"No drink, no drugs and no smoking !" he shouted turning up the music.

"That's cool" I said waving my beer bottle at him through the smokey smog.

Outside as I gasped for air I caught two Turkish teenagers lighting a huge joint who promptly disappeared citing something about police harassment. I was getting too old and now they thought I was an undercover detective. Middle age memories of my first puff on a joint flooded back and of course like a famous past President, I did not inhale but it came out of my ears as well as my nostrils. Actually I was impressed that the spliff smokers were not a part of this skateboard culture although the passive tobacco smoke was far worse to a non addicted smoker like myself. I breathed in the fresh air with several deep breaths and returned to the skateboard arena in time to catch the first run of the Skateboard King.

It was easy to see why he had an undisputed reign over the ramps as he possessed not only a pleasant and polite personality but a professional acumen far above his peers. The crowd banged their 'trucks' against the walls to acknowledge a brilliantly neat almost perfect run without any mistakes and over zealous moves. He raised his hand to the whooping crowd with a victory sign and the judges that could write scrawled out top scores. My shy children had a new role model but they didn't say anything about it until we entered the dire, outdated but decidedly hospitable Dornbirn indoor swimming pool later that evening.

As we changed into our swimming costumes in separate cabins as part of a well rehearsed family routine I overheard my two sons talking about their experience together.

"Well, I saw Goliath sitting on his board opposite. He is always at our ramps but he didn't ride this time" whispered Max to his little brother Leopold.

"Who was the one with the funny wig on ?" demanded a loud Leopold.

"Hush. I don't know but my friend, Markus, was leaning on crutches by the ramp."

"I liked Chris. He was cool!" said Leopold "Daddy says he is the Skateboard King."

"He is the Cool Skateboard King" corrected Max with some deferrential authority.

"The other one had a wig but why didn't he have a crown?" asked little Leopold.

There was no answer to that unresolved question as we did not see if Chris was crowned preferring to head for the calmer, quieter and less crowded waters of a snowbound swimming pool. I sat watching the swimming coach coping with an inadequate indoor training pool that was a sixties shoe box in comparison to the München Olympia Bad. The facilities were better than the post-war outdoor pools of the fifties when the portly but polite trainer had possibly swum for his medals. I reflected upon a skateboard t-shirt.

The white lettering had stated *'Death by Stereo'*. I now enjoyed the snow and silence.

****

No Chronicle about Vorarlberg would be complete without a trip to Austria's most inaccessible valley known as 'Klein Walsertal', so I set off with the children to rediscover the delights of this secret secluded ski resort. There are many stories associated with this small piece of Austria that is only connected by road by travelling through the neighbouring German province of Freistaat Bayern. My favourite tall tale was related to the beginning of the Euro which resulted in a sudden growth of banks there to shelter 'Black Deutsch Marks'. I am afraid that our unfortunate visit was marred by a lot of 'Red Marks' starting with the ski lift operators who pointed out that our ski passes were valid for Grosses Walsertal but not Klein Walsertal. This is something that visitors should be aware of even if the valley claims to be Austrian. It was only by the good grace of some departing Bavarians who gifted us their passes that we got to the slopes. The unsympathetic and even laughing lift operators had no intention of doing anything but milking English tourists for more cash.

It was mostly German skiers and snowboarders who were flocking to reach the slopes in a severe snow blizzard which, once again, the lift operators failed to warn us about until we stepped out into a storm with sweeping wind speeds only experienced on polar expeditions. Still, it was Sunday and the wind would give us some momentum to tackle the treacherous and extremely badly marked slopes. We really tried to ski, but it was not a family resort at all.

"What more could happen in this hidden haven of monetary madness ?" I asked my frozen daughter as we squeezed into a smoke filled restaurant full of spotty snowboarders.

"Except perhaps a mad daddy !" she replied as I halted the canteen queue.

"Look. She has charged me over two Euros for Ketchup" I said standing my ground. "You cannot be seriously expecting me to be ripped off in Klein Walsertal ?"

I complained politely to the indifferent cashier who pointed out that I was in fact in Allgäu not in Klein Walsertal as the Fellerhornbahn Mittelstation was on German soil.

"And that justifies charging more for Bavarian ketchup than for beer. That's bloody typical ! It is cheaper to drink another beer and let my children scream down your restaurant."

I was so annoyed that I really wanted to make this unpleasant lump of flabby flatulent flubber take the ketchup off the plates preferably with her flippant tongue. But 'bloody typical foreign tourist' was already stamped across my forehead and she was just doing her job upsetting customers on the border line. She knew I would never return again, unless of course I was a sadomasochist. I sat miserably with my beer, gratuitously leaving the children to spread ketchup all over the place, and contemplating painting my cheeks with the red war paint.

Fortunately the snow storm subsided and we enjoyed getting completely lost somewhere in Germany or perhaps in Austria on some of the worst prepared icy pistes in the Alps. The sun was starting to set as we skied across a sharp spur from the Gipfelstation and we were left alone to cross back over the border back into Klein Walsertal. The panoramic view was quite phenomenal. Despite the patronising people I could see that this little concealed gem was quite congenial to my frozen eyes. The pale pink sunset was somewhere on the right or the wrong side of the unmarked border and we watched the last snowboarders skimming down the soft snow on steep unmarked pistes as we descended in the ski lift.

The only thing that was well marked was a protected area for wildlife. The thought occurred to me that there was really now no real visible difference between this disconnected part of Austria as the snow had spread over this pretty little valley covering up the remaining cultural differences. We drove home over a steep winding pass into the Bregenzerwald and the headlights of the car danced between the haunting winter shadows of the snow covered fir trees. A small hotel sign had caught my attention on leaving Klein Walsertal with the flying figure of a naked man swinging on a creeper and I contemplated whether it was in fact the border sign as it summed up such a lot about this tiny wild wondrous Walser jungle.

"Well that took you a long time to get home" said my indifferent wife.

"We got a bit lost and it was just as hard to find it" I said shrugging my tired shoulders and tucking into a wonderful but belated Sunday lunch.

"We skied black runs and got lost a lot" chipped in an exhausted Leopold.

"We saw the coolest snowboarders !" said Max shovelling in another mouthful.

"It was cold and Daddy got really lost" added Emily toying with her empty plate.

"At least I know where the Klein Walsertal Ketchup border is now."

"KETCHUP BORDER"

LAUGHING IN LECH, SNOW RIDING ON HAFLINGERS AND BECK IN BRAND

There comes a point when a satirical, sarcastic and cynical middle aged chronicler is called out to complete his final verdict on Vorarlberg so I decided to make one last expedition to two diametrically different parts of this vast mountainous Alpine Lilliput. I felt that these pages were not just unbalanced due to the hormonal changes of my midlife crisis but also because I had perhaps been a little unfair to my bright young teenage daughter whom I had singularly failed to comprehend. Since she had achieved the impossible by scoring unexpectedly high school grades I felt that she should experience the high life. This was only to be found in the jet set ski resorts where I had spent some of my formative years with the same idle rich whom I had chosen so hypocritically to savagely satirise in this 'social' but not socialist chronicle.

The hidden haunt of Kings and Queens in this Alpine Lilliput was centred around Lech, Zürs and perhaps St.Anton. The latter resort was undeniably the best skiing at high altitude in Vorarlberg on the great Valluga Mountain and the Crazy Kangaroo Bar possessed some of the best 'tits' too in both the mammary meaning and the slang pejorative reference to its 'drunken' apres ski revellers. Nevertheless it was my favorite anglophile resort until I set out on my expedition to revisit some other ski resorts that I had not covered in this chronicle.

The first Email response asking to write about Lech had been very encouraging to a saucy satirical travel writer like myself but the second one was an open invitation as it had said: 'if you want to interview people, you have to do this interview yourself though- in the village or on the slopes'. This resort was obviously the home from home of film and pop stars, glamorous monarchs and fashionable monarchists, and their not-quite-so-rich-but-want-to-be-seen-to-be-famous exclusive fan club. It was like inviting a satirical fox into the chic chicken coup with a full license to cause comic chaos and laughter in luxurious Lech.

The flaking biscuit tin was a little out of puff as we strove to conquer the heady heights of high society and we were politely flashed for the first time by a chauffer driven four wheeled cavalcade doubtlessly carrying a crowned dignitary up to these luxuriant fairytale Elysian snow fields. We stopped in Stuben to pick up a well built handsome ski instructor called 'Wolfgang' who was a mine of trivial trite about his hometown and the holiday retreat of royalty like Princess Diana, Caroline of Monaco, and the royal families of Sweden, Holland and Jordan. I asked him if he had any good anecdotes but he was the sort of instructor that was so prudent as to be the very picture of discretion but he politely answered my supplementary harmless question about his favourite pop star.

"I was once in a Restaurant with a friend who was playing the guitar when Cliff Richard came over to sing with us. It was my greatest moment !" he said so ardently.

We arrived early at this resort that ran on gold standard morning meantime and to a flurry of press photographers with long lenses. My daughter was immediately star struck and she clambered out to investigate but not without imparting a question which had obviously being gnawing her inside as we climbed up the steep mountain pass.

"Daddy. Who is Cliff Richard ?" she asked with a sheepish smile.

"He's a sort of English Elvis combined with Donny Osmond" I replied.

She still looked perplexed but she slid off to find out who the press paparazzi were chasing at ten o'clock in the morning. I joined her simply to enjoy a moment of free lance journalism as their subjects slid by anonymously but glamorously behind them.

"Who are you waiting for ?" I asked a bored and cold freelance photographer.

"The Royal Family of Holland" he replied without realising who was behind him.

"I think that might have been who you were waiting for over there" I pointed.

He left to try to catch his prey and I must admit that I enjoyed sighting them throughout the morning still hunting for sporting shots. I mused that it might be easier if I attached a harpoon gun to his telephoto lense so that he could at least make the front page headlines with his eargerly awaited press 'snow-plough-skiing-royal-action-photo' instead of the gossip columns of glossy newspapers. I pondered on some of the headline captions before returning to my tourism appointment with the prettiest tourism officer in lecherous Lech.

'DUTCH ROYAL CHARACTER ASSASINATION BY ENGLISH SATIRIST'

or perhaps even 'HORNY HOLLANDER LAMPOONED BY A WILDMAN'

Of course the latter headline might be because I completely missed the Royal Family that they were looking for and perhaps I had exaggerated a bit about the person I had spotted but it certainly kept them all well occupied for the rest of the day. It is quite possible to mistake people in such a chic resort and I was perhaps not the best person for remembering faces. I had once kissed a complete stranger in a supermarket and admired the melons in her trolley on the grounds that the person was so familiar that I must know her intimately. Sometime later I was making a summer regional television programme about a country show I had helped to organise and I met the pretty presenter for an interview who was holding a horny goat. She remembered me first and promptly asked if I might like to kiss it this time rather than fondling her melons.

It must be so hard being rich and famous but somehow I liked the sound of both dirty words and it was definitely hard to look at my gorgeous interviewee who pronouced the local hiking areas of the 'Spullasee' and 'Formarinsee' with such sensuous self-satisfaction so suited to her first name of 'Samira'. I soon drifted back into the great adventures of Sindbad in the Thousand and One Night's tales which happened to be the latest fantasy book that I had accidently acquired in a local 'Flohmarkt'. I couldn't read the beautiful calligraphy in this rare German edition, but the illustrations were stories in themselves and her name seemed to suit Sindbad's stunning Princess better. The story of Ali Baba and the forty thieves also sprang to mind when I attempted to view some of the local five star hotels who charged over 11,000 Euros for the Christmas Holiday week and 800 Euros per night.

If you can afford exclusivity then I would have to recommend the rather touchy Hotel Post in Lech. This was not on account of the incredibly difficult, pedantic, pretty but typically blonde receptionist who seemed to think I was a seedy journalist. It was rather from the interview with one of its polite infamous guests whom the paparazzi had somehow missed. She kindly told me that it was the best of the six four star hotels in Lech and Zürs. Later I found out from a book that I had to hustle from the busty blonde that it coinicidentally belonged to another 'Moosbrugger' but as he had no time to see me I can only presume from his similar portly photographic characteristics and name that he might somehow be connected to the cheese baron whom Franz Michael Felder had so aptly chastised.

The tourism officer had really tried hard to offer us some skiing on the beautifully manicured motorways with lots of blue lolly pops to guide affluent and corpulent chic society from their mountain sun decks to their swimming pools, spa baths and quite inappropriate saunas. I even enjoyed the car that had been planted as a sales exhibit under the chairlift in case one of them could not manage the snowy motorway. We tried our luck at Zürs in the Hotel Zürserhof politely enquiring at the reception about this cavernous hotel on a small hillock that only opened for the golden snow and the great 'glitterati'. A rather abrupt receptionist or rather, a pompous prig called 'Rainer', looked down his long nose at us as though we were wandering waifs from the street but a character remarkably similar to an English Prince reassured us in the car park. We decided to say goodbye to high society but not without some sympathy for Felder's rebellious social democratic reforms. I wondered what he might have written about this new generation of laughable Lech long-noses. I was just a travel writer, so what did I care besides they had seventy percent repeat bookings every year. It was probably an ideal environment for pretentious pedants and ponses.

"Let's look on the bright side !" smiled Emily, "We're going to ride Haflingers in the snow and so they can go and jump off their Cliff Richard."

"Let's go and have some fun as there is little to laugh about in Lech" I retorted.

I thought of Pinochio remembering that his nose grew longer if he lied and I checked my nose in the mirror. "Lech is the best resort in Europe for skiing and summer holidays."

We left the last resort of the rich and famous and drove down to Bludenz and then back up the other side of the valley into Brandnertal. The tourism department was quite unprepared for our visit which is exactly as it should be but we could not have received a warmer and friendlier welcome. The village of Brand is in my honest opinion one of the best small all year round resorts in Vorarlberg together with perhaps Schruns, because it has a good golf course, adequate swimming pools, some tennis courts, and hiking in the summer right up onto a glacier. The skiing in winter is sufficient, although it might do better to invest in lifts that worked and in snow fields of a higher altitude as the village is only 1037 metres high.

However, if the 'white gold' snow does not come I can recommend riding on the beautiful Haflingers bred here by the charming original Walser farming family called Beck. For the uninitiated, a Haflinger pony has a white mane and nose blaise and a fox brown coat.

My daughter adored Sporthotel Beck which is designed for families and was always booked by repeat visitors, although suprisingly few English visitors have discovered it.

She fell in love with the five new foals and was soon cantering away over the snowy hills whilst I went in search of their son, the infamous but suprisingly modest ski jumper and cult snowboard champion 'Andy Beck' who was crooning over his new girlfriend in a mountain bar, wondering why an eccentric Englishman wanted to interview him on Valentine's Day.

"I'm sorry I'm late, but the bloody lift broke down so I had to walk up" I puffed.

"That's cool" he said sitting on a stool admiring his latest passion serving at the bar.

Everybody needs a teenage hero and this was the equivalent of Superman with over one hundred ski jumping and snowboarding trophies to his name. He didn't exactly wear his underpants outside his trousers but he wore a luminescent green snow jacket rather than the traditional blue tights and super hero outfit. He had a short stubbly rather than full facial beard with strategically placed studs in his lower lip, eye brow and ear lobe. His story was quite remarkable winning ski jumping competions in the early 1990's and then changing to win snowboarding championships. He was a natural athlete, although serious shoulder and knee injuries meant that now he was a singer in the band 'Working Chair' which hopefully was going to be another extraordinarily big recording label success (with a good lyric writer).

"Look Andy, I am so cruel to spotty snowborders because I can't do it and they often cause accidents" I said extremely impressed with his unpretentious sincerity.

"I teach my Snowboarders respect for all winter sports" he responded affirmatively.

We chatted about how easy it was to take up Snowboarding, which is easier than learning to ski, and that it was also a lifestyle as well as a sport.

"I don't suppose you have any advice for my son Max ?" I said hoping he wasn't going to recommend cryptonite or other super hero cultural stimulants.

"Hard work and a good diet" he said offering to sign his jump skis for luck.

"I'm converted and I promise no more spotty snowboarders wise cracks" I said starting to finally believe in this new snowboard Freeride and Freestyle culture.

"So what has the master of the Corkscrew 900 with an Indy Grab got to say that will inspire the new smooth skinned youth of today ?" I said sarcastically.

"Do whatever you wanna do. Have fun and hang loose" he said with a huge grin.

It was a stale but timeless sixties statement that satirists might poke fun at and could certainly hang him with, but I liked him. He was a convert and had knocked the spots of his sport. I finally began to understand why the craze of Snowboarding was here to stay. I skied down the slope to catch up with my daughter, politely giving way to some less capable snowborders who found the icy slopes a bit too challenging.

"I always play music to my cows" said his father, Werner Beck, as we admired his herd in their tethered winter quarters with his farming son, Wolfgang. "Sometimes I change the channel but I think they like Radio Vorarlberg."

"What is the wooden statue in the corner ?" I asked also admiring his pedigree stock.

"It's a local saint who cared for animals" he replied shovelling some silage feed.

We struck up an immediate rapport as his cattle had won several livestock prizes and he was quite typical of Walser family-orientated fathers that I had met on my travels. His charming pretty wife, Christl, ran the hotel with his other son and chef, Christian, and he ran the farm with his deeply rooted rustic son, Wolfgang, who had astutely intermarried with another farmer's daughter. This was so typical of the changes and challenges of the twenty first century Walser families farming the uplands of Vorarlberg.

We were invited to dinner. After Emily had left to go night sledging with some new found friends apart from the foals, calves and large fat fluffy ginger hotel cat that adored having it's head scratched, I chatted with Werner over a glass of wine. He told me many tales about life before tourism but my favourite story started:

"Smugglers in these parts used to cross over the Brandner glacier into Switzerland with two-way contraband for the crooked train station staff in Bludenz. The fog can suddenly engulf you up there and you can loose your way. They lost two couriers once and they found them dead with a circle of footprints in the snow and a full rucksack of provisions."

I sat listening long into the starry night with my beer in a real mountain dream world.

THE FINAL CHAPTER OF A CHRONICLER'S QUEST

The snow sloshed over the curb as I waited in lubricious limbo to cross over to the other side. It drenched me from top to bottom compounding the confusion in my absent mind. I swore at the Swiss lorry driver who couldn't hear me as he was probably busy yodelling to the Appenzellerland top ten tributes to Elvis. My extended ego at finding that so many distributors actually wanted my chronicle was most definitely dampened down by this definitive evolutionary statement. Water had brought life to the Chocolate Mountains, whirling wheels had brought civilisation and I was all washed up in the natural cycle of both of them.

"I went to the Post Office to dispatch the manuscripts and now we just have to hope that they accept me as a true satirical writer 'Schriftsteller'" I said wiping off the last brown slush which had even gone over the brim of my beloved chestnut tanned travelling hat.

"Still, you will love the house and it's all wonderful wood !" exclaimed my wife in a playful mood as things were at last coming together in our new home from home.

We alighted into our faithful four wheeled chariot and she cheerfully chatted about domestic appliances which have no real intrinsic interest to most midlife men although I could still see the romance in my coffee machine. A foolhardy local psychiatrist had once cornered me at the bar in Dornbirn on the subject of a writer's subconscious sexual libido. He finished up dragging deeply on his cigarette like a professional prostitute after a round with a rampant recently released prisoner. After relating my dirty dancing fantasy with the steamy coffee machine I wanted to ask him if it was as good for him as it most definitely was for me.

"Darling, are you listening to me at all ?" she said swerving to avoid a school bus.

"Of course. Maybe I will be able to see the bloody butter in the fridge."

There are hundreds of books on women and the menopause and this reference was designed to give the men-a-pause from the next round of beautiful but boring banter. My wife had been completely stupefying over the question of the conscious practicalities of real life whilst I regressed to politely pilot my superstitious imagination. My brilliant white angelic wings blew me up through the thermonuclear fission clouds and propelled me past the last snowy phantasmal peaks out over the sublime Bodensee. I was a jinxed, aged, atomic albatross in search of my ancient mariner so that I could 'fall out' of the heavens and contaminate him and his human kind with my adulterated and abnormal subliminal world of feckless fantasy freaks. Worse still, these feelings were far beyond any synthetic induction from pharmaceutical preparations and my musical lyrics seemed to dance off the page in a deluded delirium which the opera music composers either hated or adored.

"We are here now, so you can come off cloud nine" she said stroking my leg. "There is the phantom plumber but he is handsome and so sexy and slim."

I rubbed my eyes looking out at a busy bunch of pert bummed builders and realised that the real world whistled whilst they worked and whilst I wrote sarcastically about them. The weird thing was that literature wasn't infallible and the heavy heeled footsteps in the snow that I had imagined belonging to a corpulent conveyor of my convenience was not conveniently the characterisation that I had subconsciously conceived. He was a handsome handyman and I was a hypocritical heretic. Not only had I broken the eleventh commandment of the written word of a chronicle writer by not being true to non fiction but I had also become a character charlatan by satirising the spirit of this sex god before even seeing him. The book bores and broadcasters were going to blast my churlish chronicles and I would have to think of some publicity to persuade purchasers that it was me not the text that was at fault. I thought of my working days in the smog and grime of white collared London where I had worked for an advertising company and had been sacked from the Harrods shirts department for using the front public, rather than subterranean staff entrance after an extended lunch break. Actually, it was the serenading of an attractive but anorexic perfume girl just as the store was opening that raised the most cheers but caused me to be summoned to the basement inferno for a fire and brimstone sacking by a wise witch hunter from personnel.

"I think that working in our department store has caused a divergence of interests which unfortunately can only really be rectified by a parting of the ways" she said primly looking at me across her typewriter. "Perhaps you might try the dramatic arts."

The guilt of the lie hung over me like a sexually suspended icicle as it was something deeper than my Chocolate Mountain diaries and I dug deeper into my satirical subterranean subconsciousness. Manic marketing slogans like 'Merry Christmas from a menopausal mountain wild man' and 'Surprise Superman with a snowy, satirical but sensitive stocking filler' started to appear during my evening classes to the chagrin of my class. Then it dawned on me that my problem was probably perfectly normal and thousands of midlife men made the midlife change. Some were like chameleons changing colour cradling their comfortable beer canisters in the sauna and others combed back their colourless curls cursing their combs.

"What did you think of it all as you haven't said much" said my midlife wife.

"That phantom plumber threw me a bit. Where is the Sauna going to be ?" I replied.

"Darling sometimes you simply astonish me. I wonder what on earth you are thinking about and if you are on this planet at all" she said shrugging her shoulders.

We drove back through the deep snow and I could see the sweet sugar candy mountains behind the church tower just as the early morning sun twinkled over the high peaks. It was like a child's eye view of a far away fantasy derived from the little pictures on the miniature chocolates brought home by some smiling senior semiconductor to light up a strange new alpine world. I had finally reverted back to the naivety of natural nappy-hood and it was only one more step back into the womb to the first pumping heart beats of sublime sonorous subconsciousness. There was no more going back from here, it was onwards, upwards or downwards, but life was no longer upside down.

"Stop picking your nose ! Horrible man !" said my wife with a maternal tone.

"I am not picking my nose. I was sucking my thumb" I responded indignantly.

There was no answer to that as it was something as inborn and ingrained as the first kick in the womb as a baby floated upside down and tried to swim upright again. It was now more natural for me to swim upwards rather than downwards to breath new life again and I swore to struggle out of the deep cold chasms of my satirical fantasy world. In fact I wrote one of my better libretto love duets with these thoughts floating in my mind.

My aspirations flowered like a white winter Aurum lily lulling me with its scented sincerity in a brave new world of wonder. I was born again without the spiritual connotations and the midlife man made music with words again. My pen sprouted throughout the spring snow taking me to delicately dance with the fairies in the serene snowdrop wood of my country childhood.

"Now that you have started your second opera, I wonder whether a publisher would sponsor you to continue your crazy chronicles as it is the first time that I have ever really understood you" she said smiling at my red swollen wrinkled thumb.

"This midlife mountain wild man has received a surprising endorsement letter from the Landeshauptmann of Vorarlberg, Dr. Herbert Sausgruber, himself" I replied realising that thumb sucking was not really my cup of coffee and then laughing at how on earth she would translate that memorable mixed metaphor from my great Irish uncle who was actually a cold tea drinking Memsahib from Majorca. "I think that he has really understood me too."

The letter was for the foreword of this turbulent satirical midlife travel diary so as a pubescent podgy pedant I have placed it at the back of this book. It simply read:

Dear Robert,

I hope that your book on our chocolate mountain paradise of Vorarlberg will encourage visitors to dig a little deeper into the heart of our wonderful world of laughter and infamous alpine hospitality. I know that we have so much more to offer than skiing with sunglasses and dancing in alpine meadows as people will doubtless discover in your book.
Yours sincerely,
Landeshauptmann and Höchster

PS: I'm glad that you chose my village of Höchst to write your opera and humorous book in.

This book was inspired by a local song and the chorus line translates as:
'Oho Vorarlberg, you are indeed a dwarf of a country, small but o-ho holdrio.'

"ON PILE OF BOOKS"

THE END

IF YOU ENJOYED THIS CHOCOLATE MOUNTAIN CHRISTMAS CHRONICLE CARRY ON WITH THE NEXT:

The tale continues, but this time the intrepid wild man sets his sails to master his madness in search of something else in a fisherman's gondel on the Bodensee. He profiles more village characters like the Postman who crossdresses for Karnival as an Angel, enjoys more Karnival crusades and rides a Harley Davidson through the Alpine Meadows in search of Heidi. He steers his wooden motor boat around the sights of the Bodensee including the famous palatial gardens of the Insel Mainau and the home of the witch burning bishops of Konstanz. He prays for forgiveness for apple scrumping in Birnau and discusses the roots of the original wild men of Unteruhldingen. He takes readers on a challenging route through the classic cliché and male menopausal mixed metaphors of his travel chronicles on another wild adventure in the alps.

Here are a few loving quotes from my family when I announced my next quest:

"Daddy the Angel is off again but I hope the boat doesn't sink" said little Leopold.
"Elephants can't water ski behind that thing" saluted Max stroking the engine.
"Well it has got life jackets and a horn" chirped a safety conscious teenager, Emily.
"Don't come back without a book or at least a fish" demanded my skipper, Marina.
"I'm going to savour the still, starry nights of solitude on this sailing saveloy."
I looked at my sausage shaped 'gondel' sheltering from the snow under the extended eaves of the Mostkeller with a certain pride. The English had founded an Empire on their nautical skills and I had after all sailed down the Great Barrier Reef in a catamaran made from a fibreglass DIY kit in a Sydney back garden. But as I looked more closely at my pride and joy, I realised that something was wrong with my varnished vessel. It wasn't the motor which I was assured would start in a storm. A bright blue tarpaulin covered the boat stretched out by a long pole and it was fastened around the perimeter of the dark oak planking by little elastic toggles. I opened the cover to reveal the Spartan interior of my new floating dog kennel which looked as inviting as a freezing sauna in the snow.
"It is going to be my Chichester challenge except I am only going to sail around the Bodensee single handed" I said with due reverence to my great childhood sailing hero, Sir Francis Chichester, who had been the first person to sail around the globe single handed. His nautical feat was only just ahead of my admiralty hero, the one eyed Lord Nelson.

I recalled memories of being dressed as a white rabbit on a peaceful demonstration to save the countryside from city socialists. I had stopped to feed the famous pigeons by the lions under the great column erected as a sign of a respectful nation for the seaman's victory at Trafalgar. My son, Max, also dressed as a white rabbit, asked me who was up there on top of the huge stone pillar. I looked up at the wrong moment and caught some flying fancy pigeon excrement in my eye. It gave me time to formulate a reply suitable to my giggling son.

"He was the hero of the British Fleet who put his telescope to his blind eye and blatantly ignored orders to withdraw preferring to fight on to victory."

"Don't be silly Daddy, he was the one who asked Captain Hardy for a kiss before he died !" replied Max giving me a firm, friendly but ferocious bunny hug.

The Gondel boat was not designed to sail around the world, although that depended on which fantasy world I wanted to circumnavigate. There were no cannons to give the French warships a broadside but that did not stop me from playing ship's master of an imaginary scurvy crew press ganged into the service of the Royal Navy. Then it dawned upon me that there wasn't any sails to set as it was in fact a motor boat. My daydream of sailing on the early morning breeze skimming over choppy waters screened by the lea of snowy mountains was sinking like a lead anchor weight around my neck.

"It hasn't actually got any sails" I coughed choking on this ridiculous revelation.

"Well, never mind. Doubtless it will be powered by emotion" laughed my loving wife as she kissed me on the cheek.

I felt like Lord Nelson once again as we walked back to our wooden winter home which also seemed like a beached ship of the line. The children played warships whilst the Union Jack pennant fasted to the bow blew gently in the breeze. I winked at them with my good eye as we were off to splice the main brace and splash some ice in a gin and tonic.

CHOCOLATE MOUNTAIN CHRONICLES COMPETITION

If you would like to enter the Chocolate Mountain Chronicle Competition please write to Mackintoosh Ltd (Elsham) at Elsham Hall, Brigg, North Lincolnshire DN20 0QZ England with your answers to the following three questions and your tie breaking title for the next book. The competition closes on 5th April 2005 and all entries will be accepted only prior to this date. The competition is open to all purchasers of the Chocolate Mountain Chronicles so please also include a receipt or proof of purchase as well as writing your full name, address and postal code. The first fifty entries selected after the above date will be sent a free information package on Voralberg in Austria and a cute cow. Please note that the publishers are not responsible for receipt of entries, losses or any liability in any respect whatsoever as it is purely a fun competition not a binding contract. If you do enter we will try to judge all entries received fairly remembering that the competition panel has the final decision on all entries and any other matters relevant to the competition rules which are available separately. We can only accept one entry per book purchase or individual. Thank you for your entry in advance which we cannot acknowledge unless it is by recorded registered mail however we will endeavour without liability to enter all entries received prior to the closing date above.

1. What are the names of the two villages in Vorarlberg beginning with G and H where the author lived during the writing of the Chocolate Mountain Chronicles? *Graissau + Höchst*

2. What is the name of the chocolate beginning with 'M' that is actually made in Vorarlberg in Austria which has a lilac cow on the wrapper and inspired the title of this book? *Milka*

3. What was the name of the Irish author whose ghost was train watching with the author in Feldkirch who wrote 'Ulysses' and 'Finnegans Wake'?
James Joyce

Tie Breaker for First Prize. Please suggest a title for the next book:

Please remember to send us your details as above and book receipt. Thank you.

THE FIRST READING

Here are some of the quotations about this book at it's first reading at the Landesbibliothek of Vorarlberg in Bregenz, Austria:

'Imagine if you can being at the Royol Opera House and then being suddenly inspired to write an opera on the Queen Mum then you can understand something about this eccentric Englishman.'
Vorarlberger Nachrichten. Austria.

'To be or not to be that is the question.' William Shakespeare's Ghost.

'Let's drink to that' Ernest Hemingway's Ghost somewhere in Montafon.

'It was definitely the Orient Express you eejit.' James Joyce's Ghost.

'That's your last free colonic irrigation.' Mrs Noah, the hospital bureaucrat.

'I'll give you some more sausages next time.' Mrs Blum, the butcher's wife.

'But I'm not campanologicially challenged.' Milki the transsexual Lilac Cow.

'You forgot me again you pea brain.' The Seventh Dwarf from Bildstein.

'You made me famous at last' The modest Choir leader of Gaissau.

'Have another cigar on me.' Anonymous Smiling Smuggler.

'We do not charge duty on ketchup.' Zollamt Kleines Walsertal.

'Well they couldn't sit on me or sue me.' Michael Felder's Ghost

'A brilliant insight into my country.' Another Vorarlberg Wild Man.

'Your (chocolate mountain) project doesn't
fit our current (Milka) sponsoring profile.' Typical mean Wien Comment.

'We are pleased to have recorded it.' ORF Engineer.

'I hope ORF play it on the radio for my cows.' Mr. Beck.

ABOUT THE AUTHOR ...

Robert Elwes was born in the Lincolnshire Wolds on the edge of the River Humber where he became a self made theatre director building an award winning theatre at his family home of Elsham Hall. He has won a number of tourism and theatrical awards but was originally trained as a farmer at the Royal Agricultural College in Cirencester. He has written the libretto for 'My Little Mountain Angel' a new opera on the life of Angelica Kauffmann which is currently in musical production. His wife Marina is an Egyptologist and his children think he is completely crazy. This is the first chronicle based on his travels whilst writing his opera. He has also appeared on several television shows normally dressed as a large cuddly animal.

ABOUT THE BOOK ...

This travel chronicle charts the author's travels in Vorarlberg in Austria, Appenzellerland in Switzerland and Bayern in Germany whilst writing an opera on the infamous artist called Angelika Kauffmann. It is designed to highlight the growing problems of dyslexia as well as the escapist midlife crisis experienced by many menopausal wild men. The book varies in style to encourage readers to write diaries and read books instead of sitting in front of the square box. It is hoped that other new 'disabled' dyslexic authors will be encouraged too. The book was inspired by a local song and the chorus line translates as:
 'Oho Vorarlberg, you are indeed a dwarf of a country, small but o-ho holdrio.'

ACKNOWLEDGEMENTS ...

This book is dedicated to my loving family and extended family at home who patiently helped with this book and to the warm and friendly people of my beloved Alpine Lilliput.

DEDICATION ...

This dyslexic tome is dedicated to my late father, Captain Jeremy Elwes, for many wonderful times together in our wild fantasy heaven at Elsham Hall Country and Wildlife Park.

BIBLIOGRAPHY ...

There are so many reference books in my library mentioned in this chronicle that I can only suggest that you visit a public library or a bookshop. I used to hide under the table at Elsham.

ANGELIKA KAUFFMANN MUSICAL ...

My thanks to Teddy Maier and Rolf Aberer for their work on the musical and opera which will become as famous as the Sound of Music. I hope that one day the people of Vorarlberg will be able to show the world that they can produce great musicals like "My Little Mountain Angel."

CARTOON AND PHOTOGRAPHS ...

My thanks to those providing photographs and to Daniel Flax (www.pixelworks.at) for the cartoons. Thanks to Sascha and Marty from IRR and Wolfgang from Lustenau (www.bulu.at) for setting this book and liking Irish Whisky (www.irr.to).

PUNCTUATION ...

This Book is for radio broadcasting so the different style of punctuation is for reading aloud on air. Sorry if there are a few mistakes but this dyslexic author tries hard to please his readers. Thank you.